Second Edition

Great Jobs

for

Psychology
Majors

Julie DeGalan
Stephen Lambert

VGM Career Books

NTC/Contemporary Publishing Group

Library of Congress Cataloging-in-Publication Data

DeGalan, Julie.
    Great jobs for Psychology majors / Julie DeGalan & Stephen Lambert.—2nd ed.
        p.cm. — (Great jobs for)
    Includes index.
    ISBN 0-658-00452-2
    1. Psychology—Vocational guidance. I.Lambert, Stephen E. II. Title. III. Series.

BF76.D44 2000
150´.23´73—dc21   00-44770
                                                                                          CIP

Published by VGM Career Books
A division of NTC/Contemporary Publishing Group, Inc.
4255 West Touhy Avenue, Lincolnwood (Chicago), Illinois 60712-1975 U.S.A.
Copyright © 2001 by NTC/Contemporary Publishing Group, Inc.
Printed in the United States of America
International Standard Book Number: 0-658-00452-2
01 02 03 04 05 06 LB 15 14 13 12 11 10 9 8 7 6 5 4 3 2 1

To Matt and Fran Lambert, parents extraordinaire,
and Lari, Pat, Nick, Beau, and Olivia Hayhoe, with love.

CONTENTS

Acknowledgments

Writing the second edition of *Great Jobs for Psychology Majors* provided a wonderful opportunity to further deepen our knowledge of the career opportunities that are available today. The World Wide Web has become such an important tool in gaining information and accessing actual job listings. We encourage all readers to take a journey on the Internet to learn more about careers for psychology majors.

We want to thank our colleagues at NTC/Contemporary Publishing Group who were so helpful to and patient with us. Betsy Lancefield, Denise Betts, and Kristen Eberhard, we appreciate all your efforts!

We also want to thank Chris Myers at William M. Mercer, Inc., for providing access to salary information.

PSYCHOLOGY: A LONG PAST BUT A SHORT HISTORY

The opening chapters of your very first college psychology textbook were probably devoted to an appreciation of the principles and philosophical foundations of psychology and a brief survey of its history. You learned that psychology involves the study and understanding of how we think, feel, behave, perceive, and sense. And your ongoing studies helped you realize that psychology does indeed have a fascinating history! Some of the best historical reviews include biographies and even photographs and sketches of the pioneering women and men who carved a niche for this new science out of the disciplines of philosophy, anatomy and physiology, phrenology, biology, chemistry, and medicine. Psychology as a branch of study has a relatively short history. As a result, many of these personal histories of experimentation and brilliant discovery will have an immediacy and relevance that may surprise you.

Until the nineteenth century, psychology was very much bound together with many other branches of science and theoretical exploration, most notably philosophy. So, the history of psychology began with an attempt to "self-define," to somehow separate itself from philosophy, anatomy, biology, and other fields of investigation into what makes humans "click." It was during the nineteenth century that the work of incipient neurologists, oculists, physicists, and physiologists began to accumulate data and results that truly belonged to the new realm of psychology and not these other disciplines. A good example of this is the early work of German experimenters such as Ernst Weber and Gustav Fechner that began as investigations into ocular perception and discrimination and then led to an early understanding that we all appreciate and perceive differently.

The early French contributions were medically, rather than physiologically, oriented. The French were singularly responsible, through extensive documentation and observation of incarcerated or institutionalized cases, for the early work in psychology that helped us to understand mental illness, especially schizophrenia. Differences in symptoms and severity of cases were noted and analyzed and the beginnings of a diagnostic model were laid down. Although psychology was not part of medical training as an independent course of investigation, by the early days of the nineteenth century, most informed physicians were at least aware of the practice of hypnosis and the possibilities it held for understanding and treating mental illness.

All of this early work in the 1800s began with an emphasis on understanding our physical senses: how we hear, see, and even taste. This led directly to an understanding of our mental faculties: how we perceive, discriminate, learn, and remember. Slowly, out of this physiological background came increased understanding of the human mind and both individual behavior and group functioning. New careers for psychologists were created as psychology's history changed in form, structure, content, and methodology.

Your textbook chapter summarizing the brief history of psychology would require as much discussion of the personalities and identities of the early psychologists and how they viewed and labeled their own careers or life work, as on the content of the work itself. As individuals moved ahead in their own work and theoretical development, it became clear that psychology was a science of many, many subspecialties. During these formative years, psychology was often defined by its personalities—Freud, Jung, and Horney—or focused on the leading schools—psychoanalysis, Gestalt, Logotherapy, and behaviorism, just to name a few.

New careers from new specialities continue to appear. Expressive therapy, discussed later in this book, has strong psychodynamic roots and psychologists such as James Hillman have been instrumental in forging new careers especially for art therapists.

THE SCHOOLS OF PSYCHOLOGY

The first half of the twentieth century saw the development of a number of "schools" of psychology. These were centered around strong, influential personalities whose writings and work attracted much popular attention. Even among the general public the names of Erich Fromm, Sigmund Freud, Carl

Jung, Karen Horney, Alfred Adler, Viktor Frankl, and Abraham Maslow are well-known, though their beliefs about psychology may not be as clear to the person on the street. Many people know the schools of psychology by name, as well, though it might be hard for them to match the founding or important personalities with their schools. Many psychology careers are still built around the work of these individual schools. The most familiar schools are discussed here.

Psychoanalysis

Now, for better or for worse, completely absorbed into the mainstream of American culture, the school known as psychoanalysis is currently immersed in tremendous controversy. The concept of the unconscious, the significance of dreams, the importance and presence of conflict within our minds, and how that conflict affects our everyday life was the work of pioneers such as Sigmund Freud, Alfred Adler, and Carl Jung. They saw indications of dysfunction in all people, neuroses and behaviors that may not be healthy but do not prevent individuals from maintaining appropriateness in their lives. For these pioneers and the school of psychoanalysis there is a continuum of human experience from what is termed "healthy" to what is considered "mentally ill," and it is seamless and subtle.

Logotherapy

In *Man's Search for Meaning*, German psychologist Viktor Frankl describes his time in a concentration camp and the profound revelations that came to him about how each of us can find meaning in life. This drive to attribute meaning is at the center of Logotherapy, and its absence is what creates meaninglessness and, ultimately, poor mental health.

Humanistic Psychology

Carl Rogers, Karen Homey, Abraham Maslow, and Erich Fromm are members of a group of psychologists termed "humanistic," a reaction away from the clinical approach of the psychoanalysts. This group emphasizes the importance of culture and interpersonal relations in personality formation. It also describes the need to move toward an ideal self, to improve, to become better, to have richer, more connected experiences, and to self-actualize as the person we feel we can be.

Gestalt Psychology

This school of psychology began with discoveries about perceptions of motion and movement. Perhaps you've participated in experiments where, in a darkened room, you wave a colored fluorescent light "wand" rapidly back and forth in the air in front of you. You will actually see a "screen of light" against which it is possible to project a slide image. That image appears against this colored wall of moving light as you keep your wand in motion. Some of what you see is memory. The rapid movement of the colored wand and how you perceive the trail of light that it leaves is related to synergy; this concept of synergy has added to the understanding of learning, perception, and other areas of psychology.

Functionalism and Behaviorism

The emphasis in this school is less on mental processing and more on the outcomes of that mental activity. John Watson and B. F. Skinner believed that operant conditioning, rewards, and punishment can produce a wide variety of behavior. Strict adherents to this school make generous claims for its abilities to train organisms.

Cognitivism

Work in psychology behavior labs with rats illustrates many of the important theories of cognitivists such as E. C. Tolman. They have shown us that both animals and people can be trained to respond to rewards and incentives, and have specific drives that can be identified.

Information Processing—Computer Simulation Theory

Because of the pioneering work of Allen Newell, J. C. Shaw, and Herbert Simon we have computers that can seemingly reason. They have been programmed to mimic human thinking and can solve problems in strategy games and make guided decisions. They do not have the repository of the human mind, with its associations, memories, and synapses of cognition, but they do help us appreciate how the human mind works and how distinctive it truly is.

THE FIELD OF STUDY AND AREAS OF CONCENTRATION

The world of psychology is one of incredible diversity that can sometimes create confusion in the minds of the general public, especially in the area of careers. When we use *psychology* in everyday language, the context is often the abnormal, the aberrant, or the inappropriate in human behavior and motivation. We use many words with the *psycho* root interchangeably:

psychology, psychiatrist, psychoanalysis, psychotic. The airwaves are filled with personality psychologists who diagnose or give counseling on television or the radio. Many of these experts have Ph.D.s and M.D.s, but are equally as skilled in self-marketing.

Though these public personalities have some of the most visible psychology careers, they truly represent only the tip of the iceberg. Tens of thousands of others work far more quietly and effectively in schools, clinics, private practice, research laboratories, industry, medicine, and higher education. Some of the confusion in the general public's mind is understandable given the numerous fields that can be studied under the umbrella term *psychology*. Using any of the popular "metasearch" engines, a Web search on any school of psychology listed below will dramatically illustrate that field of inquiry. Consider the following career fields:

Clinical Psychology. Professionals in this field assess and treat people who exhibit mental or emotional disorders ranging from the expected repercussions of everyday life to extreme pathological conditions.

Community Psychology. How we function at home, at school, in our communities (neighborhoods, housing units, or group homes) is the province of this specialty, much of whose work is preventative.

Counseling Psychology. Helping people cope, make important and everyday decisions, and adjust to the stresses and strains of life through interpersonal dialogue and a variety of treatment therapies is the domain of counseling psychology.

Developmental Psychology. Human development, from birth to death, is examined in this specialty. Developmental psychology describes, measures, and explains age-related changes in behavior in terms of individual differences and universal traits.

Educational Psychology. This research-oriented branch of psychology that studies how people learn. It has important applications in schools, industry, and our growing technological society.

Environmental Psychology. Advancing theory through research to understand and to improve interactions between human behavior and the physical environment, both built and natural is the goal of environmental psychology. Architectural design, management of scarce natural resources, and effects of extreme environments on personality and behavior are some of the varied interests represented by this field.

Experimental Psychology. This much broader grouping of specialists, through research, studies basic behavioral processes including how people talk, and understand and apply what they know. Animal work is often involved as a step in understanding human behavior.

Industrial/Organizational Psychology. We spend much of our lives employed and this branch of psychology studies our relationship to work. Job productivity, development, enhancement, career counseling, retirement planning, job variety, and cross-training are all part of this branch of psychology.

Neuropsychology and Psychobiology. Understanding the relation between physical systems and behavior is the object of study in this area. The nervous system and its impact on behavior and ways to solve neurological dysfunctions are the subject of research and application in laboratories and medical settings.

Psychometrics and Quantitative Psychology. A strong background in math and data analysis is necessary for work in this area, which focuses on psychological testing and assessment. Private research firms, testing companies, colleges and universities, and government agencies employ psychometrists.

Rehabilitation Psychology. The effects of birth trauma, stroke, or other debilitating handicaps are remedied in part by the work of rehabilitation psychologists who help people overcome situational and psychological obstacles to smooth functioning in the world.

School Psychology. School psychologists assist with the emotional, psychological, and intellectual development of young people. Employed by educational systems, they counsel, work with children experiencing problems, collaborate with guidance personnel and teachers, and deliver workshops and programs on educational issues.

Social Psychology. Why are different female body types in fashion? Why does a culture revere young people? Which jobs have organizational status? All are subjects for social psychologists who are interested in our attitudes and opinions and how they are formed and changed.

Family Psychology. This relatively new field is concerned with the importance of the family as a formative structure in our lives. The prevention and treatment of marital and family problems through research and application includes a subspecialty in the prevention and treatment of sexual dysfunction.

Health Psychology. Smoking, weight gain and loss, stress management, fitness, even dental care, can have major psychological implications. This specialty is concerned with the contribution of psychology to health maintenance.

Psychology of Aging. Understanding the physical, biological, sociological, and psychological impact of aging helps us cope with the catabolic processes of growing old.

Psychology and Law and Forensic Psychology. As we become more appreciative of the devastating effects of crime on communities, victims, and even juries, we can appreciate a branch of psychology that works with the law enforcement system to bridge the understanding between these two areas of life.

Psychology of Gender. The development of gender identity, the impact of socialization on that self-identity, issues of abuse (both sexual and physical), and hormonal influences are all worthy of a separate branch of psychological study.

CURRENT ISSUES IN PSYCHOLOGY

As in any science, but perhaps more so in psychology where the number of possible presenting issues are infinite, controversies solved are quickly replaced by new ones. The merits of short-term versus long-term therapy, current practice in the use of the mood-altering drug Prozac, the continuing intrusion of politics into the health-care system, what kinds of cases and remedies are deemed worthy of third-party insurance payments, and the mainstreaming of the mentally ill into communities, neighborhoods, and workplaces are just a few of today's issues. The psychological community grapples with these issues in the press, at scholarly and scientific congresses, and in the media.

In a recent *Psychology Today* article (February 2000), Dr. David Satcher, the U.S. Surgeon General, outlines the growing prominence of mental illness as a leading cause of disability in major market economies such as the United States. Mental disorders including depression, eating disorders, bipolar illness, anxiety, attention deficit disorder, and Alzheimer's disease are as significant as cancer and heart disease in terms of premature death and lost productivity. Dr. Satcher enumerates the barriers to accessing help, including social stigmas and insurance coverage. Our understanding of mental health is becoming increasingly more sophisticated and with that growing understanding, come increased opportunities for therapists, paraprofessionals, and other employment categories in the areas related to psychology.

The disagreement about the benefits of therapy and the requisite training for effective therapists is a small controversy compared to the lack of consensus in the area of abnormal psychology or psychopathology. Just as the psychoanalysts saw a continuum of mental health, there is disagreement on what constitutes abnormal behavior or thinking. If the norms are socially determined, then psychopathology becomes an outgrowth of social enculturation—a response to society and what it believes is healthy and not a science unto itself.

The American Psychological Association's (www.apa.org) redefinition of homosexuality is certainly a good example of the social relativism of abnormal psychology. This group no longer defines homosexual behavior as a mental illness.

Our stereotypical notion of psychology, dominated as it has been by a confusion with psychiatry, with antiquated visions of Viennese clinics, Oriental rugs, and leather couches, has swung quite widely to the more recent glamorous view of psychotherapy popularized in current films, where therapy appears as a natural adjunct to urban life. The new reality is somewhere between these fanciful notions as many more Americans both take up the study of psychology in college or increase their interaction with applied psychologists in any number of professions, including the medical practice of psychiatry.

WHERE DO PSYCHOLOGY GRADUATES FIT NOW?

In the most recent past, psychology graduates on the undergraduate level seeking employment after graduation have had to make do with jobs that overly generalized their skills from psychology to simply "people" skills. Graduates were not directly using their training in psychology. Today, as this text makes patently clear, there is ample work for the psychology graduate who wants to use his or her major in the areas of therapy, human resource management, residential care, or social and human services. And each of these areas has far more byways along the possible career path than any one book could outline.

Not many years ago, a support group for men dealing with prostate cancer and its effects would have been unfathomable. Now, men dealing with issues of impotence, incontinence, and loss of self-esteem and identity are able to come together with a facilitator and discuss, in a healing and supportive way, their challenges and successes in battling this disease. Many participants dramatically credit their lives to the support group. The leader of such a group may be an individual with a bachelor's or master's degree in psychology.

Psychologists now fill many roles other than physician or psychoanalyst. They are teachers, researchers, service providers (assessing needs, providing treatment), administrators (hospitals, government agencies, schools), and consultants (advising on problems in organizations, designing surveys, and organizing new patient systems).

Graduates today want to work with their psychology degree and find more opportunities to do so in drug intervention, institutions and halfway houses for individuals with mental illnesses and/or mental handicaps, testing, group-home counseling, geriatric counseling, youth center management, employment counseling, family planning, and biofeedback.

PSYCHOLOGY: A FUTURE OF CHANGE

Any field growing as fast as psychology is going to give the appearance of disharmony or confusion as it speeds along its exponential growth curve toward some kind of maturity, if only in chronological terms. The membership of the APA grows; new organizations such as The American Psychological Society appear; the number of books and journals produced each year multiplies and so do the arguments, controversies, and legal and ethical issues that such growth naturally incurs. Specialization increases, and just as the APA counts more than thirty subspecialties among its membership, there are infinitely more areas of study in psychology, some of them extremely narrow. Within this text we discuss some of the current issues, including counselor/therapist relations, drug therapy, and the efficacy of various interventions that impact and influence career pathing in psychology.

To suggest or attempt to outline the future of a field of study as diverse as psychology would be a very foolish exercise. A fairly substantial body of work discussing this science already exists. Individuals called "psychologists" can be working on issues as diverse as sound perceptivity or the causes of depression. George Miller, quoted in Sigmund Koch and David E. Leary's *A Century of Psychology as Science*,[1] has called psychology an "intellectual zoo." Psychology is really many psychologies and as you read your introductory text and wonder where the links are between chapters and how all these disparate sciences are related, you begin to get the merest hint of the bewilderment of the psychological community itself as it struggles to find some unifying theme or umbrella philosophy to unite itself.

....
1. New York: McGraw Hill, p. 40.

Even with the continuing dialogue on self-identify, it remains clear from this discussion that psychology is a science of great fertility, exploration, and dynamic change. Not only do we keep finding new areas of exploration, but new careers continue to appear as disciplines overlap and cross-disciplinary projects appear. Regrettably, the general public is still woefully ill-informed about the career potential for a student majoring in psychology. Some of this lack of understanding is clearly due to the implicit threat many people feel in any area of study having to do with personality or the human mind. As you continue your study of psychology, you're sure to encounter the individual who, upon hearing of your career aspirations, will say, "So, can you read my mind?"

Just as the general public is confused about the job of psychologists, it is equally confused about who practices psychology. Many people believe that all psychology practitioners are doctors. While most APA members do hold a doctorate, there are tens of thousands of individuals with bachelor's and master's degrees who work in psychology. They perform testing, counseling, supervised therapy, and a variety of psychology-related tasks in schools, clinics, group homes, hospitals, and private practices.

One of the most persistent indications of the newness of the study and practice of psychology is the stigma that remains in some quarters for those undergoing any kind of treatment for mental problems. Mental health is still not part of the wellness mandala for general health. This type of illness is treated much more suspiciously by the general public than any physical ailment no matter how devastating. People understand and sympathize with those afflicted with melanomas, pancreatic cancer, Alzheimer's disease, or fibro neuroblastomas, but don't have the same compassion and understanding for those suffering from schizophrenia, obsessive compulsive disorders, melancholia, and any of a number of psychoses.

Social problems in the latter half of the twentieth century multiplied, aggravated by economic and social influences. Homelessness, alienation, the breakdown of the nuclear family, the threat of violence, and social and racial tensions have only served to increase the need for chose pursuing an education in psychology. As these symptoms multiply and the difficulties increase, the need for skilled help at all levels becomes apparent. The ability for even those with a bachelor's degree to make a contribution is evident.

A recent survey on articles in the national press reveals the following conditions impacting on the behavior and mental health of individuals and groups:

❑ Job loss

❑ Molestation

- Depression

- Alienation

- Alzheimer's disease

- Agoraphobia

- Battering

- Light affective syndrome

- AIDS

- School violence

- Drug abuse

Today's graduates face and have faced these problems in their own lives and, for many, this is part of their desire to study psychology. Consequently, today's psychology programs involve more counseling and more developmental theory courses than ever before. Courses such as psychology of sexuality, psychology of aging, psychology of personality, psychology of sports, and others focus attention on the developmental impact of life stages and life events. Each of these topics presages fieldwork possibilities for the career-minded psychology graduate.

Many, when they hear psychology, think of teachers or professors. Our mention of the controversies in the field about professional versus nonprofessional practitioners only hinted at a more serious breach that has developed between the teachers of psychology and the practitioners. For a while the division was contained within the ranks of the American Psychological Association. Finally, a breakaway group of academics formed the American Psychological Society; the split was then complete and recognized.

There is no question that psychology, by its increasing prominence in our lives, has in many cases replaced religion, ethics, and other socially established norms for acceptable human behavior. The trend of psychology toward helping human behavior is seen in curriculums with more courses offered in clinical and developmental areas than in the heretofore prominent areas of experimental or industrial/organizational psychology. Some of this shift mirrors economic changes as we move from an industrial base to a service economy and individuals face more routinization in service occupations.

The future of psychology will not be in "schools" and may not revolve around one particular individual strongly associated with one approach. Psychology increasingly is engaged in service work to alleviate human suffering and with the technology available today, research into human behavior allows us to become increasingly quantitative in our findings. Futurists talk of finding medical cures for depression, migraines, substance abuse, and other ills that have had strong psychological components. New areas such as family, forensic, and psychology of women suggest the increasing "boutiquing" of areas of study and that nothing need remain remote from psychological scrutiny.

PART ONE

THE JOB SEARCH

CHAPTER ONE

THE
SELF-ASSESSMENT

Self-assessment is the process by which you begin to acknowledge your own particular blend of education, experiences, values, needs, and goals. It provides the foundation for career planning and the entire job search process. Self-assessment involves looking inward and asking yourself what can sometimes prove to be difficult questions. This self-examination should lead to an intimate understanding of your personal traits, your personal values, your consumption patterns and economic needs, your longer-term goals, your skill base, your preferred skills, and your underdeveloped skills.

You come to the self-assessment process knowing yourself well in some of these areas, but you may still be uncertain about other aspects. You may be well aware of your consumption patterns, but have you spent much time specifically identifying your longer-term goals or your personal values as they relate to work? No matter what level of self-assessment you have undertaken to date, it is now time to clarify all of these issues and questions as they relate to the job search.

The knowledge you gain in the self-assessment process will guide the rest of your job search. In this book, you will learn about all of the following tasks:

- Writing resumes

- Exploring possible job titles

- Identifying employment sites

- Networking

- Interviewing

- Following up

- Evaluating job offers

In each of these steps, you will rely on and often return to the understanding gained through your self-assessment. Any individual seeking employment must be able and willing to express these facets of his or her personality to recruiters and interviewers throughout the job search. This communication allows you to show the world who you are so that together with employers you can determine whether there will be a workable match with a given job or career path.

HOW TO CONDUCT A SELF-ASSESSMENT

The self-assessment process goes on naturally all the time. People ask you to clarify what you mean, you make a purchasing decision, or you begin a new relationship. You react to the world and the world reacts to you. How you understand these interactions and any changes you might make because of them are part of the natural process of self-discovery. There is, however, a more comprehensive and efficient way to approach self-assessment with regard to employment.

Because self-assessment can become a complex exercise, we have distilled it into a seven-step process that provides an effective basis for undertaking a job search. The seven steps include the following:

1. Understanding your personal traits

2. Identifying your personal values

3. Calculating your economic needs

4. Exploring your longer-term goals

5. Enumerating your skill base

6. Recognizing your preferred skills

7. Assessing skills needing further development

As you work through your self-assessment, you might want to create a worksheet similar to the one shown in Exhibit 1.1 starting on the following page. Or you might want to keep a journal of the thoughts you have as you undergo this process. There will be many opportunities to revise your self-assessment as you start down the path of seeking a career.

STEP 1 Understanding Your Personal Traits
Each person has a unique personality that he or she brings to the job search process. Gaining a better understanding of your personal traits can help you

---

Exhibit 1.1

Self-Assessment Worksheet

STEP 1. Understand Your Personal Traits
The personal traits that describe me are:
(Include all of the words that describe you.)

The ten personal traits that most accurately describe
me are: *(List these ten traits.)*

STEP 2. Identify Your Personal Values
Working conditions that are important to me include:
*(List working conditions that would have to exist for
you to accept a position.)*

The values that go along with my working conditions
are:
*(Write down the values that correspond to each
working condition.)*

Some additional values I've decided to include are:
*(List those values you identify as you conduct this job
search.)*

STEP 3. Calculate Your Economic Needs
My estimated minimum annual salary requirement is:
*(Write the salary you have calculated based on your
budget.)*

Starting salaries for the positions I'm considering are:
*(List the name of each job you are considering and
the associated starting salary.)*

STEP 4. Explore Your Longer-Term Goals
My thoughts on longer-term goals right now are:
*(Jot down some of your longer-term goals as you
know them right now.)*

STEP 5. Enumerate Your Skill Base

The general skills I possess are:
(List the skills that underlie tasks you are able to complete.)

The specific skills I possess are:
(List more technical or specific skills that you possess and indicate your level of expertise.)

General and specific skills that I want to promote to employers for the jobs I'm considering are:
(List general and specific skills for each type of job you are considering.)

STEP 6. Recognize Your Preferred Skills

Skills that I would like to use on the job include:
(List skills that you hope to use on the job, and indicate how often you'd like to use them.)

STEP 7. Assess Skills Needing Further Development

Some skills that I'll need to acquire for the jobs I'm considering include:
(Write down skills listed in job advertisements or job descriptions that you don't currently possess.)

I believe I can build these skills by:
(Describe how you plan to acquire these skills.)

evaluate job and career choices. Identifying these traits and then finding employment that allows you to draw on at least some of them can create a rewarding and fulfilling work experience. If potential employment doesn't allow you to use these preferred traits, it is important to decide whether you can find other ways to express them or whether you would be better off not considering this type of job. Interests and hobbies pursued outside of work hours can be one way to use personal traits you don't have an opportunity to draw on in your work. For example, if you consider yourself an outgoing person and the kinds of jobs you are examining allow little contact with other people, you may be able to achieve the level of interaction that is comfortable for you outside of your work setting. If such a compromise seems impractical or otherwise unsatisfactory, you probably should explore only jobs that provide the interaction you want and need on the job.

Many young adults who are not very confident about their attractiveness to employers will downplay their need for income. They will say, "Money is not all that important if I love my work." But if you begin to document exactly what you need for housing, transportation, insurance, clothing, food, and utilities, you will begin to understand that some jobs cannot meet your financial needs and it doesn't matter how wonderful the job is. If you have to worry each payday about bills and other financial obligations, you won't be very effective on the job. Begin now to be honest with yourself about your needs.

Inventorying Your Personal Traits. Begin the self-assessment process by creating an inventory of your personal traits. Using the list in Exhibit 1.2, decide which of these personal traits describe you.

Exhibit 1.2

Personal Traits

Accurate	Cooperative	Flexible
Active	Courageous	Formal
Adaptable	Critical	Friendly
Adventurous	Curious	Future-oriented
Affectionate	Daring	Generous
Aggressive	Decisive	Gentle
Ambitious	Deliberate	Good-natured
Analytical	Detail-oriented	Helpful
Appreciative	Determined	Honest
Artistic	Discreet	Humorous
Brave	Dominant	Idealistic
Businesslike	Eager	Imaginative
Calm	Easygoing	Impersonal
Capable	Efficient	Independent
Caring	Emotional	Individualistic
Cautious	Empathetic	Industrious
Cheerful	Energetic	Informal
Clean	Excitable	Innovative
Competent	Expressive	Intellectual
Confident	Extroverted	Intelligent
Conscientious	Fair-minded	Introverted
Conservative	Farsighted	Intuitive
Considerate	Feeling	Inventive
Cool	Firm	Jovial

Just	Poised	Sensitive
Kind	Polite	Serious
Liberal	Practical	Sincere
Likable	Precise	Sociable
Logical	Principled	Spontaneous
Loyal	Private	Strong
Mature	Productive	Strong-minded
Methodical	Progressive	Structured
Meticulous	Quick	Subjective
Mistrustful	Quiet	Tactful
Modest	Rational	Thorough
Motivated	Realistic	Thoughtful
Objective	Receptive	Tolerant
Observant	Reflective	Trusting
Open-minded	Relaxed	Trustworthy
Opportunistic	Reliable	Truthful
Optimistic	Reserved	Understanding
Organized	Resourceful	Unexcitable
Original	Responsible	Uninhibited
Outgoing	Reverent	Verbal
Patient	Sedentary	Versatile
Peaceable	Self-confident	Wholesome
Personable	Self-controlled	Wise
Persuasive	Self-disciplined	
Pleasant	Sensible	

Focusing on Selected Personal Traits. Of all the traits you identified from the list in Exhibit 1.2, select the ten you believe most accurately describe you. If you are having a difficult time deciding, think about which words people who know you well would use to describe you. Keep track of these ten traits.

Considering Your Personal Traits in the Job Search Process. As you begin exploring jobs and careers, watch for matches between your personal traits and the job descriptions you read. Some jobs will require many personal traits you know you possess, and others will not seem to match those traits.

· ·

A residential counselor's work in a psychiatric treatment facility will draw on your reserves of patience, empathy, and energy. Residential counselors in this type of facility are important members of the treatment team and will

> interact frequently with other professionals to ensure quality care and treatment for clients. Teamwork and strong communications skills are essential. There is also a demand for strong writing skills because you will be completing process notes and evaluative summaries on those clients in your care.

·······································

Your ability to respond to changing conditions, your decision-making ability, productivity, creativity, and verbal skills all have a bearing on your success in and enjoyment of your work life. To better guarantee success, be sure to take the time needed to understand these traits in yourself.

STEP 2 Identifying Your Personal Values

Your personal values affect every aspect of your life, including employment, and they develop and change as you move through life. Values can be defined as principles that we hold in high regard, qualities that are important and desirable to us. Some values aren't ordinarily connected to work (love, beauty, color, light, relationships, family, or religion), and others are (autonomy, cooperation, effectiveness, achievement, knowledge, and security). Our values determine, in part, the level of satisfaction we feel in a particular job.

Defining Acceptable Working Conditions. One facet of employment is the set of working conditions that must exist for someone to consider taking a job.

Each of us would probably create a unique list of acceptable working conditions, but items that might be included on many people's lists are the amount of money you would need to be paid, how far you are willing to drive or travel, the amount of freedom you want in determining your own schedule, whether you would be working with people or data or things, and the types of tasks you would be willing to do. Your conditions might include statements of working conditions you will *not* accept; for example, you might not be willing to work at night or on weekends or holidays.

If you were offered a job tomorrow, what conditions would have to exist for you to realistically consider accepting the position? Take some time and make a list of these conditions.

Realizing Associated Values. Your list of working conditions can be used to create an inventory of your values relating to jobs and careers you are exploring. For example, if one of your conditions stated that you wanted to earn at least $30,000 per year, the associated value would be financial gain. If another condition was that you wanted to work with a friendly group of

---

Exhibit 1.3

Work Values

Achievement	Development	Physical activity
Advancement	Effectiveness	Power
Adventure	Excitement	Precision
Attainment	Fast pace	Prestige
Authority	Financial gain	Privacy
Autonomy	Helping	Profit
Belonging	Humor	Recognition
Challenge	Improvisation	Risk
Change	Independence	Security
Communication	Influencing others	Self-expression
Community	Intellectual stimulation	Solitude
Competition	Interaction	Stability
Completion	Knowledge	Status
Contribution	Leading	Structure
Control	Mastery	Supervision
Cooperation	Mobility	Surroundings
Creativity	Moral fulfillment	Time freedom
Decision making	Organization	Variety

---

people, the value that went along with that might be belonging or interaction with people. Exhibit 1.3 provides a list of commonly held values that relate to the work environment; use it to create your own list of personal values.

Relating Your Values to the World of Work. As you read the job descriptions in this book and in other suggested resources, think about the values associated with each position.

•••

> For example, a residential care counselor's duties would include assisting in the implementation of treatment interventions, counseling clients, organizing and supervising group activities, case management, and aftercare planning.

•••

If you were thinking about a career in this field, or any other field you're exploring, at least some of the associated values should match those you extracted from your list of working conditions. Take a second look at any values that don't match up. How important are they to you? What will happen if they are not satisfied on the job? Can you incorporate those personal values elsewhere? Your answers need to be brutally honest. As you continue your exploration, be sure to add to your list any additional values that occur to you.

STEP 3 Calculating Your Economic Needs

Each of us grew up in an environment that provided for certain basic needs, such as food and shelter, and, to varying degrees, other needs that we now consider basic, such as cable TV, E-mail, or an automobile. Needs such as privacy, space, and quiet, which at first glance may not appear to be monetary needs, may add to housing expenses and so should be considered as you examine your economic needs. For example, if you place a high value on a large, open living space for yourself, it would be difficult to satisfy that need without an associated high housing cost, especially in a densely populated city environment.

As you prepare to move into the world of work and become responsible for meeting your own basic needs, it is important to consider the salary you will need to be able to afford a satisfying standard of living. The three-step process outlined here will help you plan a budget, which in turn will allow you to evaluate the various career choices and geographic locations you are considering. The steps include (1) developing a realistic budget, (2) examining starting salaries, and (3) using a cost-of-living index.

Developing a Realistic Budget. Each of us has certain expectations for the kind of lifestyle we want to maintain. In order to begin the process of defining your economic needs, it will be helpful to determine what you expect to spend on routine monthly expenses. These expenses include housing, food, transportation, entertainment, utilities, loan repayments, and revolving charge accounts. A worksheet that details many of these expenses is shown in Exhibit 1.4. You may not currently spend anything for certain items, but you probably will have to once you begin supporting yourself. As you develop this budget, be generous in your estimates, but keep in mind any items that could be reduced or eliminated. If you are not sure about the cost

---

Exhibit 1.4

Estimated Monthly Expenses Worksheet

		Could Reduce Spending? (Yes/No)
Cable	$ _____	_____
Child care	_____	_____

		Could Reduce Spending? (Yes/No)
Clothing	$ _____	_____
Educational loan repayment	_____	_____
Entertainment	_____	_____
Food		
At home	_____	_____
Meals out	_____	_____
Gifts	_____	_____
Housing		
Rent/mortgage	_____	_____
Insurance	_____	_____
Property taxes	_____	_____
Medical insurance	_____	_____
Reading materials		
Newspapers	_____	_____
Magazines	_____	_____
Books	_____	_____
Revolving loans/charges	_____	_____
Savings	_____	_____
Telephone	_____	_____
Transportation		
Auto payment	_____	_____
Insurance	_____	_____
Parking	_____	_____
Gasoline	_____	_____
or		
Cab/train/bus fare	_____	_____
Utilities		
Electric	_____	_____
Gas	_____	_____
Water/sewer	_____	_____
Vacations	_____	_____
Miscellaneous expense 1	_____	_____
Expense: _____		
Miscellaneous expense 2	_____	_____
Expense: _____		
Miscellaneous expense 3	_____	_____
Expense: _____		

TOTAL MONTHLY EXPENSES: _____

YEARLY EXPENSES (Monthly expenses × 12): _____

INCREASE TO INCLUDE TAXES (Yearly expenses × 1.35): ___ =

MINIMUM ANNUAL SALARY REQUIREMENT: _____

of a certain item, talk with family or friends who would be able to give you a realistic estimate.

If this is new or difficult for you, start to keep a log of expenses right now. You may be surprised at how much you actually spend each month for food or stamps or magazines. Household expenses and personal grooming items can often loom very large in a budget, as can auto repairs or home maintenance.

Income taxes must also be taken into consideration when examining salary requirements. State and local taxes vary by location, so it is difficult to calculate exactly the effect of taxes on the amount of income you need to generate. To roughly estimate the gross income necessary to generate your minimum annual salary requirement, multiply the minimum salary you have calculated (see Exhibit 1.4) by a factor of 1.35. The resulting figure will be an approximation of what your gross income would need to be, given your estimated expenses.

Examining Starting Salaries. Starting salaries for each of the career tracks are provided throughout this book. These salary figures can be used in conjunction with the cost-of-living index (discussed in the next section) to determine whether you would be able to meet your basic economic needs in a given geographic location.

Using a Cost-of-Living Index. If you are thinking about trying to get a job in a geographic region other than the one where you now live, understanding differences in the cost of living will help you come to a more informed decision about making a move. By using a cost-of-living index, you can compare salaries offered and the cost of living in different locations with what you know about the salaries offered and the cost of living in your present location.

Many variables are used to calculate the cost-of-living index. Often included are housing, groceries, utilities, transportation, health care, clothing, and entertainment expenses. Right now you do not need to worry about the details associated with calculating a given index. The main purpose of this exercise is to help you understand that pay ranges for entry-level positions may not vary greatly, but the cost of living in different locations *can* vary tremendously.

. . . .

If you lived in Cleveland, Ohio, for example, and you were interested in working as a human resources generalist, you would plan on earning $29,053 annually. But let's say you're also thinking about moving to New York,

Los Angeles, or Houston. You know you can live on $29,053 in Cleveland, but you want to be able to equal that salary in the other locations you're considering. How much will you have to earn in those locations to do this? Determining the cost of living for each city will show you.

There are many websites like Home Fair's (www .homefair.com/homefair/cmr/salcalc.html) that can assist you as you undertake this research. Use any search engine and enter the keywords *cost of living index*. Several choices will appear. Choose one site and look for options like cost-of-living analysis or cost-of-living comparator. Some sites will ask you to register and/or pay for the information, but most sites are free. Follow the instructions provided and you will be able to create a table of information like the one shown below.

Job: Human Resources Generalist		
City	Base Amount	Equivalent Salary
Cleveland, OH	$29,053	
New York, NY		$32,772
Los Angeles, CA		$35,795
Minneapolis, MN		$31,738

At the time this comparison was done, you would have needed to earn $32,772 in New York, $35,795 in Los Angeles, and $31,738 in Minneapolis to match the buying power of $29,053 in Cleveland.

If you would like to determine whether it's financially worthwhile to make any of these moves, one more piece of information is needed: the salaries of human resources generalists in these other cities. One example of a website that contains job descriptions and salary information is WageWeb (www.wageweb.com). This site focuses information and services on the following fields: human resources, administration, finance, information management, engineering, health care, sales/marketing, and manufacturing. WageWeb reports the following average actual lowest salary paid for the cities being considered. These figures reflect entry-level salaries.

City	Actual Lowest Salary	Equivalent Salary Needed	Change in Buying Power
New York, NY	$33,301	$32,772	+ $529
Los Angeles, CA	$36,465	$35,795	+ $670
Minneapolis, MN	$30,895	$31,738	– $843

If you moved to New York City and secured employment as a human resources generalist you would be able to maintain a lifestyle similar to the one you lead in Cleveland. In fact, you would be able to enhance your lifestyle very modestly given the slight increase in buying power. The same would be true with a move to Los Angeles. Moving to Minneapolis from Cleveland, however, would modestly decrease your buying power. Remember, these figures change all the time, so be sure to undertake your own calculations. If you would like to see the formula used, you can visit a website like Deloitte & Touche (www.dtonline.com).

• •

You can work through a similar exercise for any type of job you are considering and for many locations when current salary information is available. It will be worth your time to undertake this analysis if you are seriously considering a relocation. By doing so you will be able to make an informed choice.

STEP 4   Exploring Your Longer-Term Goals

There is no question that when we first begin working, our goals are to use our skills and education in a job that will reward us with employment, income, and status relative to the preparation we brought with us to this position. If we are not being paid as much as we feel we should for our level of education, or if job demands don't provide the intellectual stimulation we had hoped for, we experience unhappiness and as a result often seek other employment.

Most jobs we consider "good" are those that fulfill our basic "lower-level" needs of security, food, clothing, shelter, income, and productive work. But even when our basic needs are met and our jobs are secure and productive, we as individuals are constantly changing. As we change, the demands and expectations we place on our jobs may change. Fortunately, some jobs grow and change with us, and this explains why some people are happy throughout many years in a job.

But more often people are bigger than the jobs they fill. We have more goals and needs than any job could fulfill. These are "higher-level" needs of self-esteem, companionship, affection, and an increasing desire to feel we are employing ourselves in the most effective way possible. Not all of these higher-level needs can be fulfilled through employment, but for as long as we are employed, we increasingly demand that our jobs play their part in moving us along the path to fulfillment.

Another obvious but important fact is that we change as we mature. Although our jobs also have the potential for change, they may not change as frequently or as markedly as we do. There are increasingly fewer one-job, one-employer careers; we must think about a work future that may involve voluntary or forced moves from employer to employer. Because of that very real possibility, we need to take advantage of the opportunities in each position we hold to acquire skills and competencies that will keep us viable and attractive as employees in a job market that is not only technology/computer dependent, but also is populated with more and more small, self-transforming organizations rather than the large, seemingly stable organizations of the past.

It may be difficult in the early stages of the job search to determine whether the path you are considering can meet these longer-term goals. Reading about career paths and individual career histories in your field can be very helpful in this regard. Meeting and talking with individuals further along in their careers can be enlightening as well. Older workers can provide valuable guidance on "self-managing" your career, which will become an increasingly valuable skill in the future. Some of these ideas may seem remote as you read this now, but you should be able to appreciate the need to ensure that you are growing, developing valuable new skills, and researching other employers who might be interested in your particular skills package.

....

If you are considering a position in human resources for a corporation, you would gain a better perspective on this career if you could talk to an entry-level personnel officer, a more senior and experienced staff member, and,

finally, a department head with considerable work history. Each will have a different perspective, unique concerns, and an individual set of value priorities.

••

STEP 5   Enumerating Your Skill Base

In terms of the job search, skills can be thought of as capabilities that can be developed in school, at work, or by volunteering and then used in specific job settings. Many studies have documented the kinds of skills that employers seek in entry-level applicants. For example, some of the most desired skills for individuals interested in the teaching profession include the ability to interact effectively with students one on one, to manage a classroom, to adapt to varying situations as necessary, and to get involved in school activities. Business employers have also identified important qualities, including enthusiasm for the employer's product or service, a businesslike mind, the ability to follow written or verbal instructions, the ability to demonstrate self-control, the confidence to suggest new ideas, the ability to communicate with all members of a group, an awareness of cultural differences, and loyalty, to name just a few. You will find that many of these skills are also in the repertoire of qualities demanded in your college major.

In order to be successful in obtaining any given job, you must be able to demonstrate that you possess a certain mix of skills that will allow you to carry out the duties required by that job. This skill mix will vary a great deal from job to job; to determine the skills necessary for the jobs you are seeking, you can read job advertisements or more generic job descriptions, such as those found later in this book. If you want to be effective in the job search, you must directly show employers that you possess the skills needed to be successful in filling the position. These skills will initially be described on your resume and then discussed again during the interview process.

Skills are either general or specific. General skills are those that are developed throughout the college years by taking classes, being employed, and getting involved in other related activities such as volunteer work or campus organizations. General skills include the ability to read and write, to perform computations, to think critically, and to communicate effectively. Specific skills are also acquired on the job and in the classroom, but they allow you to complete tasks that require specialized knowledge. Computer programming, drafting, language translating, and copyediting are just a few examples of specific skills that may relate to a given job.

In order to develop a list of skills relevant to employers, you must first identify the general skills you possess, then list specific skills you have to offer, and, finally, examine which of these skills employers are seeking.

Identifying Your General Skills. Because you possess or will possess a college degree, employers will assume that you can read and write, perform certain basic computations, think critically, and communicate effectively. Employers will want to see that you have acquired these skills, and they will want to know which additional general skills you possess.

One way to begin identifying skills is to write an experiential diary. An experiential diary lists all the tasks you were responsible for completing for each job you've held and then outlines the skills required to do those tasks. You may list several skills for any given task. This diary allows you to distinguish between the tasks you performed and the underlying skills required to complete those tasks. Here's an example:

Tasks	Skills
Answering telephone	Effective use of language, clear diction, ability to direct inquiries, ability to solve problems
Waiting on tables	Poise under conditions of time and pressure, speed, accuracy, good memory, simultaneous completion of tasks, sales skills

For each job or experience you have participated in, develop a worksheet based on the example shown here. On a resume, you may want to describe these skills rather than simply listing tasks. Skills are easier for the employer to appreciate, especially when your experience is very different from the employment you are seeking. In addition to helping you identify general skills, this experiential diary will prepare you to speak more effectively in an interview about the qualifications you possess.

Identifying Your Specific Skills. It may be easier to identify your specific skills because you can definitely say whether you can speak other languages, program a computer, draft a map or diagram, or edit a document using appropriate symbols and terminology.

Using your experiential diary, identify the points in your history where you learned how to do something very specific and decide whether you have a beginning, intermediate, or advanced knowledge of how to use that particular skill. Right now, be sure to list *every* specific skill you have, and don't consider whether you like using the skill. Write down a list of specific skills you have acquired and the level of competence you possess—beginning, intermediate, or advanced.

Relating Your Skills to Employers. You probably have thought about a couple of different jobs you might be interested in obtaining, and one way to begin relating the general and specific skills you possess to a potential employer's needs is to read actual advertisements for these types of positions (see Part Two for resources listing actual job openings).

••

For example, you might be interested in working as a labor relations specialist. A typical job listing might read, "Maintain records on employee attendance, compliance with contracts, eligibility for insurance and benefits. College degree required, preferably one year of experience." If you then used any one of a number of general sources of information that describe the job of labor relations specialist, you would find additional information. Labor relations specialists also do research and paperwork for individual employee grievance reports, attend grievance meetings as an assistant, and compile facts and figures for company labor negotiations.

Begin building a comprehensive list of required skills with the first job description you read. Exploring advertisements for and descriptions of several types of related positions will reveal an important core of skills that are necessary for obtaining the type of work you're interested in. In building this list, include both general and specific skills.

The following is a sample list of skills needed to be successful as a labor relations specialist. These items were extracted from both general resources and actual job listings.

Job: Labor Relations Specialist	
General Skills	Specific Skills
Perform clerical duties	Investigate complaints
Gather information	Prepare attendance
Enter data into	records
computer	Maintain good
Conduct research	employee relations
Meet deadlines	Assist in labor
Exhibit drive	negotiations

Exhibit precision	Ensure contract
Collaborate on projects	compliance
Attend meetings	Train employees
Read	

On separate sheets of paper, try to generate a comprehensive list of required skills for at least one job you are considering.

The list of general skills that you develop for a given career path will be valuable for any number of jobs you might apply for. Many of the specific skills would also be transferable to other types of positions. For example, ensuring contract compliance is a required skill for some labor management specialists, and it also would be required or some outplacement coordinators, as well.

. . . .

Now review the list of skills you developed and check off those skills that *you know you possess* and that are required for jobs you are considering. You should refer to these specific skills on the resume that you write for this type of job. See Chapter 2 for details on resume writing.

STEP 6   Recognizing Your Preferred Skills

In the previous section you developed a comprehensive list of skills that relate to particular career paths that are of interest to you. You can now relate these to skills that you prefer to use. We all use a wide range of skills (some researchers say individuals have a repertoire of about 500 skills), but we may not be particularly interested in using all of them in our work. There may be some skills that come to us more naturally or that we use successfully time and time again and that we want to continue to use; these are best described as our preferred skills. For this exercise use the list of skills that you developed for the previous section and decide which of them you are *most interested in using* in future work and how often you would like to use them. You might be interested in using some skills only occasionally, while others you would like to use more regularly. You probably also have skills that you hope you can use constantly.

As you examine job announcements, look for matches between this list of preferred skills and the qualifications described in the advertisements. These skills should be highlighted on your resume and discussed in job interviews.

STEP 7 Assessing Skills Needing Further Development

Previously you developed a list of general and specific skills required for given positions. You already possess some of these skills; those that remain to be developed are your underdeveloped skills.

If you are just beginning the job search, there may be gaps between the qualifications required for some of the jobs you're considering and skills you possess. The thought of having to admit to and talk about these underdeveloped skills, especially in a job interview, is a frightening one. One way to put a healthy perspective on this subject is to target and relate your exploration of underdeveloped skills to the types of positions you are seeking. Recognizing these shortcomings and planning to overcome them with either on-the-job training or additional formal education can be a positive way to address the concept of underdeveloped skills.

On your worksheet or in your journal, make a list of up to five general or specific skills required for the positions you're interested in that you *don't currently possess.* For each item list an idea you have for specific action you could take to acquire that skill. Do some brainstorming to come up with possible actions. If you have a hard time generating ideas, talk to people currently working in this type of position, professionals in your college career services office, trusted friends, family members, or members of related professional associations.

If, for example, you are interested in a job for which you don't have some specific required experience, you could locate training opportunities such as classes or workshops offered through a local college or university, community college, or club or association that would help you build the level of expertise you need for the job.

You will notice in this book that many excellent positions for your major demand computer skills. While basic word processing has been something you've done all through college, you may be surprised at the additional computer skills required by employers. Many positions for college graduates will ask for some familiarity with spreadsheet programming, and frequently some database-management software familiarity is a job demand as well. Desktop publishing software, graphics programs, and basic Web-page design also pop up frequently in job ads for college graduates. If your degree program hasn't introduced you to a wide variety of computer applications, what are your options? If you're still in college, take what computer courses you can before you graduate. If you've already graduated, look at evening programs, continuing education courses, or tutorial programs that may be available commercially. Developing a modest level of expertise will encourage you to be more confident in suggesting to potential employers that you can continue to add to your skill base on the job.

In Chapter 5 on interviewing, we will discuss in detail how to effectively address questions about underdeveloped skills. Generally speaking, though, employers want genuine answers to these types of questions. They want you to reveal "the real you," and they also want to see how you answer difficult questions. In taking the positive, targeted approach discussed above, you show the employer that you are willing to continue to learn and that you have a plan for strengthening your job qualifications.

USING YOUR SELF-ASSESSMENT

Exploring entry-level career options can be an exciting experience if you have good resources available and will take the time to use them. Can you effectively complete the following tasks?

1. Understand and relate your personality traits to career choices

2. Define your personal values

3. Determine your economic needs

4. Explore longer-term goals

5. Understand your skill base

6. Recognize your preferred skills

7. Express a willingness to improve on your underdeveloped skills

If so, then you can more meaningfully participate in the job search process by writing a more effective resume, finding job titles that represent work you are interested in doing, locating job sites that will provide the opportunity for you to use your strengths and skills, networking in an informed way, participating in focused interviews, getting the most out of follow-up contacts, and evaluating job offers to find those that create a good match between you and the employer. The remaining chapters in Part One guide you through these next steps in the job search process. For many job seekers, this process can take anywhere from three months to a year to implement. The time you will need to put into your job search will depend on the type of job you want and the geographic location where you'd like to work. Think of your effort as a job in itself, requiring you to set aside time each week to complete the needed work. Carefully undertaken efforts may reduce the time you need for your job search.

CHAPTER TWO

THE RESUME AND COVER LETTER

T he task of writing a resume may seem overwhelming if you are unfamiliar with this type of document, but there are some easily understood techniques that can and should be used. This section was written to help you understand the purpose of the resume, the different types of resume formats available, and how to write the sections of information traditionally found on a resume. We will present examples and explanations that address questions frequently posed by people writing their first resume or updating an old resume.

Even within the formats and suggestions given, however, there are infinite variations. True, most resumes follow one of the outlines suggested, but you should feel free to adjust the resume to suit your needs and make it expressive of your life and experience.

WHY WRITE A RESUME?

The purpose of a resume is to convince an employer that you should be interviewed. Whether you're mailing, faxing, or E-mailing this document, you'll want to present enough information to show that you can make an immediate and valuable contribution to an organization. A resume is not an indepth historical or legal document; later in the job search process you may be asked to document your entire work history on an application form and attest to its validity. The resume should, instead, highlight relevant information pertaining directly to the organization that will receive the document or to the type of position you are seeking.

We will discuss four types of resumes in this chapter: the chronological resume, functional resume, targeted resume, and the digital resume. The reasons for using one type of resume over another and the typical format for each are addressed in the following sections.

THE CHRONOLOGICAL RESUME

The chronological resume is the most common of the various resume formats and therefore the format that employers are most used to receiving. This type of resume is easy to read and understand because it details the chronological progression of jobs you have held. (See Exhibit 2.1.) It begins with your most recent employment and works back in time. If you have a solid work history or have experience that provided growth and development in your duties and responsibilities, a chronological resume will highlight these achievements. The typical elements of a chronological resume include the heading, a career objective, educational background, employment experience, activities, and references.

The Heading

The heading consists of your name, address, telephone number, and other means of contact. This may include a fax number, E-mail address, and your home-page address. If you are using a shared E-mail account or a parent's business fax, be sure to let others who use these systems know that you may receive important professional correspondence via these systems. You wouldn't want to miss a vital E-mail or fax! Likewise, if your resume directs readers to a personal home page on the Web, be certain it's a *professional* personal home page designed to be viewed and appreciated by a prospective employer. This may mean making substantial changes in the home page you currently mount on the Web.

We suggest that you spell out your full name in your resume heading and type it in all capital letters in bold type. After all, you are the focus of the resume! If you have a current as well as a permanent address and you include both in the heading, be sure to indicate until what date your current address will be valid. The two-letter state abbreviation should be the only abbreviation that appears in your heading. Don't forget to include the zip code with your address and the area code with your telephone number.

The Objective

As you formulate the wording for this part of your resume, keep the following points in mind.

Exhibit 2.1

Chronological Resume

LARI MIDDLEKAUFF

Student Apartments #17   201 East Main Road
Ball State University   Orient Heights, RI 38967
Muncie, IN 47306   (401) 555-1700
(317) 555-2336
lmiddle@xxx.com
(until May 2004)

OBJECTIVE

Entry-level position in human resources. Special interest in developing and delivering staff training programs.

EDUCATION

Bachelor of Arts in Psychology
Ball State University, Muncie, Indiana
May 2004
Minor: Business

EXPERIENCE

Resident Assistant, Ball State University, Muncie, IN, 2002–Present.
Member of a six-person staff assisting the director of a 240-resident living unit on campus. Responsible for policies, procedures, and discipline associated with campus congregate living. Developed and presented programming on a variety of subjects, including alcohol awareness, career issues, leadership, and time management.

Student Ambassador, Ball State University, Muncie, IN, 2000–01. Led campus tours for prospective students and parents. Telephoned prospective students and assisted with TGIF programs.

Projectionist/Media Coordinator, Gordon Research Conference, Bedford, IN, Summers, 2000–Present.

Provided all media needs for international conference of scientists. Worked with speakers from many different countries to provide audiovisual needs on short notice.

continued

---

continued

PRESENTATIONS

"ZAPPED! The Lightning of Empowerment," Program on value of empowering group members. Presented at NASPA conference, Hartford, CT, 2003.

"Using Type to Enhance Effectiveness," The Myers-Briggs Type Indicator as a tool in group cohesion and goal setting. Mid-Atlantic Student Professionals Conference, Baltimore, MD, Spring 2003.

"How to Be a Motivating Leader," New Resident Assistants' Retreat, Alexandria Bay, NY, Summer 2002.

ACTIVITIES

Theatre Society, active member, three years. *The Clock*, student newspaper, staff writer, three semesters. Model United Nations, conference coordinator, one year.

REFERENCES

Excellent personal and professional references are available upon request.

The Objective Focuses the Resume. Without a doubt this is the most challenging part of the resume for most resume writers. Even for individuals who have quite firmly decided on a career path, it can be difficult to encapsulate all they want to say in one or two brief sentences. For job seekers who are unfocused or unclear about their intentions, trying to write this section can inhibit the entire resume writing process.

Recruiters tell us, time and time again, that the objective creates a frame of reference for them. It helps them see how you express your goals and career focus. In addition, the statement may indicate in what ways you can immediately benefit an organization. Given the importance of the objective, every point covered in the resume should relate to it. If information doesn't relate, it should be omitted. You'll file a number of resume variations in your computer. There's no excuse for not being able to tailor a resume to individual employers or specific positions.

Choose an Appropriate Length. Because of the brevity necessary for a resume, you should keep the objective as short as possible. Although objectives of only four or five words often don't show much direction, objectives that take three full lines could be viewed as too wordy and might possibly be ignored.

Consider Which Type of Objective Statement You Will Use. There are many ways to state an objective, but generally there are four forms this statement can take: (1) a very general statement; (2) a statement focused on a specific position; (3) a statement focused on a specific industry; or (4) a summary of your qualifications. In our contacts with employers, we often hear that many resumes don't exhibit any direction or career goals, so we suggest avoiding general statements when possible.

1. General Objective Statement. General objective statements look like the following:

❑ An entry-level educational programming coordinator position

❑ An entry-level marketing position

This type of objective would be useful if you know what type of job you want but you're not sure which industries interest you.

2. Position-Focused Objective. Following are examples of objectives focusing on a specific position:

❑ To obtain the position of conference coordinator at State College

❑ To obtain a position as assistant editor at *Time* magazine

When a student applies for an advertised job opening, this type of focus can be very effective. The employer knows that the applicant has taken the time to tailor the resume specifically for this position.

3. Industry-Focused Objective. Focusing on a particular industry in an objective could be stated as follows:

❑ To begin a career as a sales representative in the cruise line industry

4. Summary of Qualifications Statement. The summary of qualifications can be used instead of an objective or in conjunction with an objective. The purpose of this type of statement is to highlight relevant qualifications gained through a variety of experiences. This type of statement is often used by individuals with extensive and diversified work experience. An example of a qualifications statement follows:

....

A degree in psychology and four years of progressively increasing job responsibility in every department of a local bank have prepared me to begin a career as a human resource management trainee with an organization that values thoroughness and attention to detail.

....

Support Your Objective. A resume that contains any one of these types of objective statements should then go on to demonstrate why you are qualified to get the position. Listing academic degrees can be one way to indicate qualifications. Another demonstration would be in the way previous experiences, both volunteer and paid, are described. Without this kind of documentation in the body of the resume, the objective looks unsupported. Think of the resume as telling a connected story about you. All the elements should work together to form a coherent picture that ideally should relate to your statement of objective.

Education

This section of your resume should indicate the exact name of the degree you will receive or have received, spelled out completely with no abbreviations. The degree is generally listed after the objective, followed by the institution name and address, and then the month and year of graduation. This section could also include your academic minor, grade point average (GPA), and appearance on the Dean's List or President's List.

If you have enough space, you might want to include a section listing courses related to the field in which you are seeking work. The best use of a "related courses" section would be to list some course work that is not traditionally associated with the major. Perhaps you took several computer courses outside your degree that will be helpful and related to the job prospects you are entertaining. Several education section examples are shown here:

....

❑ Bachelor of Arts in Interdisciplinary Studies,
a self-designed program concentrating on
Interpersonal Relations and Business,
Bristol University, Bristol, TN, May 2000

❑ Bachelor of Science Degree in Psychology
University of North Dakota, Grand Forks, ND,
December 2000 Minor: Communications

❑ Bachelor of Science Degree in Psychology
Columbia College, Columbia, IL, May 2000

An example of a format for a related courses section follows:

RELATED COURSES

Desktop Publishing	Computer Graphics
Technical Writing	Human Resource Management
Group Counseling	Organizational Communications

Experience

The experience section of your resume should be the most substantial part and should take up most of the space on the page. Employers want to see what kind of work history you have. They will look at your range of experiences, longevity in jobs, and specific tasks you are able to complete. This section may also be called "work experience," "related experience," "employment history," or "employment." No matter what you call this section, some important points to remember are the following:

1. **Describe your duties** as they relate to the position you are seeking.

2. **Emphasize major responsibilities** and indicate increases in responsibility. Include all relevant employment experiences: summer, part-time, internships, cooperative education, or self-employment.

3. **Emphasize skills**, especially those that transfer from one situation to another. The fact that you coordinated a student organization, chaired meetings, supervised others, and managed a budget leads one to suspect that you could coordinate other things as well.

4. **Use descriptive job titles** that provide information about what you did. A "Student Intern" should be more specifically stated as, for example, "Magazine Operations Intern." "Volunteer" is also too general; a title such as "Peer Writing Tutor" would be more appropriate.

5. **Create word pictures** by using active verbs to start sentences. Describe *results* you have produced in the work you have done.

A limp description would say something like the following: "My duties included helping with production, proofreading, and editing. I used a word-processing package to alter text." An action statement would be stated as follows: "Coordinated and assisted in the creative marketing of brochures and seminar promotions, becoming proficient in Word."

Remember, an accomplishment is simply a result, a final measurable product that people can relate to. A duty is not a result, it is an obligation—every job holder has duties. For an effective resume, list as many results as you can. To make the most of the limited space you have and to give your description impact, carefully select appropriate and accurate descriptors from the list of action words in Exhibit 2.2.

Exhibit 2.2

Resume Action Verbs

Achieved	Developed	Introduced
Acted	Directed	Learned
Administered	Documented	Lectured
Advised	Drafted	Led
Analyzed	Edited	Maintained
Assessed	Eliminated	Managed
Assisted	Ensured	Mapped
Attained	Established	Marketed
Balanced	Estimated	Met
Budgeted	Evaluated	Modified
Calculated	Examined	Monitored
Collected	Explained	Negotiated
Communicated	Facilitated	Observed
Compiled	Finalized	Obtained
Completed	Generated	Operated
Composed	Handled	Organized
Conceptualized	Headed	Participated
Condensed	Helped	Performed
Conducted	Identified	Planned
Consolidated	Illustrated	Predicted
Constructed	Implemented	Prepared
Controlled	Improved	Presented
Converted	Increased	Processed
Coordinated	Influenced	Produced
Corrected	Informed	Projected
Created	Initiated	Proposed
Decreased	Innovated	Provided
Defined	Instituted	Qualified
Demonstrated	Instructed	Quantified
Designed	Integrated	Questioned
Determined	Interpreted	Realized

continued

<table>
<tr><td colspan="3">continued</td></tr>
<tr><td>Received</td><td>Scheduled</td><td>Studied</td></tr>
<tr><td>Recommended</td><td>Selected</td><td>Submitted</td></tr>
<tr><td>Recorded</td><td>Served</td><td>Summarized</td></tr>
<tr><td>Reduced</td><td>Showed</td><td>Systematized</td></tr>
<tr><td>Reinforced</td><td>Simplified</td><td>Tabulated</td></tr>
<tr><td>Reported</td><td>Sketched</td><td>Tested</td></tr>
<tr><td>Represented</td><td>Sold</td><td>Transacted</td></tr>
<tr><td>Researched</td><td>Solved</td><td>Updated</td></tr>
<tr><td>Resolved</td><td>Staffed</td><td>Verified</td></tr>
<tr><td>Reviewed</td><td>Streamlined</td><td></td></tr>
</table>

Here are some traits that employers tell us they like to see:

- Teamwork
- Energy and motivation
- Learning and using new skills
- Demonstrated versatility
- Critical thinking
- Understanding how profits are created
- Displaying organizational acumen
- Communicating directly and clearly, in both writing and speaking
- Risk taking
- Willingness to admit mistakes
- Manifesting high personal standards

SOLUTIONS TO FREQUENTLY ENCOUNTERED PROBLEMS

Repetitive Employment with the Same Employer

EMPLOYMENT: The Foot Locker, Portland, Oregon. Summer 2001, 2002, 2003. Initially employed in high school as salesclerk. Due to successful performance, asked to return next two summers at higher pay with added responsibility. Ranked as the #2 salesperson the first summer and #1 the next two summers. Assisted in arranging eye-catching retail displays; served as manager of other summer workers during owner's absence.

A Large Number of Jobs

EMPLOYMENT: Recent Hospitality Industry Experience: Affiliated with four upscale hotel/restaurant complexes (September 2001–February 2004), where I worked part- and full-time as a waiter, bartender, disc jockey, and bookkeeper to produce income for college.

Several Positions with the Same Employer

EMPLOYMENT: Coca-Cola Bottling Co., Burlington, VT, 2001–2004. In four years, I received three promotions, each with increased pay and responsibility.

Summer Sales Coordinator: Promoted to hire, train, and direct efforts of add-on staff of fifteen college-age route salespeople hired to meet summer peak demand for product.

Sales Administrator: Promoted to run home office sales desk, managing accounts and associated delivery schedules for professional sales force of ten people. Intensive phone work, daily interaction with all personnel, and strong knowledge of product line required.

Route Salesperson: Summer employment to travel and tourism industry sites that use Coke products. Met specific schedule demands, used good communication skills with wide variety of customers, and demonstrated strong selling skills. Named salesperson of the month for July and August of that year.

QUESTIONS RESUME WRITERS OFTEN ASK

How Far Back Should I Go in Terms of Listing Past Jobs?

Usually, listing three or four jobs should suffice. If you did something back in high school that has a bearing on your future aspirations for employment, by all means list the job. As you progress through your college career, high school jobs may be replaced on the resume by college employment.

Should I Differentiate Between Paid and Nonpaid Employment?

Most employers are not initially concerned about how much you were paid. They are anxious to know how much responsibility you held in your past employment. There is no need to specify that your work was volunteer if you had significant responsibilities.

How Should I Represent My Accomplishments or Work-Related Responsibilities?

Succinctly, but fully. In other words, give the employer enough information to arouse curiosity, but not so much detail that you leave nothing to the imagination. Besides, some jobs merit more lengthy explanations than others. Be sure to convey any information that can give an employer a better understanding of the depth of your involvement at work. Did you supervise others? How many? Did your efforts result in a more efficient operation? How much did you increase efficiency? Did you handle a budget? How much? Were you promoted in a short time? Did you work two jobs at once or fifteen hours per week after high school? Where appropriate, quantify.

Should the Work Section Always Follow the Education Section on the Resume?

Always lead with your strengths. If your education closely relates to the employment you now seek, put this section after the objective. Or, if you are weak on the academic side but have a surplus of good work experiences, consider reversing the order of your sections to lead with employment, followed by education.

How Should I Present My Activities, Honors, Awards, Professional Societies, and Affiliations?

This section of the resume can add valuable information for an employer to consider if used correctly. The rule of thumb for information in this section is to include only those activities that are in some way relevant to the objective stated on your resume. If you can draw a valid connection between your activities and your objective, include them; if not, leave them out.

Granted, this is hard to do. Playing center on the championship basketball team or serving as coordinator of the biggest homecoming parade ever held are roles that have meaning for you and represent personal accomplishments you'd like to share. But the resume is a brief document, and the information you provide on it should help the employer make a decision about your job eligibility. Including personal details can be confusing and could hurt your candidacy. Limiting your activity list to a few very significant experiences can be very effective.

If you are applying for a position as a safety officer, your certificate in Red Cross lifesaving skills or CPR would be related and valuable. You would want to include it. If, however, you are applying for a job as a junior account executive in an advertising agency, that information would be unrelated and superfluous. Leave it out.

Professional affiliations and honors should *all* be listed; especially important are those related to your job objective. Social clubs and activities need not be a part of your resume unless you hold a significant office or you are looking for a position related to your membership. Be aware that most prospective employers' principal concerns are related to your employability, not your social life. If you have any, publications can be included as an addendum to your resume.

The focus of the resume is your experience and education. It is not necessary to describe your involvement in activities. However, if your resume needs to be lengthened, this section provides the freedom either to expand on or mention only briefly the contributions you have made. If you have made significant contributions (e.g., an officer of an organization or a particularly long tenure with a group), you may choose to describe them in more detail. It is not always necessary to include the dates of your memberships with your activities the way you would include job dates.

There are a number of different ways in which to present additional information. You may give this section a number of different titles. Assess what you want to list, and then use an appropriate title. Do not use "extracurricular activities." This terminology is scholastic, not professional, and therefore not appropriate. The following are two examples:

❑ ACTIVITIES: Society for Technical Communication, Student Senate, Student Admissions Representative, Senior Class Officer

❑ ACTIVITIES:
  • Society for Technical Communication Member
  • Student Senator
  • Student Admissions Representative
  • Senior Class Officer

The position you are looking for will determine what you should or should not include. *Always* look for a correlation between the activity and the prospective job.

How Should I Handle References?

The use of references is considered a part of the interview process, and they should never be listed on a resume. You would always provide references to a potential employer if requested to, so it is not even necessary to include this section on the resume if room does not permit. If space is available, it is acceptable to include one of the following statements:

❏ REFERENCES: Furnished upon request.

❏ REFERENCES: Available upon request.

Individuals used as references must be protected from unnecessary contacts. By including names on your resume, you leave your references unprotected. Overuse and abuse of your references will lead to less-than-supportive comments. Protect your references by giving out their names only when you are being considered seriously as a candidate for a given position.

THE FUNCTIONAL RESUME

The functional resume departs from a chronological resume in that it organizes information by specific accomplishments in various settings: previous jobs, volunteer work, associations, and so forth. This type of resume permits you to stress the substance of your experiences rather than the position titles you have held. (See Exhibit 2.3.) You should consider using a functional resume if you have held a series of similar jobs that relied on the same skills or abilities.

Exhibit 2.3

Functional Resume

TABITHA A. KEEFE

Mary Lyons Hall   12 River Road
Cleveland State University   Rocky River, OH 44116
Cleveland, OH 44115   (216) 555-6666
(216) 555-7799
tkeefe@xxx.com
(until May 2003)

OBJECTIVE
A position with a human services or community-based social service organization where I could use my counseling, networking, and referral skills to help clients become more self-sustaining.

CAPABILITIES
- Empathic listener
- Skilled at connecting people in need to sources of help and support
- Grounded realist with "save the world" aspirations!

continued

continued

SPECIFIC ACCOMPLISHMENTS

COUNSELING: Experienced with two distinct populations: women seeking short-term residence in a battered women's shelter and men incarcerated in state prison for a variety of offenses. Developed excellent listening skills, attending behavior, and record-keeping experience, including process notes. Both positions under strict clinical supervision.

NETWORKING: Developed considerable skill and creativity in bringing together a variety of traditional and nontraditional sources of support for clients in need of housing, financial assistance, furniture, clothing, education, and job retraining. Excellent telephone skills, persuasive ability, and public presentation technique.

WRITING: Co-authored a successful funding grant proposal and numerous brochures, information leaflets, and fact sheets for a variety of projects. Experienced in handling significant amounts of professional correspondence and fluent in many word-processing softwares.

AWARDS

Student Humanitarian of the Year, 2001
Maintained Dean's list six consecutive semesters
Nominated to *Who's Who in American Colleges and Universities*

EMPLOYMENT HISTORY

Vincennes Women's Shelter, Bridge Street, Cleveland, OH, 2001–Present.
Ohio State Penitentiary, Cleveland, OH, 2002–Present.
Student Counselor, Cleveland State University, OH, 2000.

EDUCATION

Bachelor of Science in Psychology with honors
Pace University, New York, NY
May 2003

REFERENCES

Provided upon request

The Objective

A functional resume begins with an objective that can be used to focus the contents of the resume.

Specific Accomplishments

Specific accomplishments are listed on this type of resume. Examples of the types of headings used to describe these capabilities might include research, computer skills, teaching, communication, production, management, marketing, or writing. The headings you choose will directly relate to your experience and the tasks that you carried out. Each accomplishment section contains statements related to your experience in that category, regardless of when or where it occurred. Organize the accomplishments and the related tasks you describe in their order of importance as related to the position you seek.

Experience or Employment History

Your actual work experience is condensed and placed after the specific accomplishments section. It simply lists dates of employment, position titles, and employer names.

Education

The education section of a functional resume is identical to that of the chronological resume, but it does not carry the same visual importance because it is placed near the bottom of the page.

References

Because actual reference names are never listed on a resume, a statement of reference availability is optional if space does not permit.

THE TARGETED RESUME

The targeted resume focuses on specific work-related capabilities you can bring to a given position within an organization. (See Exhibit 2.4.) It should be sent to an individual within the organization who makes hiring decisions about the position you are seeking.

The Objective

The objective on this type of resume should be targeted to a specific career or position. It should be supported by the capabilities, accomplishments, and achievements documented in the resume.

Exhibit 2.4

Targeted Resume

RICHARD T. HAGE

Geneva Smith Hall, 7708
University of Denver
Denver, CO 80201
(303) 555-0909
rhage@xxx.com
(until May 2004)

RR 2, Box 71
Poughkeepsie, NY 12601
(914) 555-4456

Activities therapist, member of multidisciplinary psychiatric team

CAPABILITIES
- Skilled in a variety of therapeutic recreation modalities
- Proven team skills
- Excellent communicator, both written and verbal
- Strong quantitative skills; practiced in research techniques
- Familiar with a variety of computer software, including spreadsheets

ACHIEVEMENTS
- Student peer advocate/counselor for four years
- Founding member of college wellness board of governors
- Successfully advocated for three new recreational offerings at my college
- Coached both men's and women's tennis and basketball

WORK HISTORY
2002–present (part-time)
Recreation Therapist, Havenwood Retirement Community, Milton, CO
- Design and deliver evening recreation programs

2001–2002
Coach/Trainer, University of Denver, CO
- Men's and Women's basketball and tennis

2000 (150 hrs)
Observation, Milton Memorial Hospital, CO
- Structured observation of therapy departments

continued

continued

2000–2002 Summers	Counselor, Poughkeepsie Park and Recreation Dept., NY
	• Increasing responsibilities at children's day camp

EDUCATION

Bachelor of Science in Psychology, 2004
University of Denver
Minor: Recreation

Capabilities

Capabilities should be statements that illustrate tasks you believe you are capable of based on your accomplishments, achievements, and work history. Each should relate to your targeted career or position. You can stress your qualifications rather than your employment history. This approach may require research to obtain an understanding of the nature of the work involved and the capabilities necessary to carry out that work.

Accomplishments/Achievements

This section relates the various activities you have been involved in to the job market. These experiences may include previous jobs, extracurricular activities at school, internships, and part-time summer work.

Experience

Your work history should be listed in abbreviated form and may include position title, employer name, and employment dates.

Education

Because this type of resume is directed toward a specific job target and an individual's related experience, the education section is not prominently located at the top of the resume as is done on the chronological resume.

DIGITAL RESUMES

Today's employers have to manage an enormous number of resumes. One of the most frequent complaints the writers of this series hear from students is the failure of employers to even acknowledge the receipt of a resume and cover letter. Frequently, the reason for this poor response or nonresponse is the volume of applications received for every job. In an attempt to better manage the considerable labor investment involved in processing large numbers of resumes, many employers are requiring digital submission of resumes. There are two types of digital resumes: those that can be E-mailed or posted to a website, called *electronic resumes,* and those that can be "read" by a computer, commonly called *scannable resumes.* Though the format may be a bit different than the traditional "paper" resume, the goal of both types of digital resumes is the same—to get you an interview! These resumes must be designed to be "technologically friendly." What that basically means to you is that they should be free of graphics and fancy formatting.

Electronic Resumes

Sometimes referred to as plain-text resumes, electronic resumes are designed to be E-mailed to an employer or posted to a commercial Internet database such as CareerMosaic.com, America's Job Bank (www.ajb.dni.us), or Monster.com.

Some technical considerations:

- Electronic resumes must be written in American Standard Code for Information Interchange (ASCII), which is simply a plain-text format. These characters are universally recognized so that every computer can accurately read and understand them. To create an ASCII file of your current resume, open your document, then save it as a text or ASCII file. This will eliminate all formatting. Edit as needed using your computer's text editor application.

- Use a standard-width typeface. Courier is a good choice because it is the font associated with ASCII in most systems.

- Use a font size of 11 to 14 points. A 12-point font is considered standard.

- Your margin should be left-justified.

- Do not exceed sixty-five characters per line, because the word-wrap function doesn't operate in ASCII.

- Do not use boldface, italics, underlining, bullets, and various font sizes. Instead, use asterisks, plus signs, and all capital letters when you want to emphasize something.

- Avoid graphics and shading.

- Use as many "keywords" as you possibly can. These are words or phrases usually relating to skills or experience that are either specifically used in the job announcement or are popular buzzwords in the industry.

- Minimize abbreviations. One exception is B.S. or B.A. for your degree.

- Your name should be the first line of text.

- Conduct a "test run" by E-mailing your resume to yourself and a friend before you send it to the employer. See how it transmits, and make any changes you need to. Continue to test it until it's exactly how you want it to look.

- Unless an employer specifically requests that you send the resume in the form of an attachment, don't. Employers can encounter problems opening a document as an attachment, and there are always viruses to consider.

- Don't forget your cover letter. Send it along with your resume as a single message.

Scannable Resumes

Some companies are relying on technology to narrow the candidate pool for available job openings. Electronic Applicant Tracking uses imaging to scan, sort, and store resume elements in a database. Then, through OCR (Optical Character Recognition) software, the computer scans the resumes for keywords and phrases. To have the best chance at getting an interview, you want to increase the number of "hits"—matches of your skills, abilities, experience, and education to those the computer is scanning for—your resume will get. You can see how critical using the right keywords is for this type of resume.

Technical considerations include:

- Again, do not use boldface (newer systems may read this OK, but many older ones won't), italics, underlining, bullets, shading, graphics, and multiple font sizes. Instead, for emphasis, use asterisks, plus signs, and all capital letters. Minimize abbreviations.

- Use a popular typeface such as Courier, Helvetica, Ariel, or Palatino. Avoid decorative fonts.

- Font size should be between 11 and 14 points.

- Do not compress the spacing between letters.

- Use horizontal and vertical lines sparingly; the computer may misread them as the letters L or I.

- Left-justify the text.

- Do not use parentheses or brackets around telephone numbers, and be sure your phone number is on its own line of text.
- Your name should be the first line of text and on its own line. If your resume is longer than one page, be sure to put your name on the top of all pages.
- Use a traditional resume structure. The chronological format may work best.
- Use nouns that are skill-focused, such as *management, writer,* and *programming.* This is different from traditional paper resumes, which use action-oriented verbs.
- Laser printers produce the finest copies. Avoid dot-matrix printers.
- Use standard, light-colored paper with text on one side only. Since the higher the contrast the better, your best choice is black ink on white paper.
- Always send original copies. If you must fax, set the fax on fine mode, not standard.

Exhibit 2.5

DIGITAL RESUME

SARAH MCDOUGLE — Put your name at the top
117 Stetson Avenue on its own line.
Small School, MA 02459 — Put your phone number
859-425-5478 — on its own line.
saramc@xxx.com — Use a standard-width
typeface—like Courier.

KEYWORD SUMMARY
B.S. Computer Science, 2002, C++, Visual
Basic, Assemble, FORTRAN, TUTOR, Keywords make your
HTML, CAD, PATRAN, Oracle, MS Office, resume easier to find in a
IBM 630-670, Windows NT, UNIX, database.
Programmer

EDUCATION — Capital letters emphasize
Bachelor of Science, Computer Science, headings.
2002
Small State College, Small School,
Massachusetts

continued

continued
Minor: Graphic Design
G.P.A.: 3.0/4.0

Related Courses
Database Design, Compiler Design,
System Architecture, Operating Systems,
Data Structures

No line should exceed
sixty-five characters.

COMPUTER SKILLS
Languages: C/C++, Visual Basic, Assembly,
FORTRAN, TUTOR, HTML
Software: CAD, PATRAN, Oracle, MS
Office
Systems: IBM 360/370, Windows NT,
UNIX

EXPERIENCE
Support desk, Small State College, 2001–02

End each line by hitting
the ENTER key.

* Maintained computer systems in
computer lab
* Installed application and performed
troubleshooting
* Instructed students on application and
systems

Programmer (intern), Large Company, 2001
* Wrote instructional programs using
TUTOR language

Use a space between
asterisk and text.

* Corrected errors in prewritten
programs using C++
* Altered existing programs to fit user
needs

Data-entry clerk, XYZ Sales, Winter 2000
* Updated inventory and sales data

COMMUNICATION SKILLS
Served as a vice president of Computer Science Society
Received As in technical writing and speech class

REFERENCES
Available upon request
++ Willing to relocate ++

Asterisks and plus signs
replace bullets.

- Do not staple or fold your resume. This can confuse the computer.
- Before you send your scannable resume, be certain the employer uses this technology. If you can't determine this, you may want to send two versions (scannable and traditional) to be sure your resume gets considered.

RESUME PRODUCTION AND OTHER TIPS

An ink-jet printer is the preferred option for printing your resume. Begin by printing just a few copies. You may find a small error or you may simply want to make some changes, and this is less frustrating and less expensive if you print in small batches.

Resume paper color should be carefully chosen. You should consider the types of employers who will receive your resume and the types of positions for which you are applying. Use white or ivory paper for traditional or conservative employers or for higher-level positions.

Black ink on sharp white paper can be harsh on the reader's eyes. Think about an ivory or cream paper that will provide less contrast and be easier to read. Pink, green, and blue tints should generally be avoided.

Many resume writers buy packages of matching envelopes and cover sheet stationery that, although not absolutely necessary, do convey a professional impression.

If you'll be producing many cover letters at home, be sure you have high quality printing equipment. Learn standard envelope formats for business and retain a copy of every cover letter you send out. You can use the copies to take notes of any telephone conversations that may occur.

If attending a job fair, either carry a briefcase or place your resume in a nicely covered legal-size pad holder.

THE COVER LETTER

The cover letter provides you with the opportunity to tailor your resume by telling the prospective employer how you can be a benefit to the organization. It will allow you to highlight aspects of your background that are not already discussed in your resume and that might be especially relevant to the organization you are contacting or to the position you are seeking. Every resume should have a cover letter enclosed when you send it out. Unlike the resume, which may be mass-produced, a cover letter is most effective when it is individually typed and focused on the particular requirements of the organization in question.

A good cover letter should supplement the resume and motivate the reader to review the resume. The format shown in Exhibit 2.6 is only a suggestion to help you decide what information to include in writing a cover letter.

Exhibit 2.6

Cover Letter Format

Your Name
Your Street Address
Your Town, State, Zip
Phone Number
Fax Number
E-mail

Date

Name
Title
Organization
Address

Dear _____:

First Paragraph. In this paragraph state the reason for the letter, name the specific position or type of work you are applying for, and indicate from which resource (career services office, website, newspaper, contact, employment service) you learned of this opening. The first paragraph can also be used to inquire about future openings.

Second Paragraph. Indicate why you are interested in this position, the company, its products or services, and what you can do for the employer. If you are a recent graduate, explain how your academic background makes you a qualified candidate. Try not to repeat the same information found in the resume.

Third Paragraph. Refer the reader to the enclosed resume for more detailed information.

continued

---

continued

Fourth Paragraph. In this paragraph say what you will do to follow up on your letter. For example, state that you will call by a certain date to set up an interview or to find out if the company will be recruiting in your area. Finish by indicating your willingness to answer any questions they may have. Be sure you have provided your phone number.

Sincerely,

Type your name

Enclosure

Begin the cover letter with your street address twelve lines down from the top. Leave three to five lines between the date and the name of the person to whom you are addressing the cover letter. Make sure you leave one blank line between the salutation and the body of the letter and between paragraphs. After typing "Sincerely," leave four blank lines and type your name. This should leave plenty of room for your signature. A sample cover letter is shown in Exhibit 2.7.

Exhibit 2.7

Sample Cover Letter

85 Greengate #17D
Falmouth, MA 02540
(508) 540-1633
cglass@xxx.com
April 8, 2002

Amy Phillips
Director of Personnel
Youth, Inc.
279 Main Street
Shreveport, LA 71130

Dear Ms. Phillips:

continued

continued

In May of 2002 I will graduate from Louisiana State University with a bachelor of arts degree in psychology. I read of your opening for a residential counselor in your group home for adolescent girls in *The Times* last Sunday, and I am very interested in the possibilities it offers. I am writing to explore the opportunity for employment with Youth, Inc.

The advertisement indicated that you were looking for someone capable of working with a clinical team, experienced in counseling and case management, and with a psychology degree. I believe my resume outlines a work and education history that you will find interesting and relevant. Beginning with camp counseling at an all-girls camp for two years early in high school, I have continued to add one-on-one counseling experiences in my school's women's center and at a local teen drop-in evening held in my hometown library community room. Courses in development theory and counseling techniques have added richness to these hands-on experiences that I hope to continue in my professional career. My counseling style is still evolving but is characterized by empathy, sensitivity, and a solution focus.

As you will see by my enclosed resume, I have enjoyed a number of team and collaborative experiences, and some of my references will speak specifically about my team performance and contributions. I do not, as of yet, have experience with case management but can assure you of my attention to detail, excellent record-keeping skills, and a communications style that is open and engages others.

I would like to meet with you to discuss how my education and experience would be consistent with your needs. I will contact your office next week to discuss the possibility of an interview. In the meantime, if you have any questions or require additional information, please contact me at my home, (508) 540-1633.

Sincerely,

Constance Glass
Enclosure

The following guidelines will help you write good cover letters:

1. Be sure to type your letter; ensure there are no misspellings.

2. Avoid unusual typefaces, such as script.

3. Address the letter to an individual, using the person's name and title. To obtain this information, call the company. If answering a blind newspaper advertisement, address the letter "To Whom It May Concern" or omit the salutation.

4. Be sure your cover letter directly indicates the position you are applying for and tells why you are qualified to fill it.

5. Send the original letter, not a photocopy, with your resume. Keep a copy for your records.

6. Make your cover letter no more than one page.

7. Include a phone number where you can be reached.

8. Avoid trite language and have someone read the letter over to react to its tone, content, and mechanics.

9. For your own information, record the date you send out each letter and resume.

CHAPTER THREE

RESEARCHING CAREERS

••

Many psychology majors will say they loved their degree work, but "What can I do with it?" It's a common question for career counselors. Psychology majors have learned *about* psychology, they have not learned how to *do* psychology in any way. Unlike your college classmates in applied fields like teaching, computer science, and business, you may be confused about what kinds of jobs you can do with your degree and what kinds of organizations will hire you. Sure, a marketing major goes into sales, and a public administration major heads for a city planner's job. But what does the psychology major become?

••

WHAT DO THEY CALL THE JOB YOU WANT?

There is every reason to be unaware. One reason for confusion is perhaps a mistaken assumption that a college education provides job training. In most cases it does not. Of course, applied fields such as engineering, management, or education provide specific skills for the workplace, whereas most liberal arts degrees simply provide an education. A liberal arts education exposes you to numerous fields of study and teaches you quantitative reasoning, critical thinking, writing, and speaking, all of which can be successfully applied to a number of different job fields. But it still remains up to you to choose a job field and to learn how to articulate the benefits of your education in a way the employer will appreciate.

As indicated in Chapter 1 on self-assessment, your first task is to understand and value what parts of that education you enjoyed and were good at and would continue to enjoy in your life's work. Did your writing courses encourage you in your ability to express yourself in writing? Did you enjoy the research process, and did you find your work was well received? Did you enjoy any of your required quantitative subjects such as algebra or calculus?

The answers to questions such as these provide clues to skills and interests you bring to the employment market over and above the credential of your degree. In fact, it is not an overstatement to suggest that most employers who demand a college degree immediately look beyond that degree to you as a person and your own individual expression of what you like to do and think you can do for them, regardless of your major.

Collecting Job Titles

The world of employment is a big place, and even seasoned veterans of the job hunt can be surprised about what jobs are to be found in what organizations. You need to become a bit of an explorer and adventurer and be willing to try a variety of techniques to begin a list of possible occupations that might use your talents and education. Once you have a list of possibilities that you are interested in and qualified for, you can move on to find out what kinds of organizations have these job titles.

●●●

Not every employer seeking to hire a community or social service professional may be equally desirable to you. Some employment environments may be more attractive to you than others. A psychology major considering community or social service work could do that in a local senior citizen's center, in a teen drop-in center for sexual awareness, in an area home for battered or abused women, or in some association with the court system. Each environment presents a different "culture" with associated norms in the pace of work, the clients' presenting issues, and the background and training of those you'll be working alongside. Your job title might be the same in each situation, but not all locations may present the same "fit" for you.

If you majored in psychology and enjoyed your studies and work with human development, you might think about doing graduate work specifically in this field. But psychology majors with this interest also go to work in human resources, management, medicine, public relations, sales, systems analysis, and counseling. Each job title in this list can be found in a variety of settings.

. . . .

Take training, for example. Trainers write policy and procedural manuals and actively teach to assist all levels of employees in mastering various tasks and work-related systems. Trainers exist in all large corporations, banks, consumer goods manufacturers, medical diagnostic equipment firms, sales organizations, and any organization that has processes or materials that need to be presented to and learned by the staff.

In reading job descriptions or want ads for any of these positions, you would find your four-year degree a "must." However, the academic major might be less important than your own individual skills in critical thinking, analysis, report writing, public presentations, and interpersonal communication. Even more important than thinking or knowing you have certain skills is your ability to express those skills concretely and the examples you use to illustrate them to an employer.

The best beginning to a job search is to create a list of job titles you might want to pursue, learn more about the nature of the jobs behind those titles, and then discover what kinds of employers hire for those positions. In the following section we'll teach you how to build a job title directory to use in your job search.

Developing a Job Title Directory That Works for You

A job title directory is simply a complete list of all the job titles you are interested in, are intrigued by, or think you are qualified for. Combining the understanding gained through self-assessment with your own individual interests and the skills and talents you've acquired with your degree, you'll soon start to read and recognize a number of occupational titles that seem right for you. There are several resources you can use to develop your list, including computer searches, books, and want ads.

Computerized Interest Inventories. One way to begin your search is to identify a number of jobs that call for your degree and the particular skills and interests you identified as part of the self-assessment process. There are excellent interactive computer career guidance programs on the market to help you produce such selected lists of possible job titles. Most of these are available at high schools and colleges and at some larger town and city libraries. Two of the industry leaders are sigi and DISCOVER. Both allow you to enter interests, values, educational background, and other information to produce lists of possible occupations and industries. Each of the resources listed here will produce different job title lists. Some job titles will appear again and again, while others will be unique to a particular source. Investigate them all!

Reference Books. Books on the market that may be available through your local library, bookstore, or career counseling office also suggest various occupations related to a number of majors. The following are only two of the many good books on the market: *Occupational Outlook Handbook (OOH)* and *Occupational Projections and Training Data*, both put out annually by the U.S. Department of Labor, Bureau of Labor Statistics (www.bls.gov). The *OOH* describes hundreds of job titles under several broad categories such as Executive, Administrative, and Managerial Occupations and also identifies those jobs by their *Dictionary of Occupational Titles (DOT)* code. (See the following discussion.)

· ·

Many college and university career office Web pages offer some great information on what you can do with specific majors. Several of the best we've seen are from Florida State University (www.fus.edu/~career/match_match), Georgia Southern University (www2.gasou.edu/sta/career), and the University of North Carlina at Wilmington (www.uncwil.edu/stuaff/career). In addition to potential job titles and/or employers, these sites will provide you with further related resources to explore, including websites.

· ·

Each job title deserves your consideration. Like the layers of an onion, the search for job titles can go on and on! As you spend time doing this activity, you are actually learning more about the value of your degree. What's important in your search at this point is not to become critical or selective, but rather to develop as long a list of possibilities as you can. Every source used will help you add new and potentially exciting jobs to your growing list.

Want Ads. It has been well publicized that newspaper want ads represent only about 10 to 15 percent of the current job market. However, with the current high state of employment as this book goes to press, the percentage of jobs advertised in the newspapers and on-line is rising dramatically, so don't ignore these sources.

Read the Sunday want ads in a major market newspaper for several Sundays in a row. Save any and all ads that interest you and seem to call for something close to your education and experience. Remember, because want ads are written for what an organization *hopes* to find, you don't have to meet absolutely every criterion. However, if certain requirements are stated as absolute minimums and you cannot meet them, it's best not to waste your time.

A recent examination of *The Boston Sunday Globe* (www.boston.com) reveals the following possible occupations for a liberal arts major with some computer skills and limited prior work experience. (This is only a partial list of what was available.)

- Admissions representative
- Salesperson
- Compliance director
- Assistant principal gifts writer
- Public relations officer
- Technical writer
- Personnel trainee
- GED examiner
- Direct mail researcher
- Associate publicist

After performing this exercise for a few Sundays, you'll find you have collected a new library of job titles.

The Sunday want ad exercise is important because these jobs are out in the marketplace. They truly exist, and people with your qualifications are being sought to apply. What's more, many of these advertisements describe the duties and responsibilities of the job advertised and give you a beginning sense of the challenges and opportunities such a position presents. Some will indicate salary, and that will be helpful as well. This information will better define the jobs for you and provide some good material for possible interviews in that field.

If you are able to be mobile in your job search, you may want to search other newspapers in other cities for their classified sections. This is now possible on-line. A good source for this search is the site called www.look smart.com. Using the keywords "newspaper classifieds" will lead you to their site where you can search by state alphabetically. It's an excellent source for want ads.

Exploring Job Descriptions

Once you've arrived at a solid list of possible job titles that interest you and for which you believe you are somewhat qualified, it's a good idea to do some research on each of these jobs. The preeminent source for such job information is the *Dictionary of Occupational Titles,* or *DOT* (www.wave .net/upg/immigration/dot_index.html). This directory lists every conceivable job and provides excellent up-to-date information on duties and responsibilities, interactions with associates, and day-to-day assignments and tasks. These descriptions provide a thorough job analysis, but they do not consider the possible employers or the environments in which a job may be performed. So, although a position as public relations officer may be well defined in terms of duties and responsibilities, it does not explain the differences in doing public relations work in a college or a hospital or a factory or a bank. You will need to look somewhere else for work settings.

Learning More About Possible Work Settings

After reading some job descriptions, you may choose to edit and revise your list of job titles once again, discarding those you feel are not suitable and keeping those that continue to hold your interest. Or you may wish to keep your list intact and see where these jobs may be located. For example, if you are interested in public relations and you appear to have those skills and the requisite education, you'll want to know what organizations do public relations. How can you find that out? How much income does someone in public relations make a year and what is the employment potential for the field of public relations?

To answer these and many other good questions about your list of job titles, we recommend you try any of the following resources: *Careers Encyclopedia,* a career information center site such as that provided by the American Marketing Association at www.amaboston.org/jobs.htm; *College to Career: The Guide to Job Opportunities*; and the *Occupational Outlook Handbook* (http://stats.bls.gov/ocohome.htm). Each of these resources, in a different way, will help to put the job titles you have selected into an employer context. *VGM's Handbook of Business and Management Careers* contains detailed career descriptions for more than fifty fields. Entries include complete information on duties and responsibilities for individual careers and detailed entry-level requirements. There is information on working conditions and promotional opportunities as well. Salary ranges and career outlook projections are also provided. Perhaps the most extensive discussion is found in the *Occupational Outlook Handbook,* which gives a thorough presentation of the nature of the work, the working conditions, employment statistics, training, other qualifications, and advancement possibilities as well as job outlook and earnings. Related occupations are also detailed, and a select bibliography is provided to help you find additional information.

Continuing with our public relations example, your search through these reference materials would teach you that the public relations jobs you find attractive are available in larger hospitals, financial institutions, most corporations (both consumer goods and industrial goods), media organizations, and colleges and universities.

Networking to Get the Complete Story

You now have not only a list of job titles but also, for each of these job titles, a description of the work involved and a general list of possible employment settings in which to work. You'll want to do some reading and keep talking to friends, colleagues, teachers, and others about the possibilities. Don't neglect to ask if the career office at your college maintains some kind of alumni network. Often such alumni networks will connect you with another graduate from the college who is working in the job title or industry you are seeking information about. These career networkers offer what assistance they can. For some it is a full day "shadowing" the alumnus as he or she goes about the job. Others offer partial-day visits, tours, informational interviews, resume reviews, job postings, or, if distance prevents a visit, telephone interviews. As fellow graduates, they'll be frank and informative about their own jobs and prospects in their field.

Take them up on their offer and continue to learn all you can about your own personal list of job titles, descriptions, and employment settings. You'll probably continue to edit and refine this list as you learn more about the realities of the job, the possible salary, advancement opportunities, and supply and demand statistics.

In the next section we'll describe how to find the specific organizations that represent these industries and employers so that you can begin to make contact.

WHERE ARE THESE JOBS, ANYWAY?

Having a list of job titles that you've designed around your own career interests and skills is an excellent beginning. It means you've really thought about who you are and what you are presenting to the employment market. It has caused you to think seriously about the most appealing environments to work in, and you have identified some employer types that represent these environments.

The research and the thinking that you've done thus far will be used again and again. They will be helpful in writing your resume and cover letters, in talking about yourself on the telephone to prospective employers, and in answering interview questions.

Now is a good time to begin to narrow the field of job titles and employment sites down to some specific employers to initiate the employment contact.

Finding Out Which Employers Hire People Like You

This section will provide tips, techniques, and specific resources for developing an actual list of specific employers that can be used to make contacts. It is only an outline that you must be prepared to tailor to your own particular needs and according to what you bring to the job search. Once again, it is important to stress the need to communicate with others along the way exactly what you're looking for and what your goals are for the research you're doing. Librarians, employers, career counselors, friends, friends of friends, business contacts, and bookstore staff will all have helpful information on geographically specific and new resources to aid you in locating employers who'll hire you.

Identifying Information Resources

Your interview wardrobe and your new resume may have put a dent in your wallet, but the resources you'll need to pursue your job search are available for free (although you might choose to copy materials on a machine instead of taking notes by hand). The categories of information detailed here are not hard to find and are yours for the browsing.

Numerous resources described in this section will help you identify actual employers. Use all of them or any others that you identify as available in your geographic area. As you become experienced in this process, you'll quickly figure out which information sources are helpful and which are not. If you live in a rural area, a well-planned day trip to a major city that includes a college career office, a large college or city library, state and federal employment centers, a chamber of commerce office, and a well-stocked bookstore can produce valuable results.

There are many excellent resources available to help you identify actual job sites. They are categorized into employer directories (usually indexed by product lines and geographic location), geographically based directories (designed to highlight particular cities, regions, or states), career-specific directories (e.g., *Sports Market Place,* which lists tens of thousands of firms involved with sports), periodicals and newspapers, targeted job posting publications, and videos. This is by no means meant to be a complete list of resources, but rather a starting point for identifying useful resources.

Working from the more general references to highly specific resources, we will provide a basic list to help you begin your search. Many of these you'll find easily available. In some cases reference librarians and others will suggest even better materials for your particular situation. Start to create your own customized bibliography of job search references. Use copying services to save time and to allow you to carry away information about organizations' missions, locations, company officers, phone numbers, and addresses.

Employer Directories. There are many employer directories available to give you the kind of information you need for your job search. Some of our favorites are listed here, but be sure to ask the professionals you are working with to make additional suggestions.

❑ *America's Corporate Families*
(www.apsu.edu/~careers/res3.htm), the website of the Austin Peay State University in Clarksville, Tennessee, has an excellent directory of corporate affiliations, parent companies, and subsidiaries. It has several search links for corporate families.

❑ *Million Dollar Directory: America's Leading Public and Private Companies* lists about 160,000 companies.

❑ *Moody's* (www.moodys.com) various manuals are intended as guides for investors, so they contain a history of each company. Each manual contains a classification of companies by industries and products.

❑ *Standard and Poor's Register of Corporations*
(www.stockinfo.standardpoor.com) contains listings for 45,000 businesses, some of which are not listed in the *Million Dollar Directory*.

❑ *Job Seekers Guide to Private and Public Companies*
(www.tomah.com/jobseeker) profiles 15,000 employers in four volumes, each covering a different geographic region. Company entries include contact information, business descriptions, and application procedures.

❑ *The Career Guide: Dun's Employment Opportunities Directory* includes more than 5,000 large organizations, including hospitals and local governments. Profiles include an overview and history of the employer as well as opportunities, benefits, and contact names. It contains geographic and industrial indexes and indexes by discipline or internship availability. This guide also includes a state-by-state list of professional personnel consultants and their specialties.

❑ *Professional's Job Finder/Government Job Finder/Non-Profits Job Finder* (http://einsys.einpgh.org) is the general website that will ultimately lead you to specific directories of job services, salary surveys, and periodical listings in which advertisements for jobs in the professional, government, or not-for-profit sector are found. Search under the icon "Title" for each of these directories.

❑ *The 100 Best Companies to Work for in America* rates organizations on several factors including opportunities, job security, and pay.

❑ *Infotrac cd-rom Business Index* (http://infotrac.galegroup.com) covers business journals and magazines as well as news magazines and can provide information on public and private companies.

❑ *ABI/Inform On Disc* (cd-rom) indexes articles in more than 800 journals.

Geographically Based Directories. The Job Bank series published by Bob Adams, Inc. (www.aip.com) contains detailed entries on each area's major employers, including business activity, address, phone number, and hiring contact name. Many listings specify educational backgrounds being sought in potential employees. Each volume contains a solid discussion of each city's or state's major employment sectors. Organizations are also indexed by industry. Job Bank volumes are available for the following places: Atlanta, Boston, Chicago, Denver, Dallas–Ft. Worth, Florida, Houston, Ohio, St. Louis, San Francisco, Seattle, Los Angeles, New York, Detroit, Philadelphia, Minneapolis, the Northwest, and Washington, D.C.

National Job Bank (www.careercity.com) lists employers in every state, along with contact names and commonly hired job categories. Included are many small companies often overlooked by other directories. Companies are also indexed by industry. This publication provides information on educational backgrounds sought and lists company benefits.

Career-Specific Directories. VGM (www.ntccpg.com) publishes a number of excellent series detailing careers for college graduates. In the Professional Career series are guides to careers in a range of fields, among them:

❑ Advertising

❑ Business

❑ Communications

❑ Computers

❑ Health Care

❑ High Tech

Each of these books is titled *Careers in . . .* and provides an excellent discussion of the industry, educational requirements for jobs, salary ranges, duties, and projected outlooks for the field.

Another VGM series, *Opportunities in . . .* , has an equally wide range of titles relating to specific majors, such as the following:

❑ *Opportunities in Education Careers*

❑ *Opportunities in Film Careers*

❑ *Opportunities in Insurance Careers*

❑ *Opportunities in Journalism Careers*

❑ *Opportunities in Law Careers*

❑ *Opportunities in Nursing Careers*

❑ *Opportunities in Government Careers*

❑ *Opportunities in Teaching Careers*

❑ *Opportunities in Technical Writing Careers*

Sports Market Place (Sportsguide) lists organizations by sport. It also describes trade/professional associations, college athletic organizations, multisport publications, media contacts, corporate sports sponsors, promotion/event/athletic management services, and trade shows.

Periodicals and Newspapers. Several sources are available to help you locate which journals or magazines carry job advertisements in your field. Other resources help you identify opportunities in other parts of the country.

❑ *The Helping Professions: A Career Sourcebook* contains a periodical matrix organized by academic discipline and highlights periodicals containing job listings.

❑ *National Business Employment Weekly* (www.nbew.com) compiles want ads from four regional editions of the *Wall Street Journal* (http://interactive.wsj.com). Most are business and management positions.

❑ *National Ad Search* (www.nationaladsearch.com) reprints ads from seventy-five metropolitan newspapers across the country. Although the focus is on management positions, technical and professional postings are also included. *Caution*: Watch deadline dates carefully on listings because deadlines may have already passed by the time the ad is printed.

❑ *The Federal Jobs Digest* (www.jobsfed.com) and *Federal Career Opportunities* list government positions.

❑ *World Chamber of Commerce Directory* (www.chamberofcommerce .com) lists addresses for chambers worldwide, state boards of tourism, convention and visitors' bureaus, and economic development organizations.

This list is certainly not exhaustive; use it to begin your job search work.

Targeted Job Posting Publications. Although the resources that follow are national in scope, they are either targeted to one medium of contact (telephone), focused on specific types of jobs, or are less comprehensive than the sources previously listed.

❑ *Job Hotlines USA* (www.careers.org/topic01_002.html) pinpoints more than 1,000 hard-to-find telephone numbers for companies and government agencies that use prerecorded job messages and listings. Very few of the telephone numbers listed are toll-free, and sometimes recordings are long, so callers beware!

❑ *The Job Hunter* (www.jobhunter.com) is a national biweekly newspaper listing business, arts, media, government, human services, health, community-related, and student services job openings.

❑ *Current Jobs for Graduates* (www.graduatejobs.com) is a national employment listing for liberal arts professions, including editorial positions, management opportunities, museum work, teaching, and nonprofit work.

❑ *Environmental Opportunities* (www.ecojobs.com) serves environmental job interests nationwide by listing administrative, marketing, and human resources positions along with education-related jobs and positions directly related to a degree in an environmental field.

❑ *Y National Vacancy List* (www.ymcahrm.ns.ca/employed/jobleads.html) shows YMCA professional vacancies, including development, administration, programming, membership, and recreation postings.

❑ *ARTSearch* is a national employment service bulletin for the arts, including administration, managerial, marketing, and financial management jobs.

❑ *Community Jobs* is an employment newspaper for the nonprofit sector that provides a variety of listings, including project manager, canvas director, government relations specialist, community organizer, and program instructor.

❑ *College Placement Council Annual: A Guide to Employment Opportunities for College Graduates* is an annual guide containing solid job-hunting information and, more important, displaying ads from large corporations actively seeking recent college graduates in all majors. Company profiles provide brief descriptions and available employment opportunities. Contact names and addresses are given. Profiles are indexed by organization name, geographic location, and occupation.

Videos. You may be one of the many job seekers who like to get information via a medium other than paper. Many career libraries, public libraries, and career centers in libraries carry an assortment of videos that will help you learn new techniques and get information helpful in the job search.

Locating Information Resources

An essay by John Case that appeared in the *Boston Globe* alerts both new and seasoned job seekers that the job market is changing, and the old guarantees of lifelong employment no longer hold true. Some of our major corporations, which were once seen as the most prestigious of employment destinations, are now laying off thousands of employees. Middle management is especially hard hit in downsizing situations. On the other side of the coin, smaller, more entrepreneurial firms are adding employees and realizing enormous profit margins. The geography of the new job market is unfamiliar, and the terrain is much harder to map. New and smaller firms can mean different kinds of jobs and new job titles. The successful job seeker will keep an open mind about where he or she might find employment and what that employment might be called.

In order to become familiar with this new terrain, you will need to undertake some research, which can be done at any of the following locations:

❑ Public libraries

❑ Business organizations

❑ Employment agencies

❑ Bookstores

❑ Career libraries

Each one of these places offers a collection of resources that will help you get the information you need.

As you meet and talk with service professionals at all these sites, be sure to let them know what you're doing. Inform them of your job search, what you've already accomplished, and what you're looking for. The more people who know you're job seeking, the greater the possibility that someone will have information or know someone who can help you along your way.

Public Libraries. Large city libraries, college and university libraries, and even well-supported town library collections contain a variety of resources to help you conduct a job search. It is not uncommon for libraries to have separate "vocational choices" sections with books, tapes, computer terminals, and associated materials relating to job search and selection. Some are now even making resume creation software available for use by patrons.

Some of the publications we name throughout this book are expensive reference items that are rarely purchased by individuals. In addition, libraries carry a wide range of newspapers and telephone Yellow Pages as well as the usual array of books. If resources are not immediately available, many libraries have loan arrangements with other facilities and can make information available to you relatively quickly.

Take advantage not only of the reference collections, but also the skilled and informed staff. Let them know exactly what you are looking for, and they'll have their own suggestions. You'll be visiting the library frequently, and the reference staff will soon come to know who you are and what you're working on. They'll be part of your job search network!

Business Organizations. Chambers of Commerce, Offices of New Business Development, Councils on Business and Industry, Small Business Administration (SBA) offices, and professional associations can all provide geographically specific lists of companies and organizations that have hiring needs. They also have an array of other available materials, including visitors' guides and regional fact books that provide additional employment information.

These agencies serve to promote local and regional businesses and ensure their survival and success. Although these business organizations do not advertise job openings or seek employees for their members, they may be very aware of staffing needs among their member firms. In your visits to each of these locations, spend some time with the personnel, getting to know who they are and what they do. Let them know of your job search and your intentions regarding employment. You may be surprised and delighted at the information they may provide.

Employment Agencies. Employment agencies (including state and federal employment offices), professional "headhunters" or executive search firms, and some private career counselors can provide direct leads to job openings. Don't overlook these resources. If you are mounting a complete job search program and want to ensure that you are covering the potential market for employers, consider the employment agencies in your territory. Some of these organizations work contractually with several specific firms and may have access that is unavailable to you. Others may be particularly well-informed about supply and demand in particular industries or geographic locations.

In the case of professional (commercial) employment agencies, which include those executive recruitment firms labeled "headhunters," you should be cautious about entering into any binding contractual agreement. Before doing so, be sure to get the information you need to decide whether their services can be of use to you. Questions to ask include the following: Who pays the fee when employment is obtained? Are there any other fees or costs associated with this service? What is their placement rate? Can you see a list of previous clients and can you talk to any for references? Do they typically work with entry-level job seekers? Do they tend to focus on particular kinds of employment or industries?

A few cautions are in order, however, when you work with professional agencies. Remember, the professional employment agency is, in most cases, paid by the hiring organization. Naturally, their interest and attention is largely directed to the employer, not to the candidate. Of course, they want to provide good candidates to guarantee future contracts, but they are less interested in the job seeker than the employer.

For teacher candidates there are a number of good placement firms that charge the prospective teacher, not the employer. This situation has evolved over time as a result of supply and demand and financial structuring of most school systems, which cannot spend money on recruiting teachers. Usually these firms charge a nonrefundable administrative fee and, upon successful placement, require a fee based on a percentage of salary, which may range from 10 to 20 percent of annual compensation. Often, this can be repaid over a number of months. Check your contract carefully.

State and federal employment offices are no-fee services that maintain extensive "job boards" and can provide detailed specifications for each job advertised and help with application forms. Because government employment application forms are detailed, keep a master copy along with copies of all additional documentation (resumes, educational transcripts, military discharge papers, proof of citizenship, and so forth). Successive applications may require separate filings. Visit these offices as frequently as you can because most deal with applicants on a "walk-in" basis and will not telephone prospective candidates or maintain files of job seekers. Check your telephone book for the address of the nearest state and federal offices.

The Web is also a great source of job listings for teachers, especially for entry-level positions. A good search tactic on the Web is to use a "metaengine" that combines several search engines in one. Dogpile.com is an example of a metasearch engine. Using search string descriptors such as "teacher recruitment," "teacher supply," or "K12 jobs," you will discover job boards with current postings. At the time of publication, three excellent sites were: www.teachersatwork.com, www.K12jobs.com/jobfinder, and www.edweek .org, which has listings by region.

One type of employment service that causes much confusion among job seekers is the outplacement firm. Their advertisements tend to suggest they will put you in touch with the "hidden job market." They use advertising phrases such as "We'll work with you until you get that job" or "Maximize your earnings and career opportunities." In fact, if you read the fine print on these ads, you will notice these firms must state they are "Not an employment agency." These firms are, in fact, corporate and private outplacement counseling agencies whose work involves resume editing, counseling to provide leads for jobs, interview skills training, and all the other aspects of hiring preparation. They do this for a fee, sometimes in the thousands of dollars range, which is paid by you, the client. Some of these firms have good reputations and provide excellent materials and techniques. Most, however, provide a service you as a college student or graduate can receive free from your alma mater or through a reciprocity agreement between your college and a college or university located closer to your current address.

Bookstores. Any well-stocked bookstore will carry some job search books that are worth buying. Some major stores will even have an extensive section devoted to materials, including excellent videos, related to the job search process. You will also find copies of local newspapers and business magazines. The one advantage that is provided by resources purchased at a bookstore is that you can read and work with the information in the comfort of your own home and do not have to conform to the hours of operation of a library, which can present real difficulties if you are working full-time as you seek employment. A few minutes spent browsing in a bookstore might be a beneficial break from your job search activities and turn up valuable resources.

Career Libraries. Career libraries, which are found in career centers at colleges and universities and sometimes within large public libraries, contain a unique blend of the job search resources housed in other settings. In addition, career libraries often purchase a number of job listing publications, each of which targets a specific industry or type of job. You may find job listings specifically for entry-level positions for your specific major. Ask about job posting newsletters or newspapers specifically focused on careers in the area that most interests you. Each center will be unique, but you are certain to discover some good sources of jobs.

Most college career libraries now hold growing collections of video material on specific industries and on aspects of your job search process, including dress and appearance, how to manage the luncheon or dinner interview, how to be effective at a job fair, and many other specific titles. Some larger corporations produce handsome video materials detailing the variety of career paths and opportunities available in their organizations.

Some career libraries also house computer-based career planning and information systems. These interactive computer programs help you to clarify your values and interests and will combine that with your education to provide possible job titles and industry locations. Some even contain extensive lists of graduate school programs.

One specific kind of service a career library will be able to direct you to is computerized job search services. These services, of which there are many, are run by private companies, individual colleges, or consortiums of colleges. They attempt to match qualified job candidates with potential employers. The candidate submits a resume (or an application) to the service. This information (which can be categorized into hundreds of separate "fields" of data) is entered into a computer database. Your information is then compared with the information from employers about what they desire in a prospective employee. If there is a "match" between what they want and what you have indicated you can offer, the job search service or the employer will contact you directly to continue the process.

Computerized job search services can complement an otherwise complete job search program. They are *not*, however, a substitute for the kinds of activities described in this book. They are essentially passive operations that are random in nature. If you have not listed skills, abilities, traits, experiences, or education *exactly* as an employer has listed its needs, there is simply no match.

Consult with the staff members at the career libraries you use. These professionals have been specifically trained to meet the unique needs you present. Often you can just drop in and receive help with general questions, or you may want to set up an appointment to speak one-on-one with a career counselor to gain special assistance.

Every career library is different in size and content, but each can provide valuable information for the job search. Some may even provide some limited counseling. If you have not visited the career library at your college or alma mater, call and ask if these collections are still available for your use. Be sure to ask about other services that you can use as well.

If you are not near your own college as you work on your job search, call the career office and inquire about reciprocal agreements with other colleges that are closer to where you live. Very often, your own alma mater can arrange for you to use a limited menu of services at another school. This typically would include access to a career library and job posting information and might include limited counseling.

CHAPTER FOUR

NETWORKING

Networking is the process of deliberately establishing relationships to get career-related information or to alert potential employers that you are available for work. Networking is critically important to today's job seeker for two reasons: it will help you get the information you need, and it can help you find out about *all* of the available jobs.

Getting the Information You Need

Networkers will review your resume and give you feedback on its effectiveness. They will talk about the job you are looking for and give you a candid appraisal of how they see your strengths and weaknesses. If they have a good sense of the industry or the employment sector for that job, you'll get their feelings on future trends in the industry as well. Some networkers will be very forthcoming about salaries, job-hunting techniques, and suggestions for your job search strategy. Many have been known to place calls right from the interview desk to friends and associates who might be interested in you. Each networker will make his or her own contribution, and each will be valuable.

Because organizations must evolve to adapt to current global market needs, the information provided by decision makers within various organizations will be critical to your success as a new job market entrant. For example, you might learn about the concept of virtual organizations from a networker. Virtual organizations coordinate economic activity to deliver value to customers using resources outside the traditional boundaries of the organization. This concept is being discussed and implemented by chief executive officers of many organizations, including Ford Motor, Dell, and IBM.

Networking can help you find out about this and other trends currently affecting the industries under your consideration.

Finding Out About All of the Available Jobs

Not every job that is available at this very moment is advertised for potential applicants to see. This is called the *hidden job market*. Only 15 to 20 percent of all jobs are formally advertised, which means that 80 to 85 percent of available jobs do not appear in published channels. Networking will help you become more knowledgeable about all the employment opportunities available during your job search period.

Although someone you might talk to today doesn't know of any openings within his or her organization, tomorrow or next week or next month an opening may occur. If you've taken the time to show an interest in and knowledge of their organization, if you've shown the company representative how you can help achieve organizational goals and that you can fit into the organization, you'll be one of the first candidates considered for the position.

Networking: A Proactive Approach

Networking is a proactive rather than a reactive approach. You, as a job seeker, are expected to initiate a certain level of activity on your own behalf; you cannot afford to simply respond to jobs listed in the newspaper. Being proactive means building a network of contacts that includes informed and interested decision makers who will provide you with up-to-date knowledge of the current job market and increase your chances of finding out about employment opportunities appropriate for your interests, experience, and level of education.

An old axiom of networking says "You are only two phone calls away from the information you need." In other words, by talking to enough people, you will quickly come across someone who can offer you help. Start with your professors. Each of them probably has a wide circle of contacts. In their work and travel they might have met someone who can help you or direct you to someone who can.

Control and the Networking Process

In deliberately establishing relationships, the process of networking begins with you in control—*you* are contacting specific individuals. As your network expands and you establish a set of professional relationships, your search for information or jobs will begin to move outside of your total control. A part of the networking process involves others assisting you by gathering information for you or recommending you as a possible job candidate.

As additional people become a part of your networking system, you will have less knowledge about activities undertaken on your behalf; you will undoubtedly be contacted by individuals whom you did not initially approach. If you want to function effectively in surprise situations, you must be prepared at all times to talk with strangers about the informational or employment needs that motivated you to become involved in the networking process.

PREPARING TO NETWORK

In deliberately establishing relationships, maximize your efforts by organizing your approach. Five specific areas in which you can organize your efforts include reviewing your self-assessment, reviewing your research on job sites and organizations, deciding who it is you want to talk to, keeping track of all your efforts, and creating your self-promotion tools.

Review Your Self-Assessment

Your self-assessment is as important a tool in preparing to network as it has been in other aspects of your job search. You have carefully evaluated your personal traits, personal values, economic needs, longer-term goals, skill base, preferred skills, and underdeveloped skills. During the networking process you will be called upon to communicate what you know about yourself and relate it to the information or job you seek. Be sure to review the exercises that you completed in the self-assessment section of this book in preparation for networking. We've explained that you need to assess what skills you have acquired from your major that are of general value to an employer and to be ready to express those in ways employers can appreciate as useful in their own organizations.

Review Research on Job Sites and Organizations

In addition, individuals assisting you will expect that you'll have at least some background information on the occupation or industry of interest to you. Refer to the appropriate sections of this book and other relevant publications to acquire the background information necessary for effective networking. They'll explain how to identify not only the job titles that might be of interest to you, but also what kinds of organizations employ people to do that job. You will develop some sense of working conditions and expectations about duties and responsibilities—all of which will be of help in your networking interviews.

Decide Who It Is You Want to Talk To

Networking cannot begin until you decide who it is that you want to talk to and, in general, what type of information you hope to gain from your contacts. Once you know this, it's time to begin developing a list of contacts. Five useful sources for locating contacts are described here.

College Alumni Network. Most colleges and universities have created a formal network of alumni and friends of the institution who are particularly interested in helping currently enrolled students and graduates of their alma mater gain employment-related information.

· ·

Because psychology is and has been the most popular undergraduate major for many years, you'll find an abundance of psychology graduates spanning the full spectrum of possible employment settings. Just the diversity of employment within a list of your college's alumni should be both encouraging and informative to you. Among such a diversified group, there are likely to be scores of people you would enjoy talking with and perhaps meeting.

· ·

It is usually a simple process to make use of an alumni network. You need only visit the alumni or career office at your college or university and follow the procedure that has been established. Often, you will simply complete a form indicating your career goals and interests and you will be given the names of appropriate individuals to contact. In many cases staff members will coach you on how to make the best use of the limited time these alumni contacts may have available for you.

Alumni networkers may provide some combination of the following services: day-long shadowing experiences, telephone interviews, in-person interviews, information on relocating to given geographic areas, internship information, suggestions on graduate school study, and job vacancy notices.

· ·

What a valuable experience. Perhaps you are interested in providing therapy or working in a clinical setting but you are unsure about what you might contribute or if you'd like it or not. Spending a day with an alumnus in a clinical setting is a good way to resolve some of those questions. Asking your alumni contact about his or her academic preparation and the role of a psychology education in the current job, as well as observing firsthand the dynamics of a day in a clinical setting will be a far better decision-making tool for you than any reading on the subject could possibly provide.

••

Present and Former Supervisors. If you believe you are on good terms with present or former job supervisors, they may be an excellent resource for providing information or directing you to appropriate resources that would have information related to your current interests and needs. Additionally, these supervisors probably belong to professional organizations that they might be willing to utilize to get information for you.

••

If, for example, you were interested in working in industrial psychology, perhaps for a large manufacturing company, and you were currently working on the wait staff of a local restaurant, talk to your supervisor or the owner. They probably belong to the local chamber of commerce and can put you in touch with other chamber members who are affiliated with manufacturing firms in the area. You would probably be able to obtain the names and telephone numbers of these people, which would allow you to begin the networking process.

••

Employers in Your Area. Although you may be interested in working in a geographic location different from the one where you currently reside, don't overlook the value of the knowledge and contacts those around you are able to provide. Use the local telephone directory and newspaper to identify the types of organizations you are thinking of working for or professionals who have the kinds of jobs you are interested in. Recently, a call made to a local hospital's financial administrator for information on working in health-care financial administration yielded more pertinent information on training seminars, regional professional organizations, and potential employment sites than a national organization was willing to provide.

Employers in Geographic Areas Where You Hope to Work. If you are thinking about relocating, identifying prospective employers or informational contacts in your new location will be critical to your success. Here are some tips for on-line searching. First, use a metasearch engine to get the most out of your search. Metasearch engines combine several engines into one powerful tool. The authors frequently use www.dogpile.com and www.metasearch.com for this purpose. Try using the city and state as your keywords in a search. *New Haven, Connecticut* will bring you to the city's website with links to the chamber of commerce, member businesses, and other valuable resources. By using www.looksmart.com, you can locate newspapers in any area and they, too, provide valuable insight before relocating. Of course, both dogpile and metasearch can lead you to Yellow Page and white page directories in areas you are considering.

Professional Associations and Organizations. Professional associations and organizations can provide valuable information in several areas: career paths that you may not have considered, qualifications relating to those career choices, publications that list current job openings, and workshops or seminars that will enhance your professional knowledge and skills. They can also be excellent sources for background information on given industries: their health, current problems, and future challenges.

There are several excellent resources available to help you locate professional associations and organizations that would have information to meet your needs. Two especially useful publications are the *Encyclopedia of Associations* and *National Trade and Professional Associations of the United States.*

Keep Track of All Your Efforts

It can be difficult, almost impossible, to remember all the details related to each contact you make during the networking process, so you will want to develop a record-keeping system that works for you. Formalize this process by using your computer to keep a record of the people and organizations you want to contact. You can simply record the contact's name, address, telephone number, and what information you hope to gain. Each entry might look something like this:

Contact Name	Address/E-mail	Phone #	Purpose
Mr. Tim Keefe	Wrigley Bldg.	(P) (312) 555-8906	resume
Dir. of Mines	Suite 72	(F) (312) 555-9806	screen
	tkeefe@mail.com		

You could record this as a simple Word document and you could still use the *find* function if you were trying to locate some data and could only recall the firm's name or the contact's name. If you're comfortable with database management and have some database software on your computer, then you can put information at your fingertips even if you have only the zip code! The point here is not technological sophistication but good record keeping.

Once you have created this initial list, it will be helpful to keep more detailed information as you begin to actually make the contacts. Using the Network Contact Record form in Exhibit 4.1 will help you keep good information on all your network contacts. They'll appreciate your recall of details of your meetings and conversations, and the information will help you to focus your networking efforts.

Exhibit 4.1

Network Contact Record

Name: Be certain your spelling is absolutely correct.

Title: Pick up a business card to be certain of the correct title.

Employing organization: Note any parent company or subsidiaries.

Business mailing address: This is often different from the street address.

Business E-mail address:

Business telephone number: Include area code and alternative numbers.

Business fax number:

Source for this contact: Who referred you, and what is their relationship to the contact?

Date of call or letter: Use plenty of space here to record multiple phone calls or visits, other employees you may have met, names of secretaries/ receptionists, and so forth.

Content of discussion: Keep enough notes here to remind you of the substance of your visits and telephone conversations in case some time elapses between contacts.

Follow-up necessary to continue working with this contact:
Your contact may request that you send him or her some materials or direct you to contact an associate. Note any such instructions or assignments in this space.

Name of additional networker: Here you would record the
Address: names and phone numbers of
E-Mail: additional contacts met at this
Phone: employer's site. Often you will
Fax: be introduced to many people,
Name of additional networker: some of whom may indicate
Address: a willingness to help in your
E-mail: job search.
Phone:
Fax:
Name of additional networker:
Address:
E-mail:
Phone:
Fax:

Date thank-you note written: May help to date your next contact.

Follow-up action taken: Phone calls, visits, additional notes

Other miscellaneous notes: Record any other additional interaction you think may be important to remember in working with this networking client. You will want this form in front of you when telephoning or just before and after a visit.

Create Your Self-Promotion Tools

There are two types of promotional tools that are used in the networking process. The first is a resume and cover letter, and the second is a one-minute "infomercial," which may be given over the telephone or in person.

Techniques for writing an effective resume and cover letter are discussed in Chapter 2. Once you have reviewed that material and prepared these important documents, you will have created one of your self-promotion tools.

The one-minute infomercial will demand that you begin tying your interests, abilities, and skills to the people or organizations you want to network with. Think about your goal for making the contact to help you understand what you should say about yourself. You should be able to express yourself easily and convincingly. If, for example, you are contacting an alumnus of your institution to obtain the names of possible employment sites in a distant city, be prepared to discuss why you are interested in moving to that location, the types of jobs you are interested in, and the skills and abilities you possess that will make you a qualified candidate.

To create a meaningful one-minute infomercial, write it out, practice it as if it will be a spoken presentation, rewrite it, and practice it again if necessary until expressing yourself comes easily and is convincing.

Here's a simplified example of an infomercial for use over the telephone:

> Hello, Ms. Regan? My name is Ruth Fowler. I am a recent graduate of Polytechnic University, and I hope to enter the field of human resources. I was a psychology major and feel confident that I have many of the skills valued in HR, such as writing, speaking, and preparing and delivering effective presentations. What's more, I work well under pressure. I have read that can be a real advantage in your field!
>
> Ms. Regan, I'm calling you because I still need more information about the HR field. I'm hoping you'll have time to sit down with me for about half an hour and discuss your perspective on HR careers. There are so many possible places to work in human resources, and I am seeking some advice on which of those settings might be the best for my particular combination of skills and experiences.
>
> Would you be willing to do that for me? I would greatly appreciate it. I am available most mornings, if that's convenient for you.

It very well may happen that your employer contact wishes you to communicate by E-mail. The infomercial quoted above could easily be rewritten for an E-mail message. You should "cut and paste" your resume right into the E-mail text itself.

Other effective self-promotion tools include portfolios for those in the arts, writing professions, or teaching. Portfolios show examples of work, photographs of projects or classroom activities, or certificates and credentials that are job related. There may not be an opportunity to use the portfolio during an interview, and it is not something that should be left with the organization. It is designed to be explained and displayed by the creator. However, during some networking meetings, there may be an opportunity to illustrate a point or strengthen a qualification by exhibiting the portfolio.

BEGINNING THE NETWORKING PROCESS

Set the Tone for Your Contacts

It can be useful to establish "tone words" for any communications you embark upon. Before making your first telephone call or writing your first letter, decide what you want your contact to think of you. If you are networking to try to obtain a job, your tone words might include words such as *genuine, informed,* and *self-knowledgeable.* When trying to acquire information, your tone words may have a slightly different focus, such as *courteous, organized, focused,* and *well-spoken.* Use the tone words you establish for your contacts to guide you through the networking process.

Honestly Express Your Intentions

When contacting individuals, it is important to be honest about your reasons for making the contact. Establish your purpose in your own mind and be able and ready to articulate it concisely. Determine an initial agenda, whether it be informational questioning or self-promotion, present it to your contact, and be ready to respond immediately. If you don't adequately prepare before initiating your contacts, you may find yourself at a disadvantage if you're asked to immediately begin your informational interview or self-promotion during the first phone conversation or visit.

Start Networking Within Your Circle of Confidence

Once you have organized your approach—by utilizing specific researching methods, creating a system for keeping track of the people you will contact, and developing effective self-promotion tools—you are ready to begin networking. The best way to begin networking is by talking with a group of people you trust and feel comfortable with. This group is usually made up of your family, friends, and career counselors. No matter who is in this inner circle, they will have a special interest in seeing you succeed in your job search. In addition, because they will be easy to talk to, you should try taking some risks in terms of practicing your information-seeking approach. Gain confidence in talking about the strengths you bring to an organization and the underdeveloped skills you feel hinder your candidacy. Be sure to review the section on self-assessment for tips on approaching each of these areas. Ask for critical but constructive feedback from the people in your circle of confidence on the letters you write and the one-minute infomercial you have developed. Evaluate whether you want to make the changes they suggest, then practice the changes on others within this circle.

Stretch the Boundaries of Your Networking Circle of Confidence

Once you have refined the promotional tools you will use to accomplish your networking goals, you will want to make additional contacts. Because you will not know most of these people, it will be a less comfortable activity to undertake. The practice that you gained with your inner circle of trusted friends should have prepared you to now move outside of that comfort zone.

It is said that any information a person needs is only two phone calls away, but the information cannot be gained until you (1) make a reasonable guess about who might have the information you need and (2) pick up the telephone to make the call. Using your network list that includes alumni, instructors, supervisors, employers, and associations, you can begin preparing your list of questions that will allow you to get the information you need. Review the question list that follows and then develop a list of your own.

Questions You Might Want to Ask

1. In the position you now hold, what do you do on a typical day?

2. What are the most interesting aspects of your job?

3. What part of your work do you consider dull or repetitious?

4. What were the jobs you had that led to your present position?

5. How long does it usually take to move from one step to the next in this career path?

6. What is the top position to which you can aspire in this career path?

7. What is the next step in *your* career path?

8. Are there positions in this field that are similar to your position?

9. What are the required qualifications and training for entry-level positions in this field?

10. Are there specific courses a student should take to be qualified to work in this field?

11. What are the entry-level jobs in this field?

12. What types of training are provided to persons entering this field?

13. What are the salary ranges your organization typically offers to entry-level candidates for positions in this field?

14. What special advice would you give a person entering this field?

15. Do you see this field as a growing one?

16. How do you see the content of the entry-level jobs in this field changing over the next two years?

17. What can I do to prepare myself for these changes?

18. What is the best way to obtain a position that will start me on a career in this field?

19. Do you have any information on job specifications and descriptions that I may have?

20. What related occupational fields would you suggest I explore?

21. How could I improve my resume for a career in this field?

22. Who else would you suggest I talk to, both in your organization and in other organizations?

Questions You Might Have to Answer

In order to communicate effectively, you must anticipate questions that will be asked of you by the networkers you contact. Review the list below and see if you can easily answer each of these questions. If you cannot, it may be time to revisit the self-assessment process.

1. Where did you get my name, or how did you find out about this organization?

2. What are your career goals?

3. What kind of job are you interested in?

4. What do you know about this organization and this industry?

5. How do you know you're prepared to undertake an entry-level position in this industry?

6. What course work have you done that is related to your career interests?

7. What are your short-term career goals?

8. What are your long-term career goals?

9. Do you plan to obtain additional formal education?

10. What contributions have you made to previous employers?

11. Which of your previous jobs have you enjoyed the most and why?

12. What are you particularly good at doing?

13. What shortcomings have you had to face in previous employment?

14. What are your three greatest strengths?

15. Describe how comfortable you feel with your communication style.

General Networking Tips

Make Every Contact Count. Setting the tone for each interaction is critical. Approaches that will help you communicate in an effective way include politeness, being appreciative of time provided to you, and being prepared and thorough. Remember, *everyone* within an organization has a circle of influence, so be prepared to interact effectively with each person you encounter in the networking process, including secretarial and support staff. Many information or job seekers have thwarted their own efforts by being rude to some individuals they encountered as they networked because they made the incorrect assumption that certain persons were unimportant.

Sometimes your contacts may be surprised at their ability to help you. After meeting and talking with you, they might think they have not offered much in the way of help. A day or two later, however, they may make a contact that would be useful to you and refer you to it.

With Each Contact, Widen Your Circle of Networkers. Always leave an informational interview with the names of at least two more people who can help you get the information or job that you are seeking. Don't be shy about asking for additional contacts; networking is all about increasing the number of people you can interact with to achieve your goals.

Make Your Own Decisions. As you talk with different people and get answers to the questions you pose, you may hear conflicting information or get conflicting suggestions. Your job is to listen to these "experts" and decide what information and which suggestions will help you achieve *your* goals. Only implement those suggestions that you believe will work for you.

SHUTTING DOWN YOUR NETWORK

As you achieve the goals that motivated your networking activity—getting the information you need or the job you want—the time will come to inactivate all or parts of your network. As you do so, be sure to tell your primary supporters about your change in status. Call or write to each one of them and give them as many details about your new status as you feel is necessary to maintain a positive relationship.

Because a network takes on a life of its own, activity undertaken on your behalf will continue even after you cease your efforts. As you get calls or are contacted in some fashion, be sure to inform these networkers about your change in status, and thank them for assistance they have provided.

Information on the latest employment trends indicates that workers will change jobs or careers several times in their lifetime. Networking, then, will be a critical aspect in the span of your professional life. If you carefully and thoughtfully conduct your networking activities during your job search, you will have a solid foundation of experience when you need to network the next time around.

CHAPTER FIVE

INTERVIEWING

*C*ertainly, there can be no one part of the job search process more fraught with anxiety and worry than the interview. Yet seasoned job seekers welcome the interview and will often say, "Just get me an interview and I'm on my way!" They understand that the interview is crucial to the hiring process and equally crucial for them, as job candidates, to have the opportunity of a personal dialogue to add to what the employer may already have learned from a resume, cover letter, and telephone conversations.

Believe it or not, the interview is to be welcomed, and even enjoyed! It is a perfect opportunity for you, the candidate, to sit down with an employer and express yourself and display who you are and what you want. Of course, it takes thought and planning and a little strategy; after all, it *is* a job interview! But it can be a positive, if not pleasant, experience and one you can look back on and feel confident about your performance and effort.

For many new job seekers, a job, any job, seems a wonderful thing. But seasoned interview veterans know that the job interview is an important step for both sides—the employer and the candidate—to see what each has to offer and whether there is going to be a "fit" of personalities, work styles, and attitudes. And it is this concept of balance in the interview, that both sides have important parts to play, that holds the key to success in mastering this aspect of the job search strategy.

Try to think of the interview as a conversation between two interested and equal partners. You both have important, even vital, information to deliver and to learn. Of course, there's no denying the employer has some leverage, especially in the initial interview for recruitment or any interview scheduled by the candidate and not the recruiter. That should not prevent the interviewee from seeking to play an equal part in what should be a fair exchange of information. Too often the untutored candidate allows the interview to become one-sided. The employer asks all the questions and the candidate simply responds. The ideal would be for two mutually interested parties to sit down and discuss possibilities for each. This is a *conversation of significance,* and it requires pre-interview preparation, thought about the tone of the interview, and planning of the nature and details of the information to be exchanged.

PREPARING FOR THE INTERVIEW

Most initial interviews are about thirty minutes long. Given the brevity, the information that is exchanged ought to be important. The candidate should be delivering material that the employer cannot discover on the resume and, in turn, the candidate should be learning things about the employer that he or she could not otherwise find out. After all, if you have only thirty minutes, why waste time on information that is already published? The information exchanged is more than just factual, and both sides will learn much from what they see of each other, as well. How the candidate looks, speaks, and acts is important to the employer. The employer's attention to the interview and awareness of the candidate's resume, the setting, and the quality of information presented are important to the candidate.

Just as the employer has every right to be disappointed when a prospect is late for the interview, looks unkempt, and seems ill-prepared to answer fairly standard questions, the candidate may be disappointed with an interviewer who isn't ready for the meeting, hasn't learned the basic resume facts, and is constantly interrupted for telephone calls. In either situation there's good reason to feel let down.

There are many elements to a successful interview, and some of them are not easy to describe or prepare for. Sometimes there is just a chemistry between interviewer and interviewee that brings out the best in both, and a good exchange takes place. But there is much the candidate can do to pave the way for success in terms of his or her resume, personal appearance, goals, and interview strategy—each of which we will discuss. However, none of this preparation is as important as the time and thought the candidate gives to personal self-assessment.

Self-Assessment

Neither a stunning resume nor an expensive, well-tailored suit can compensate for candidates who do not know what they want, where they are going, or why they are interviewing with a particular employer. Self-assessment, the process by which we begin to know and acknowledge our own particular blend of education, experiences, needs, and goals, is not something that can be sorted out the weekend before a major interview. Of all the elements of interview preparation, this one requires the longest lead time and cannot be faked.

Because the time allotted for most interviews is brief, it is all the more important for job candidates to understand and express succinctly why they are there and what they have to offer. This is not a time for undue modesty (or for braggadocio either); it is a time for a compelling, reasoned statement of why you feel that you and this employer might make a good match. It means you have to have thought about your skills, interests, and attributes; related those to your life experiences and your own history of challenges and opportunities; and determined what that indicates about your strengths, preferences, values, and areas needing further development.

A common complaint of employers is that many candidates didn't take advantage of the interview time, didn't seem to know why they were there or what they wanted. When candidates are asked to talk about themselves and their work-related skills and attributes, employers don't want to be faced with shyness or embarrassed laughter; they need to know about you so they can make a fair determination of you and your competition. If you lose the opportunity to make a case for your employability, you can be certain the person ahead of you has or the person after you will, and it will be on the strength of those impressions that the employer will hire.

If you need some assistance with self-assessment issues, refer to Chapter 1. Included are suggested exercises that can be done as needed, such as making up an experiential diary and extracting obvious strengths and weaknesses from past experiences. These simple assignments will help you look at past activities as collections of tasks with accompanying skills and responsibilities. Don't overlook your high school or college career office. Many offer personal counseling on self-assessment issues and may provide testing instruments such as the Myers-Briggs Type Indicator (MBTI), the Harrington-O'Shea Career Decision Making System (CDM), the Strong Interest Inventory (SII), or any of a wide selection of assessment tools that can help you clarify some of these issues prior to the interview stage of your job search.

The Resume

Resume preparation has been discussed in detail, and some basic examples of various types were provided. In this section we want to concentrate on how best to use your resume in the interview. In most cases the employer will have seen the resume prior to the interview and, in fact, it may well have been the quality of that resume that secured the interview opportunity.

An interview is a conversation, however, and not an exercise in reading. So, if the employer hasn't seen your resume and you have brought it along to the interview, wait until asked or until the end of the interview to offer it. Otherwise, you may find yourself staring at the back of your resume and simply answering "yes" and "no" to a series of questions drawn from that document.

Sometimes an interviewer is not prepared and does not know or recall the contents of the resume and may use the resume to a greater or lesser degree as a "prompt" during the interview. It is for you to judge what that may indicate about the individual doing the interview or the employer. If your interviewer seems surprised by the scheduled meeting, relies on the resume to an inordinate degree, and seems otherwise unfamiliar with your background, this lack of preparation for the hiring process could well be a symptom of general management disorganization or may simply be the result of poor planning on the part of one individual. It is your responsibility as a potential employee to be aware of these signals and make your decisions accordingly.

··

In any event, it is perfectly acceptable for you to get the conversation back to a more interpersonal style by saying something like, "Mr. Smith, you might be interested in some recent counseling experience I gained in a volunteer position at our state prison that is not detailed on my resume. May I tell you about it?" This can return the interview to two people talking to each other, not one reading and the other responding.

··

By all means, bring at least one copy of your resume to the interview. Occasionally, at the close of an interview, an interviewer will express an interest in circulating a resume to several departments, and you could then offer the copy you brought. Sometimes, an interview appointment provides an opportunity to meet others in the organization who may express an interest in you and your background, and it may be helpful to follow up with a copy of your resume. Our best advice, however, is to keep it out of sight until needed or requested.

Appearance

Although many of the absolute rules that once dominated the advice offered to job candidates about appearance have now been moderated significantly, conservative is still the watchword unless you are interviewing in a fashion-related industry. For men, conservative translates into a well-cut dark suit with appropriate tie, hosiery, and dress shirt. A wise strategy for the male job seeker looking for a good but not expensive suit would be to try the men's department of a major department store. They usually carry a good range of sizes, fabrics, and prices; offer professional sales help; provide free tailoring; and have associated departments for putting together a professional look.

For women, there is more latitude. Business suits are still popular, but they have become more feminine in color and styling with a variety of jacket and skirt lengths. In addition to suits, better-quality dresses are now worn in many environments and, with the correct accessories, can be most appropriate. Company literature, professional magazines, the business section of major newspapers, and television interviews can all give clues about what is being worn in different employer environments.

Both men and women need to pay attention to issues such as hair, jewelry, and makeup; these are often what separates the candidate in appearance from the professional workforce. It seems particularly difficult for the young job seeker to give up certain hairstyles, eyeglass fashions, and jewelry habits, yet those can be important to the employer who is concerned with your ability to successfully make the transition into the organization. Candidates often find the best strategy is to dress conservatively until they find employment. Once employed and familiar with the norms within your organization, you can begin to determine a look that you enjoy, works for you, and fits your organization.

Choose clothes that suit your body type, fit well, and flatter you. Feel good about the way you look! The interview day is not the best for a new hairdo, a new pair of shoes, or any other change that will distract you or cause you to be self-conscious. Arrive a bit early to avoid being rushed, and ask the receptionist to direct you to a restroom for any last-minute adjustments of hair and clothes.

Employer Information

Whether your interview is for graduate school admission, an overseas corporate position, or a reporter position with a local newspaper, it is important to know something about the employer or the organization. Keeping in mind that the interview is relatively brief and that you will hopefully have other interviews with other organizations, it is important to keep your research in proportion. If secondary interviews are called for, you will have additional time to do further research. For the first interview, it is helpful to know the organization's mission, goals, size, scope of operations, and so forth. Your research may uncover recent areas of challenge or particular successes that may help to fuel the interview. Use the "What Do They Call the Job You Want?" section of Chapter 3, your library, and your career or guidance office to help you locate this information in the most efficient way possible. Don't be shy in asking advice of these counseling and guidance professionals on how best to spend your preparation time. With some practice, you'll soon learn how much information is enough and which kinds of information are most useful to you.

INTERVIEW CONTENT

We've already discussed how it can help to think of the interview as an important conversation—one that, as with any conversation, you want to find pleasant and interesting and to leave you with a good feeling. But because this conversation is especially important, the information that's exchanged is critical to its success. What do you want them to know about you? What do you need to know about them? What interview technique do you need to particularly pay attention to? How do you want to manage the close of the interview? What steps will follow in the hiring process?

Except for the professional interviewer, most of us find interviewing stressful and anxiety-provoking. Developing a strategy before you begin interviewing will help you relieve some stress and anxiety. One particular strategy that has worked for many and may work for you is interviewing by objective. Before you interview, write down three to five goals you would like to achieve for that interview. They may be technique goals: smile a little more, have a firmer handshake, be sure to ask about the next stage in the interview process before leaving. They may be content-oriented goals: find out about the company's current challenges and opportunities; be sure to speak of your recent research, writing experiences, or foreign travel; and so on. Whatever your goals, jot down a few of them as goals for each interview.

Most people find that, in trying to achieve these few goals, their interviewing technique becomes more organized and focused. After the interview, the most common question friends and family ask is "How did it go?" With this technique, you have an indication of whether you met *your* goals for the meeting, not just some vague idea of how it went. Chances are, if you accomplished what you wanted to, it improved the quality of the entire interview. As you continue to interview, you will want to revise your goals to continue improving your interview skills.

Now, add to the concept of the significant conversation the idea of a beginning, a middle, and a closing and you will have two thoughts that will give your interview a distinctive character. Be sure to make your introduction warm and cordial. Say your full name (and if it's a difficult-to-pronounce name, help the interviewer to pronounce it) and make certain you know your interviewer's name and how to pronounce it. Most interviews begin with some "soft talk" about the weather, chat about the candidate's trip to the interview site, or national events. This is done as a courtesy to relax both you and the interviewer, to get you talking, and to generally try to defuse the atmosphere of excessive tension. Try to be yourself, engage in the conversation, and don't try to second-guess the interviewer. This is simply what it appears to be—casual conversation.

Once you and the interviewer move on to exchange more serious information in the middle part of the interview, the two most important concerns become your ability to handle challenging questions and your success at asking meaningful ones. Interviewer questions will probably fall into one of three categories: personal assessment and career direction, academic assessment, and knowledge of the employer. The following are some examples of questions in each category:

Personal Assessment and Career Direction

1. How would you describe yourself?

2. What motivates you to put forth your best effort?

3. In what kind of work environment are you most comfortable?

4. What do you consider to be your greatest strengths and weaknesses?

5. How well do you work under pressure?

6. What qualifications do you have that make you think you will be successful in this career?

7. Will you relocate? What do you feel would be the most difficult aspect of relocating?

8. Are you willing to travel?

9. Why should I hire you?

Academic Assessment

1. Why did you select your college or university?

2. What changes would you make at your alma mater?

3. What led you to choose your major?

4. What subjects did you like best and least? Why?

5. If you could, how would you plan your academic study differently? Why?

6. Describe your most rewarding college experience.

7. How has your college experience prepared you for this career?

8. Do you think that your grades are a good indication of your ability to succeed with this organization?

9. Do you have plans for continued study?

Knowledge of the Employer

1. If you were hiring a graduate of your school for this position, what qualities would you look for?

2. What do you think it takes to be successful in an organization like ours?

3. In what ways do you think you can make a contribution to our organization?

4. Why did you choose to seek a position with this organization?

The interviewer wants a response to each question but is also gauging your enthusiasm, preparedness, and willingness to communicate. In each response you should provide some information about yourself that can be related to the employer's needs. A common mistake is to give too much information. Answer each question completely, but be careful not to run on too long with extensive details or examples.

Questions About Underdeveloped Skills

Most employers interview people who have met some minimum criteria of education and experience. They interview candidates to see who they are, to learn what kind of personality they exhibit, and to get some sense of how this person might fit into the existing organization. It may be that you are asked about skills the employer hopes to find and that you have not documented. Maybe it's grant-writing experience, knowledge of the European political system, or a knowledge of the film world.

To questions about skills and experiences you don't have, answer honestly and forthrightly and try to offer some additional information about skills you do have. For example, perhaps the employer is disappointed you have no grant-writing experience. An honest answer may be as follows:

> No, unfortunately, I was never in a position to acquire those skills. I do understand something of the complexities of the grant-writing process and feel confident that my attention to detail, careful reading skills, and strong writing would make grants a wonderful challenge in a new job. I think I could get up on the learning curve quickly.

The employer hears an honest admission of lack of experience but is reassured by some specific skill details that do relate to grant writing and a confident manner that suggests enthusiasm and interest in a challenge.

For many students, questions about their possible contribution to an employer's organization can prove challenging. Because your education has probably not included specific training for a job, you need to review your academic record and select capabilities you have developed in your major that an employer can appreciate. For example, perhaps you read well and can analyze and condense what you've read into smaller, more focused pieces. That could be valuable. Or maybe you did some serious research and you know you have valuable investigative skills. Your public speaking might be highly developed and you might use visual aids appropriately and effectively. Or maybe your skill at correspondence, memos, and messages is effective. Whatever it is, you must take it out of the academic context and put it into a new, employer-friendly context so your interviewer can best judge how you could help the organization.

Exhibiting knowledge of the organization will, without a doubt, show the interviewer that you are interested enough in the available position to have done some legwork in preparation for the interview. Remember, it is not necessary to know every detail of the organization's history, but rather to have a general knowledge about why it is in business and how the industry is faring.

Sometime during the interview, generally after the midway point, you'll be asked if you have any questions for the interviewer. Your questions will tell the employer much about your attitude and your desire to understand the organization's expectations so you can compare it to your own strengths. The following are some selected questions you might want to ask:

1. What are the main responsibilities of the position?

2. What are the opportunities and challenges associated with this position?

3. Could you outline some possible career paths beginning with this position?

4. How regularly do performance evaluations occur?

5. What is the communication style of the organization? (meetings, memos, and so forth.)

6. What would a typical day in this position be like for me?

7. What kinds of opportunities might exist for me to improve my professional skills within the organization?

8. What have been some of the interesting challenges and opportunities your organization has recently faced?

Most interviews draw to a natural closing point, so be careful not to prolong the discussion. At a signal from the interviewer, wind up your presentation, express your appreciation for the opportunity, and be sure to ask what the next stage in the process will be. When can you expect to hear from them?

Will they be conducting second-tier interviews? If you're interested and haven't heard, would they mind a phone call? Be sure to collect a business card with the name and phone number of your interviewer. On your way out, you might have an opportunity to pick up organizational literature you haven't seen before.

With the right preparation—a thorough self-assessment, professional clothing, and employer information—you'll be able to set and achieve the goals you have established for the interview process.

CHAPTER SIX

NETWORKING OR INTERVIEW FOLLOW-UP

Quite often there is a considerable time lag between interviewing for a position and being hired or, in the case of the networker, between your phone call or letter to a possible contact and the opportunity of a meeting. This can be frustrating. "Why aren't they contacting me?" "I thought I'd get another interview, but no one has telephoned." "Am I out of the running?" You don't know what is happening.

CONSIDER THE DIFFERING PERSPECTIVES

Of course, there is another perspective—that of the networker or hiring organization. Organizations are complex, with multiple tasks that need to be accomplished each day. Hiring is but one discrete activity that does not occur as frequently as other job assignments. The hiring process might have to take second place to other, more immediate organizational needs. Although it may be very important to you, and it is certainly ultimately significant to the employer, other issues such as fiscal management, planning and product development, employer vacation periods, or financial constraints may prevent an organization or individual within that organization from acting on your employment or your request for information as quickly as you or they would prefer.

USE YOUR COMMUNICATION SKILLS

Good communication is essential here to resolve any anxieties, and the responsibility is on you, the job or information seeker. Too many job seekers and networkers offer as an excuse that they don't want to "bother" the organization by writing letters or calling. Let us assure you here and now, once and for all, that if you are troubling an organization by over-communicating, someone will indicate that situation to you quite clearly. If not, you can only assume you are a worthwhile prospect and the employer appreciates being reminded of your availability and interest in them. Let's look at follow-up practices in both the job interview process and the networking situation separately.

FOLLOWING UP ON THE EMPLOYMENT INTERVIEW

A brief thank-you note following an interview is an excellent and polite way to begin a series of follow-up communications with a potential employer with whom you have interviewed and want to remain in touch. It should be just that—a thank you for a good meeting. If you failed to mention some fact or experience during your interview that you think might add to your candidacy, you may use this note to do that. However, this should be essentially a note whose overall tone is appreciative and, if appropriate, indicative of a continuing interest in pursuing any opportunity that may exist with that organization. It is one of the few pieces of business correspondence that may be handwritten, but always use plain, good quality, standard-size paper.

If, however, at this point you are no longer interested in the employer, the thank-you note is an appropriate time to indicate that. You are under no obligation to identify any reason for not continuing to pursue employment with that organization, but if you are so inclined to indicate your professional reasons (pursuing other employers more akin to your interests, looking for greater income production than this employer can provide, a different geographic location than is available), you certainly may. It should not be written with an eye to negotiation for it will not be interpreted as such.

As part of your interview closing, you should have taken the initiative to establish lines of communication for continuing information about your candidacy. If you asked permission to telephone, wait a week following your thank-you note, then telephone your contact simply to inquire how things are progressing on your employment status. The feedback you receive here should be taken at face value. If your interviewer simply has no information, he or she will tell you so and indicate whether you should call again and when. Don't be discouraged if this should continue over some period of time.

If during this time something occurs that you think improves or changes your candidacy (some new qualification or experience you may have had), including any offers from other organizations, by all means telephone or write to inform the employer about this. In the case of an offer from a competing but less desirable or equally desirable organization, telephone your contact, explain what has happened, express your real interest in the organization, and inquire whether some determination on your employment might be made before you must respond to this other offer. If the organization is truly interested in you, they may be moved to make a decision about your candidacy. Equally possible is the scenario in which they are not yet ready to make a decision and so advise you to take the offer that has been presented. Again, you have no ethical alternative but to deal with the information presented in a straightforward manner.

When accepting other employment, be sure to contact any employers still actively considering you and inform them of your new job. Thank them graciously for their consideration. There are many other job seekers out there just like you who will benefit from having their candidacy improved when others bow out of the race. Who knows, you might at some future time have occasion to interact professionally with one of the organizations with whom you sought employment. How embarrassing to have someone remember you as the candidate who failed to notify them of taking a job elsewhere!

In all of your follow-up communications, keep good notes of whom you spoke with, when you called, and any instructions that were given about return communications. This will prevent any misunderstandings and provide you with good records of what has transpired.

FOLLOWING UP ON THE NETWORK CONTACT

Far more common than the forgotten follow-up after an interview is the situation where a good network contact is allowed to lapse. Good communications are the essence of a network, and follow-up is not so much a matter of courtesy here as it is a necessity. In networking for job information and contacts, you are the active network link. Without you, and without continual contact from you, there is no network. You and your need for employment is often the only shared element between members of the network. Because network contacts were made regardless of the availability of any particular employment, it is incumbent upon the job seeker, if not simple common sense, that unless you stay in regular communication with the network, you will not be available for consideration should some job become available in the future.

This brings up the issue of responsibility, which is likewise very clear. The job seeker initiates network contacts and is responsible for maintaining those contacts; therefore, the entire responsibility for the network belongs with him or her. This becomes patently obvious if the network is left unattended. It very shortly falls out of existence because it cannot survive without careful attention by the networker.

A variety of ways are open to you to keep the lines of communication open and to attempt to interest the network in you as a possible employee. You are limited only by your own enthusiasm for members of the network and your creativity. However, you as a networker are well advised to keep good records of whom you have met and contacted in each organization. Be sure to send thank-you notes to anyone who has spent any time with you, be it an E-mail message containing information or advice, a quick tour of a department, or a sit-down informational interview. All of these communications should, in addition to their ostensible reason, add some information about you and your particular combination of strengths and attributes.

You can contact your network at any time to convey continued interest, to comment on some recent article you came across concerning an organization, to add information about your training or changes in your qualifications, to ask advice or seek guidance in your job search, or to request referrals to other possible network opportunities. Sometimes just a simple note to network members reminding them of your job search, indicating that you have been using their advice, and noting that you are still actively pursuing leads and hope to continue to interact with them is enough to keep communications alive.

The Internet has opened up the world of networking. You may be able to find networkers who graduated from your high school or from the college you're attending, who live in a geographic region where you hope to work, or who are employed in a given industry. The Internet makes it easy to reach out to many people, but don't let this perceived ease lull you into complacency. Internet networking demands the same level of preparation as the more traditional forms of networking do.

Because networks have been abused in the past, it's important that your conduct be above reproach. Networks are exploratory options, they are not backdoor access to employers. The network works best for someone who is exploring a new industry or making a transition into a new area of employment and who needs to find information or to alert people to his or her search activity. Always be candid and direct with contacts in expressing the purpose of your E-mail, call, or letter and your interest in their help or information about their organization. In follow-up contacts keep the tone professional and direct. Your honesty will be appreciated, and people will respond as best they can if your qualifications appear to meet their forthcoming needs. The network does not owe you anything, and that tone should be clear to each person you meet.

FEEDBACK FROM FOLLOW-UPS

A network contact may prove to be miscalculated. Perhaps you were referred to someone and it became clear that your goals and his or her particular needs did not make a good match. Or the network contact may simply not be in a position to provide you with the information you are seeking. Or in some unfortunate situations, the contact may become annoyed by being contacted for this purpose. In such a situation, many job seekers simply say "Thank you" and move on.

If the contact is simply not the right connection, but the individual you are speaking with is not annoyed by the call, it might be a better tactic to express regret that the contact was misplaced and then tell the person what you are seeking and ask for his or her advice or possible suggestions as to a next step. The more people who are aware you are seeking employment, the better your chances of connecting, and that is the purpose of a network. Most people in a profession have excellent knowledge of their field and varying amounts of expertise on areas near to or tangent to their own. Use their expertise and seek some guidance before you dissolve the contact. You may be pleasantly surprised.

Occasionally, networkers will express the feeling that they have done as much as they can or provided all the information that is available to them. This may be a cue that they would like to be released from your network. Be alert to such attempts to terminate, graciously thank the individual by letter, and move on in your network development. A network is always changing, adding, and losing members, and you want the network to be composed only of those who are actively interested in supporting you.

A FINAL POINT ON
NETWORKING FOR PSYCHOLOGY MAJORS

In any field a psychology major might consider as a potential career path, your contacts will be critically evaluating all of your written and verbal communications. For many jobs drawing on your psychology background, how you connect and communicate with others will be of paramount importance. Your choice of major carries with it a very legitimate assumption that you know something about how people work and how they behave. The quality of your own communications will be a crucial part of the criteria by which you are judged.

In your telephone communications, interview presentations, follow-up correspondence, and in dealing with negative feedback, your communication style will be part of the portfolio of impressions you create in those you meet along the way.

....

CHAPTER SEVEN

JOB OFFER CONSIDERATIONS

for many recent college graduates, the thrill of their first job and, for some, the most substantial regular income they have ever earned seems an excess of good fortune coming at once. To question that first income or to be critical in any way of the conditions of employment at the time of the initial offer seems like looking a gift horse in the mouth. It doesn't seem to occur to many new hires even to attempt to negotiate any aspect of their first job. And, as many employers who deal with entry-level jobs for recent college graduates will readily confirm, the reality is that there simply isn't much movement in salary available to these new college recruits. The entry-level hire generally does not have an employment track record on a professional level to provide any leverage for negotiation. Real negotiations on salary, benefits, retirement provisions, and so forth, come to those with significant employment records at higher income levels.

Of course, the job offer is more than just money. It can be composed of geographic assignment, duties and responsibilities, training, benefits, health and medical insurance, educational assistance, car allowance or company vehicle, and a host of other items. All of this is generally detailed in the formal letter that presents the final job offer. In most cases this is a follow-up to a personal phone call from the employer representative who has been principally responsible for your hiring process.

That initial telephone offer is certainly binding as a verbal agreement, but most firms follow up with a detailed letter outlining the most significant parts of your employment contract. You may certainly choose to respond immediately at the time of the telephone offer (which would be considered a binding oral contract), but you will also be required to formally answer the letter of offer with a letter of acceptance, restating the salient elements of the employer's description of your position, salary, and benefits. This ensures that both parties are clear on the terms and conditions of employment and remuneration and any other outstanding aspects of the job offer.

IS THIS THE JOB YOU WANT?

Most new employees will write this letter of acceptance back, glad to be in the position to accept employment. If you've worked hard to get the offer and the job market is tight, other offers may not be in sight, so you will say, "Yes, I accept!" What is important here is that the job offer you accept be one that does fit your particular needs, values, and interests as you've outlined them in your self-assessment process. Moreover, it should be a job that will not only use your skills and education, but also challenge you to develop new skills and talents.

Jobs are sometimes accepted too hastily, for the wrong reasons, and without proper scrutiny by the applicant. For example, an individual might readily accept a sales job only to find the continual rejection by potential clients unendurable. An office worker might realize within weeks the constraints of a desk job and yearn for more activity. Employment is an important part of our lives. It is, for most of our adult lives, our most continuous productive activity. We want to make good choices based on the right criteria.

If you have a low tolerance for risk, a job based on commission will certainly be very anxiety-provoking. If being near your family is important, issues of relocation could present a decision crisis for you. If you're an adventurous person, a job with frequent travel would provide needed excitement and be very desirable. The importance of income, the need to continue your education, your personal health situation—all of these have an impact on whether the job you are considering will ultimately meet your needs. Unless you've spent some time understanding and thinking about these issues, it will be difficult to evaluate offers you do receive.

More important, if you make a decision that you cannot tolerate and feel you must leave that job, you will then have both unemployment and self-esteem issues to contend with. These will combine to make the next job search tough going, indeed. So make your acceptance a carefully considered decision.

NEGOTIATING YOUR OFFER

It may be that there is some aspect of your job offer that is not particularly attractive to you. Perhaps there is no relocation allotment to help you move your possessions, and this presents some financial hardship for you. It may be that the medical and health insurance is less than you had hoped. Your initial assignment may be different from what you expected, either in its location or in the duties and responsibilities that comprise it. Or it may simply be that the salary is less than you anticipated. Other considerations may be your official starting date of employment, vacation time, evening hours, dates of training programs or schools, and other concerns.

If you are considering not accepting the job because of some item or items in the job offer "package" that do not meet your needs, you should know that most employers emphatically wish that you would bring that issue to their attention. It may be that the employer can alter it to make the offer more agreeable for you. In some cases it cannot be changed. In any event the employer would generally like to have the opportunity to try to remedy a difficulty rather than risk losing a good potential employee over an issue that might have been resolved. After all, they have spent time and funds in securing your services, and they certainly deserve an opportunity to resolve any possible differences.

Honesty is the best approach in discussing any objections or uneasiness you might have over the employer's offer. Having received your formal offer in writing, contact your employer representative and indicate your particular dissatisfaction in a straightforward manner. For example, you might explain that, while very interested in being employed by this organization, the salary (or any other benefit) is less than you have determined you require. State the terms you do need, and listen to the response. You may be asked to put this in writing, or you may be asked to hold off until the firm can decide on a response. If you are dealing with a senior representative of the organization, one who has been involved in hiring for some time, you may get an immediate response or a solid indication of possible outcomes.

Perhaps the issue is one of relocation. Your initial assignment is in the Midwest, and because you had indicated a strong West Coast preference, you are surprised at the actual assignment. You might simply indicate that, while you understand the need for the company to assign you based on its needs, you are disappointed and had hoped to be placed on the West Coast. You could inquire if that were still possible and, if not, would it be reasonable to expect a West Coast relocation in the future.

If your request is presented in a reasonable way, most employers will not see this as jeopardizing your offer. If they can agree to your proposal, they will. If not, they will simply tell you so, and you may choose to continue your candidacy with them or remove yourself from consideration as a possible employee. The choice will be up to you.

Some firms will adjust benefits within their parameters to meet the candidate's need if at all possible. If a candidate requires a relocation cost allowance, he or she may be asked to forgo tuition benefits for the first year to accomplish this adjustment. An increase in life insurance may be adjusted by some other benefit trade-off; perhaps a family dental plan is not needed. In these decisions you are called upon, sometimes under time pressure, to know how you value these issues and how important each is to you.

Many employers find they are more comfortable negotiating for candidates who have unique qualifications or who bring especially needed expertise to the organization. Employers hiring large numbers of entry-level college graduates may be far more reluctant to accommodate any changes in offer conditions. They are well supplied with candidates with similar education and experience, so that if rejected by one candidate, they can draw new candidates from an ample labor pool.

COMPARING OFFERS

The conditions of the economy, the job seekers' academic major and particular geographic job market, and their own needs and demands for certain employment conditions may not provide more than one job offer at a time. Some job seekers may feel that no reasonable offer should go unaccepted for the simple fear there won't be another.

In a tough job market, or if the job you seek is not widely available, or when your job search goes on too long and becomes difficult to sustain financially and emotionally, it may be necessary to accept an offer. The alternative is continued unemployment. Even here, when you feel you don't have a choice, you can at least understand that in accepting this particular offer, there may be limitations and conditions you don't appreciate. At the time of acceptance, there were no other alternatives, but the new employee can begin to use that position to gain the experience and talent to move toward a more attractive position.

Sometimes, however, more than one offer is received at one time, and the candidate has the luxury of choice. If the job seeker knows what he or she wants and has done the necessary self-assessment honestly and thoroughly, it may be clear that one of the offers conforms more closely to those expressed wants and needs.

However, if, as so often happens, the offers are similar in terms of conditions and salary, the question then becomes which organization might provide the necessary climate, opportunities, and advantages for your professional development and growth. This is the time when solid employer research and astute questioning during the interviews really pays off. How much did you learn about the employer through your own research and skillful questioning? When the interviewer asked during the interview "Do you have any questions?" did you ask the kinds of questions that would help resolve a choice between one organization and another? Just as an employer must decide among numerous applicants, so must the applicant learn to assess the potential employer. Both are partners in the job search.

RENEGING ON AN OFFER

An especially disturbing occurrence for employers and career counseling professionals is when a job seeker formally (either verbally or by written contract) accepts employment with one organization and later reneges on the agreement and goes with another employer.

There are all kinds of rationalizations offered for this unethical behavior. None of them satisfies. The sad irony is that what the job seeker is willing to do to the employer—make a promise and then break it—he or she would be outraged to have done to them—have the job offer pulled. It is a very bad way to begin a career. It suggests the individual has not taken the time to do the necessary self-assessment and self-awareness exercises to think and judge critically. The new offer taken may, in fact, be no better or worse than the one refused. Job candidates should be aware that there have been incidents of legal action following job candidates reneging on an offer. This adds a very sour note to what should be a harmonious beginning of a lifelong adventure.

CHAPTER EIGHT

THE GRADUATE SCHOOL CHOICE

The reasons for continuing one's education in graduate school can be as varied and unique as the individuals electing this course of action. Many continue their studies at an advanced level because they simply find it difficult to end the educational process. They love what they are learning and want to learn more and continue their academic exploration.

. . . .

Maybe you had a practicum experience or internship in your psychology program that had you intrigued about the possibilities of community practice. You saw first-hand the valuable contributions that individual psychotherapy and psychoanalysis made and felt strongly that you could make a contribution, perhaps in child or adolescent psychology or in group psychology. Some psychology majors have enjoyed their academic work but feel they want to know more than their undergraduate degree provided.

Others go to graduate school for purely practical reason; they have examined employment prospects in their field of study, and all indications are that a graduate degree is requisite. Certainly, in psychology, a graduate degree is required for clinical supervision responsibility, for jobs in therapeutic modalities, psychodiagnostics, for research, publication, and for teaching at the college level. Without a graduate degree, as some of the career paths in this book suggest, you will be using your psychology background as an ancillary skill.

If that is not enough for you and you feel you want to make your livelihood in psychology, then you might begin by reviewing jobs in the areas mentioned and their advanced degree requirements. Alumni working in college teaching, therapy, and clinical settings will be a wonderful source of what degree level is needed for certain jobs. Ask at your career office for some alumni names and give those people a telephone call or send them an E-mail. Prepare some questions on specific job prospects in their field at each degree level. A thorough examination of the marketplace and talking to employers and professionals will give you a sense of the scope of employment for a bachelor's degree, master's degree, or doctorate.

CONSIDER YOUR MOTIVES

The answer to the question of "Why graduate school?" is a personal one for each applicant. Nevertheless, it is important to consider your motives carefully. Graduate school involves additional time out of the employment market, a high degree of critical evaluation, significant autonomy as you pursue your studies, and considerable financial expenditure. For some students in doctoral programs, there may be additional life choice issues, such as relationships, marriage, and parenthood, that may present real challenges while in a program of study. You would be well advised to consider the following questions as you think about your decision to continue your studies.

Are You Postponing Some Tough Decisions by Going to School?

Graduate school is not a place to go to avoid life's problems. There is intense competition for graduate school slots and for the fellowships, scholarships, and financial aid available. This competition means extensive interviewing, resume submission, and essay writing that rivals corporate recruitment. Likewise, the graduate school process is a mentored one in which faculty stay aware of and involved in the academic progress of their students and continually challenge the quality of their work. Many graduate students are called upon to participate in teaching and professional writing and research as well.

In other words, this is no place to hide from the spotlight. Graduate students work very hard and much is demanded of them individually. If you elect to go to graduate school to avoid the stresses and strains of the "real world," you will find no safe place in higher academics. Vivid accounts, both fictional and nonfictional, have depicted quite accurately the personal and professional demands of graduate school work.

The selection of graduate studies as a career option should be a positive choice—something you *want* to do. It shouldn't be selected as an escape from other, less attractive or more challenging options, nor should it be selected as the option of last resort (i.e., "I can't do anything else; I'd better just stay in school."). If you're in some doubt about the strength of your reasoning about continuing in school, discuss the issues with a career counselor. Together you can clarify your reasoning, and you'll get some sound feedback on what you're about to undertake.

On the other hand, staying on in graduate school because of a particularly poor employment market and a lack of jobs at entry-level positions has proven to be an effective "stalling" strategy. If you can afford it, pursuing a graduate degree immediately after your undergraduate education gives you a year or two to "wait out" a difficult economic climate while at the same time acquiring a potentially valuable credential.

Have You Done Some "Hands-On" Reality Testing?

There are experiential options available to give some reality to your decision-making process about graduate school. Internships or work in the field can give you a good idea about employment demands, conditions, and atmosphere.

••

Perhaps as a psychology major, you're considering a graduate program in clinical psychology. A summer job or internship that puts you in contact with practicing clinicians may help to define for you exactly what clinical psychologists do. Even with the experience of only one employment setting, you have a stronger concept of the pace of the job, interaction with colleagues, subject matter, opportunities for personal development, and the amount of paperwork required. Talking to people and asking questions are invaluable as exercises to help you better understand the objecting of your graduate study.

For psychology majors especially, the opportunity to do this kind of reality testing is invaluable. It demonstrates far more authoritatively than any other method what your real-world skills are, how they can be put to use, and what aspects of your academic preparation you rely on. It has been well documented that psychology majors do well in their occupations once they identify them. Internships, practica, and co-op experiences speed that process up and prevent the frustrating and expensive process of investigation many graduates begin only after graduation.

....

Do You Need an Advanced Degree to Work in Your Field?

Certainly there are fields such as law, psychiatry, medicine, and college teaching that demand advanced degrees. Is the field of employment you're considering one that also puts a premium on an advanced degree? You may be surprised. Read job ads on the Internet and in a number of major Sunday newspapers for positions you would enjoy. How many of those require an advanced degree?

Retailing, for example, has always put a premium on what people can do, rather than how much education they have had. Successful people in retailing come from all academic preparations. A Ph.D. in your field may bring only more prestige to a job, but it may not bring a more senior position or better pay. In fact, it may disqualify you for some jobs because an employer might believe you will be unhappy to be overqualified for a particular position. Or your motives in applying for the work may be misconstrued, and the employer might think you will only be working at this level until something better comes along. None of this may be true for you, but it comes about because you are working outside of the usual territory for that degree level.

When economic times are especially difficult, we tend to see stories featured about individuals with advanced degrees doing what is considered unsuitable work, such as the Ph.D. in psychology driving a cab or the Ph.D. in chemistry waiting tables. Actually, this is not particularly surprising when you consider that as your degree level advances, the job market narrows appreciably. At any one time, regardless of economic circumstances, there are only so many jobs for your particular level of expertise. If you cannot find employment for your advanced degree level, chances are you will be considered suspect for many other kinds of employment and may be forced into temporary work far removed from your original intention.

Before making an important decision such as graduate study, learn your options and carefully consider what you want to do with your advanced degree. Ask yourself whether it is reasonable to think you can achieve your goals. Will there be jobs when you graduate? Where will they be? What will they pay? How competitive will the market be at that time, based on current predictions?

If you're uncertain about the degree requirements for the fields you're interested in, you should check a publication such as the U.S. Department of Labor's *Occupational Outlook Handbook* (www.bls.gov). Each entry has a section on training and other qualifications that will indicate what the minimum educational requirement is for employment, what degree is the standard, and what employment may be possible without the required credential.

For example, for physicists and astronomers a doctoral degree in physics or a closely related field is essential. Certainly this is the degree of choice in academic institutions. However, the *Occupational Outlook Handbook* also indicates what kinds of employment may be available to individuals holding a master's or even a bachelor's degree in physics.

Have You Compared Your Expectations of What Graduate School Will Do for You with What It Has Done for Alumni of the Program You're Considering?

Most colleges and universities perform some kind of postgraduate survey of their students to ascertain where they are employed, what additional education they have received, and what levels of salary they are enjoying. Ask to see this information either from the university you are considering applying to or from your own alma mater, especially if it has a similar graduate program. Such surveys often reveal surprises about occupational decisions, salaries, and work satisfaction. This information may affect your decision.

The value of self-assessment (the process of examining and making decisions about your own hierarchy of values and goals) is especially important in this process of analyzing the desirability of possible career paths involving graduate education. Sometimes a job requiring advanced education seems to hold real promise but is disappointing in salary potential or number of opportunities available. Certainly it is better to research this information before embarking on a program of graduate studies. It may not change your mind about your decision, but by becoming better informed about your choice, you become better prepared for your future.

Have You Talked with People in Your Field to Explore What You Might Be Doing After Graduate School?

In pursuing your undergraduate degree, you will have come into contact with many individuals trained in the field you are considering. You might also have the opportunity to attend professional conferences, workshops, seminars, and job fairs where you can expand your network of contacts. Talk to them all! Find out about their individual career paths, discuss your own plans and hopes, get their feedback on the reality of your expectations, and heed their advice about your prospects. Each will have a unique tale to tell, and each will bring a different perspective on the current marketplace for the credentials you are seeking. Talking to enough people will make you an expert on what's out there.

Are You Excited by the Idea of Studying the Particular Field You Have in Mind?

This question may be the most important one of all. If you are going to spend several years in advanced study, perhaps engendering some debt or postponing some lifestyle decisions for an advanced degree, you simply ought to enjoy what you're doing. Examine your work in the discipline so far. Has it been fun? Have you found yourself exploring various paths of thought? Do you read in your area for fun? Do you enjoy talking about it, thinking about it, and sharing it with others? Advanced degrees often are the beginning of a lifetime's involvement with a particular subject. Choose carefully a field that will hold your interest and your enthusiasm.

It is fairly obvious by now that we think you should give some careful thought to your decision and take some action. If nothing else, do the following:

- Talk and question (remember to listen!)
- Reality test
- Soul-search by yourself or with a person you trust

FINDING THE RIGHT PROGRAM FOR YOU: SOME CONSIDERATIONS

There are several important factors in coming to a sound decision about the right graduate program for you. You'll want to begin by locating institutions that offer appropriate programs, examining each of these programs and their requirements, undertaking the application process by reviewing catalogs and obtaining application materials, visiting campuses if possible, arranging for letters of recommendation, writing your application statement, and, finally, following up on your applications.

Locate Institutions with Appropriate Programs

Once you decide on a particular advanced degree, it's important to develop a list of schools offering such a degree program. Perhaps the best source of graduate program information is Peterson's. Their website (www.petersons .com) and their printed *Guides to Graduate Study* allow you to search for information by institution name, location, or academic area. The website also allows you to do a keyword search. Use their website and guides to build your list. In addition, you may want to consult the College Board's *Index of Majors and Graduate Degrees,* which will help you find graduate programs offering the degree you seek. It is indexed by academic major and then categorized by state.

Now, this may be a considerable list. You may want to narrow the choices down further by a number of criteria: tuition, availability of financial aid, public versus private institutions, United States versus international institutions, size of student body, size of faculty, application fee, and geographic location. This is only a partial list; you will have your own important considerations. Perhaps you are an avid scuba diver and you find it unrealistic to think you could pursue graduate study for a number of years without being able to ocean dive from time to time. Good! That's a decision and it's honest. Now, how far from the ocean is too far, and what schools meet your other needs? In any case, and according to your own criteria, begin to build a reasonable list of graduate schools that you are willing to spend time investigating.

Examine the Degree Programs and Their Requirements

Once you've determined the criteria by which you want to develop a list of graduate schools, you can begin to examine the degree program requirements, faculty composition, and institutional research orientation. Again, using resources such as Peterson's website or guides can reveal an amazingly rich level of material by which to judge your possible selections.

In addition to degree programs and degree requirements, entries will include information about application fees, entrance test requirements, tuition, percentage of applicants accepted, numbers of applicants receiving financial aid, gender breakdown of students, numbers of full- and part-time faculty, and often gender breakdown of faculty as well. Numbers graduating in each program and research orientations of departments are also included in some entries. There is information on graduate housing; student services; and library, research, and computer facilities. A contact person, phone number, and address are also standard pieces of information in these listings.

It can be helpful to draw up a chart and enter relevant information about each school you are considering in order to have a ready reference on points of information that are important to you.

Undertake the Application Process

Program Information. Once you've decided on a selection of schools, obtain program information and applications. Nearly every school has a website that contains most of the detailed information you need to narrow your choices. In addition, applications can be printed from the site. If, however, you don't want to print out lots of information, you can request that a copy of the catalog and application materials be sent to you.

When you have your information in hand, give it all a careful reading and make notes of issues you might want to discuss via E-mail, on the telephone, or in a personal interview.

··

> If you are interested in graduate work in experimental psychology, for example, in addition to graduate courses in conditioning and learning, are there additional courses in memory, cognition, physiological, psychological assessment, and others?

··

What is the ratio of faculty to the required number of courses for your degree? How often will you encounter the same faculty member as an instructor?

If, for example, your program offers a practicum or off-campus experience, who arranges this? Does the graduate school select a site and place you there, or is it your responsibility? What are the professional affiliations of the faculty? Does the program merit any outside professional endorsement or accreditation?

Critically evaluate the catalogs of each of the programs you are considering. List any questions you have and ask current or former teachers and colleagues for their impressions as well.

The Application. Preview each application thoroughly to determine what you need to provide in the way of letters of recommendation, transcripts from undergraduate schools or any previous graduate work, and personal essays that may be required. Make a notation for each application of what you need to complete that document.

Additionally, you'll want to determine entrance testing requirements for each institution and immediately arrange to register for appropriate tests. Information can be obtained from associated websites, including www.ets.org (GRE, GMAT, TOEFL, PRAXIS, SLS, Higher Education Assessment), www.lsat.org (LSAT), and www.tpcweb.com/mat (MAT). Your college career office should also be able to provide you with advice and additional information.

Visit the Campus if Possible

If time and finances allow, a visit, interview, and tour can help make your decision easier. You can develop a sense of the student body, meet some of the faculty, and hear up-to-date information on resources and the curriculum. You will have a brief opportunity to "try out" the surroundings to see if they fit your needs. After all, it will be home for a while. If a visit is not possible but you have questions, don't hesitate to call and speak with the dean of the graduate school. Most are more than happy to talk to candidates and want them to have the answers they seek. Graduate school admission is a very personal and individual process.

Arrange for Letters of Recommendation

This is also the time to begin to assemble a group of individuals who will support your candidacy as a graduate student by writing letters of recommendation or completing recommendation forms. Some schools will ask you to provide letters of recommendation to be included with your application or sent directly to the school by the recommender. Other graduate programs will provide a recommendation form that must be completed by the recommender. These graduate school forms vary greatly in the amount of space provided for a written recommendation. So that you can use letters as you need to, ask your recommenders to address their letters "To Whom It May Concern," unless one of your recommenders has a particular connection to one of your graduate schools or knows an official at the school.

Choose recommenders who can speak authoritatively about the criteria important to selection officials at your graduate school. In other words, choose recommenders who can write about your grasp of the literature in your field of study, your ability to write and speak effectively, your class performance, and your demonstrated interest in the field outside of class. Other characteristics that graduate schools are interested in assessing include your emotional maturity, leadership ability, breadth of general knowledge, intellectual ability, motivation, perseverance, and ability to engage in independent inquiry.

When requesting recommendations, it's especially helpful to put the request in writing. Explain your graduate school intentions and express some of your thoughts about graduate school and your appreciation for their support. Don't be shy about "prompting" your recommenders with some suggestions of what you would appreciate being included in their comments. Most recommenders will find this direction helpful and will want to produce a statement of support that you can both stand behind. Consequently, if your interaction with one recommender was especially focused on research projects, he or she might be best able to speak of those skills and your critical thinking ability. Another recommender may have good comments to make about your public presentation skills.

Give your recommenders plenty of lead time in which to complete your recommendation, and set a date by which they should respond. If they fail to meet your deadline, be prepared to make a polite call or visit to inquire if they need more information or if there is anything you can do to move the process along.

Whether or not you are providing a graduate school form or asking for an original letter to be mailed, be sure to provide an envelope and postage if the recommender must mail the form or letter directly to the graduate school.

Each recommendation you request should provide a different piece of information about you for the selection committee. It might be pleasant for letters of recommendation to say that you are a fine, upstanding individual, but a selection committee for graduate school will require specific information. Each recommender has had a unique relationship with you, and their letters should reflect that. Think of each letter as helping to build a more complete portrait of you as a potential graduate student.

Write Your Application Statement

....

For a psychology major, the application and personal essay should be a welcome opportunity to express your deep interest in pursuing graduate study. Your understanding of the challenges ahead, your commitment to the work involved, and your expressed self-awareness will weigh heavily in the decision process of the graduate school admissions committee.

....

An excellent source to help in thinking about writing this essay is *How to Write a Winning Personal Statement for Graduate and Professional School,* by Richard J. Stelzer. It has been written from the perspective of what graduate school selection committees are looking for when they read these essays. It provides helpful tips to keep your essay targeted on the kinds of issues and criteria that are important to selection committees and that provide them · with the kind of information they can best utilize in making their decision.

Follow Up on Your Applications

After you have finished each application and mailed it along with your transcript requests and letters of recommendation, be sure to follow up on the progress of your file. For example, call the graduate school administrative staff to see whether your transcripts have arrived. If the school required your recommenders to fill out a specific recommendation form that had to be mailed directly to the school, you will want to ensure that they have all arrived in good time for the processing of your application. It is your responsibility to make certain that all required information is received by the institution.

RESEARCHING FINANCIAL AID
SOURCES, SCHOLARSHIPS, AND FELLOWSHIPS

Financial aid information is available from each graduate school. You may be eligible for federal, state, and/or institutional support. There are lengthy forms to complete, and some of these will vary by school, type of school (public versus private), and state. Be sure to note the deadline dates on each form.

There are many excellent resources available to help you explore all of your financial aid options. Visit your college career office or local public library to find out about the range of materials available. Two excellent resources are Peterson's website (www.petersons.com) and its book *Grants for Graduate Students.* Another good reference is the Foundation Center's *Foundation Grants to Individuals.* These types of resources generally contain information that can be accessed by indexes including field of study, specific eligibility requirements, administering agency, and geographic focus.

EVALUATING ACCEPTANCES

If you apply to and are accepted at more than one school, it is time to return to your initial research and self-assessment to evaluate your options and select the program that will best help you achieve the goals you set for pursuing graduate study. You'll want to choose a program that will allow you to complete your studies in a timely and cost-effective way. This may be a good time to get additional feedback from professors and career professionals who are familiar with your interests and plans. Ultimately, the decision is yours, so be sure you get answers to all the questions you can think of.

SOME NOTES ABOUT REJECTION

Each graduate school is searching for applicants who appear to have the qualifications necessary to succeed in its program. Applications are evaluated on a combination of undergraduate grade point average, strength of letters of recommendation, standardized test scores, and personal statements written for the application.

A carelessly completed application is one reason many applicants are denied admission to a graduate program. To avoid this type of needless rejection, be sure to carefully and completely answer all appropriate questions on the application form, focus your personal statement given the instructions provided, and submit your materials well in advance of the deadline. Remember that your test scores and recommendations are considered a part of your application, so they must also be received by the deadline.

If you are rejected by a school that especially interests you, you may want to contact the dean of graduate studies to discuss the strengths and weaknesses of your application. Information provided by the dean will be useful in reapplying to the program later on or applying to other, similar programs.

PART TWO

THE CAREER PATHS

CHAPTER NINE

INTRODUCTION TO THE PSYCHOLOGY CAREER PATHS

D o you remember using a special graphic feature in your anatomy textbook? It included a basic illustration of the human body and a series of transparent overlays for the venous system, the arterial system, the nervous system, and other important systems that are a part of the human anatomy. Laying one on top of the other, you began to build a comprehensive picture of how the human body works.

The anatomy of a career path in psychology can be described in much the same way. We begin by defining the outline of a career path with the broadest of brush strokes. Think about workers overseeing congregate living in a residential setting. People in organizations managing human resources. Teachers in the classroom educating students. Case managers working with clients to promote health and well-being in social and human services. Therapists using a variety of techniques to heal someone with a physical or mental illness through therapy.

There may be just a spark of intuitive interest in teaching or a preference for the humanistic outreach of social and community services. Some prefer the role modeling and direct assistance opportunities afforded by group living, while others feel a deep need to assist individuals struggling with mental problems that might be alleviated through any of a number of interventions.

Read each of the paths included in this book and follow your instinct. That choice, which you may change many times, will become the basic illustration of your career anatomy. Thinking about some employment conditions (the overlays) will affect how you see your choice. You will have the outline of your original choice but you'll gain a more complex, more complete understanding as you add layers of information and facts. Each successive overlay will refine and further define the career path for you by choices you make about location, specialization, and your own needs and life goals. All these decisions help you in making choices.

The first overlay will be a template of your skills, interests, and abilities. You'll want to do a serious self-assessment like the one suggested at the opening of this book to think about the education requirements of each path. Does this career path make the best use of your skills and interests? For example, if you're a strong team builder and team player and enjoy working closely with many colleagues, therapy or social and human services provide more opportunities in that direction than residential care or even teaching.

The next important overlay might be that of the possible client populations we've discussed: undergraduate or graduate students, individuals of different ages with mental illnesses or handicaps, seriously ill clients, or those having difficulty coping with life's stresses and strains. Each will make different demands on you. Which will you work with best and most effectively? Which population offers you the scope, growth, and, maybe, "stretch" we all need in an occupation?

Your third overlay has to do with the nature of the activity you want to primarily engage in. Teaching involves reading, research, lecturing, grading papers, and serving on committees. Therapy means intimate, sometimes physical work with clients to work toward healing. Residential care involves all the tasks involved in managing a home with the additional supervision and responsibility for your patient group. Social and human services work involves counseling, using the telephone, significant paperwork, and lots of negotiation. Human resources requires listening skills, data analysis, decision making, and public-presentation ability.

Other overlays are up to you. Financial reward may be important to you or even necessary if you are graduating with significant debt burden. Each of these jobs has a salary range, and some paths pay more than others. If your salary is critical or if you have specific income thresholds you must meet, then by all means, investigate possible salary differences for each path and add that overlay to your illustration

Status, privacy or lack thereof, geographic location, supply and demand for jobs, promotion possibilities, and opportunities for professional growth are all individual concerns, and each constitutes another overlay as you build your composite picture of the best career path choice. You may choose to do this exercise for each path that follows until you have a solid understanding of the pluses and minuses of each career choice.

PSYCHOLOGY AS EDUCATION RATHER THAN TRAINING

The four-year degree is very often an entrance hurdle required to enter many segments of the job market today. Interestingly enough, aside from technical positions, most organizations are willing to and do train their entry-level college graduate employees for any number of management positions. The Japanese major becomes a university official, the geography major becomes a counselor, the English major is a salesperson, and the sociology major does telemarketing. The employer tends to see many liberal arts degrees as guarantees of "trainability" and not guarantees of subject area expertise. Some graduates end up in what they find, not in what they planned for.

BEGIN PLANNING YOUR CAREER

One of the principal reasons liberal arts graduates get sidetracked from their major when they enter the job market is because they soon learn that their time in college was not job training. Unlike the business major, the education major, or the computer science graduate, the psychology major has been learning *about* psychology, not how to *do* psychology. And yet, as these paths demonstrate, if you prepare yourself and plan your career, many employers will be willing to take you on in jobs with a very direct use of your psychology background. You'll use every course you had and learn so much more.

The remaining sections of this book will be devoted to outlining five possible career paths you can follow with your degree in psychology. These five individual paths have been carefully selected to draw deeply on your psychology education. Many graduates who have liberal arts degrees say they don't need a four-year degree to do their work. The accounting major in sales or the English major in retail, the biology major in restaurant management all have the .same lament, "What did I get my degree for?" But the psychology majors will see, in reading the paths presented here, that they can directly use what they learned in earning their degree.

The five career paths outlined in this book are worth all the planning you can give them, because they depend upon and continue to build on the foundation of an excellent education in psychology. These career paths and the many actual jobs illustrated for each all hold the promise of being able to enhance and enrich the time and effort you have spent in achieving your degree and launch you on a career of unlimited possibilities, because they all involve human development and behavior.

WHAT PATHS CAN YOU TAKE TO BEGIN WITH?

The five career paths chosen for psychology are:

1. Residential Care

2. Social and Human Services

3. Human Resources

4. Therapy

5. Teaching

These paths are described in detail in Chapters 10–14, and each of them can help you create a complete set of overlays for specific careers that draw on your psychology background. They are offered as realistic and achievable suggestions, and they are presented to stimulate your thinking about possible *directions* as you enter the workforce following graduation. The text of each is sprinkled with many actual job listings, so you can match your resume or degree aspirations against what is being requested. Many travelers begin on the same road using the same basic career outline, because entry-level jobs, even with different organizations, seem remarkably similar. Soon, however, the road divides, and each person begins to acquire different skills and experiences in his or her life's work—creating unique overlays. It is the detail contained on each overly and the layering of them that will determine your career direction.

CHAPTER TEN

PATH 1: RESIDENTIAL CARE

As a psychology major, you have come to understand a number of issues that affect American society. Human development and its stages and transitions are manifest in the familiar issues and concerns of American culture: midlife crisis, body image, aging, eating disorders, sexual orientation, depression, anxiety, and a thousand and one issues that influence our individual and collective mental health. The popularization of psychology, begun by an over-the-counter glossy magazine that was first published in 1968, was a visible manifestation of our concern with things psychological.

From your classwork, your reading, and your professors you know enough to be suspicious of this attention. America is a great nation for fads, and psychology may be the beneficiary of that attention. We have seen a resurgence of the psychobiography, declared majors in undergraduate colleges, and an enormous increase in types of therapy and in individuals enrolling in such therapy. Psychotherapeutic drug prescriptions are on the increase, and particular drugs, such as Prozac, have become the subject of intense debate among physicians, psychologists, ethicists, and the person on the street.

Has anything changed? Are we more sensitive to mental health issues? Are our overall goals for health and well-being advancing? In the area of residential care, the answer must be a qualified "yes." Increasing provision of residential care, the growing quality of residential care facilities, and the corresponding increase in professionalism and training of residential-care staff and administration have created an awareness and an appreciation in the general public for the advantages and therapeutic rewards of noninstitutional care.

At an earlier and more naive time in our history of dealing with individuals who, either temporarily or permanently, varied from socially imposed norms, our solution was institutionalization. The social service, medical, legal, and humanitarian communities locked away everyone from psychotics to orphans. Hospitals, sanitariums, state hospitals (a well-known euphemism for mental institutions), homes (which, ironically, were closer to prisons), and prisons held people who were blind, mentally retarded or handicapped, epileptic, without speech, criminally insane, chronically depressed, or schizophrenic, as well as individuals with cerebral palsy, polio, multiple sclerosis, and cystic fibrosis.

No longer. Dramatic discoveries and improvements in drug therapy in areas such as schizophrenia and depression, the Community Mental Health Centers Act of 1963 (essentially eliminating mental hospitals), and increasing acceptance of people who are mentally and physically challenged in the workplace have spurred the creation of a variety of residential-care options.

Even in the criminal justice system, the range of options in correctional institutions and prisons has expanded enormously. Day programs outside the institution, halfway houses that more closely resemble attractive rooming houses than prison facilities, and work-release programs all improve rehabilitation. They speed the reintroduction of the offender into society, reduce recidivism through retraining, and avoid the conditioning effects of incarceration. Ultimately, the cost to the tax-paying public is lowered.

Trying to define residential care is a challenge. You could be working as an overnight counselor in a small group home for delinquent adolescent boys. Or you could be a recreation therapist working nine to five in a luxury facility for older adults. Both are residential-care positions, though the responsibilities, working conditions, and patient population are dramatically different.

To begin to define residential care, we can make the following general statements:

- Residents participate, to some degree, in their own care and maintenance (chores, shopping, group decisions, personal care).

- Both short-term and long-term living situations are available.

- There is an attempt to duplicate, insofar as possible, homelike conditions.

- Medical treatment is off-site.

- Generally, staff do not wear uniforms.

- A variety of therapies may be offered: general counseling, milieu therapy, recreational therapy, expressive therapies, and in some specific situations (substance abuse recovery) drug and alcohol abuse treatments are provided.

THE GROWING IMPORTANCE OF RESIDENTIAL CARE

Several factors have played roles in the growing importance of residential care for a wide range of clients. First, the deinstitutionalization movement that began in the 1960s has resulted in a growing number of community-integrated homes and apartment-suite living situations for people with mental retardation or a mental handicap. Second, a host of other social issues are being addressed by government agencies, nonprofit organizations, and private, for-profit facilities, and residential care is a factor in their solutions. The various types of residential-care facilities include group homes. They house people with various needs: recovering drug and substance abusers, young boys who are acting out different types of emotional and/or physical trauma, delinquents of both genders, and battered and abused women and children. The group home or psychiatric halfway house can accommodate any of the changing issues that society presents. Health-care professionals have found that when clients can be brought together in a more homelike environment with caring role models they do far better than in the institutional settings of the past.

Besides making therapeutic sense, these residential-care facilities make economic sense. One reason for lower costs is that these homes are based on group and individual therapy in a community milieu. Also, some clients can contribute more to their own care in a residential setting than they can in an institution. Maintenance, cooking, cleaning, and recreation can be self-managed in some group homes. A recent U.S. government General Accounting Office report on the efficacy of residential care for youth engaged in high-risk behaviors (substance abuse, delinquency, unprotected sex, and related issues) demonstrated that, in some programs, this destructive cycle can be broken. By removing youth to a protected, structured program that teaches new life skills, this high-risk behavior can be altered, although further study is indicated and results are expressed cautiously.

DEFINITION OF THE CAREER PATH

An oft-heard complaint of the newly minted psychology graduate is that all the jobs demand far more experience than the graduate has. You want to work in psychology and use your education, but where do you start?

The short answer to this very valid question is residential-care facilities, also known as psychiatric halfway houses, community residences for the mentally ill, group homes, shelters, and transitional living. These residences provide a noninstitutional, homelike setting for patients with a variety of presenting issues.

Kinds of Residential Care

Residential care can be defined using a number of discriminants. **Duration of Residence:** You can classify residential care by the average stay of clients, either short term or long term. **Structure:** You can define residential care by the amount of structure and/or therapeutic treatment that occurs in the residence. Drug rehab care is very strict and ordered with many rigid routines and protocols to foster success and responsible behavior. Some residential-care settings for employed individuals with mental handicaps are not essentially different than group apartment living. **Presenting Issues:** Others legitimately want to categorize residential care by the population served: the aged, adolescent delinquents, recovering drug abusers, battered women, or pregnant teenage girls. Each of these categorizations has implications for you and your employment suitability.

Duration of Residence.   How long your clients stay at the residential-care facility may be important to you because it affects your interaction with clients. At one end of the spectrum, in short-term residences, you may have a constantly changing population of clients and little time to effect much change. You can provide comfort, counseling, sustenance, security, and many basic needs. There may be time for some referrals but generally not for long-term follow-up. The pace may be rapid with much diversity, and there may be little closure. On the other hand, long-term facilities allow you to work intensively with clients and mark progress over time. Therapeutic options for connection with your clients increase with duration of residence, as do the options. There can be, as well, a corresponding static quality, with little dramatic change day to day.

Structure.   How involved you want to be in working with your clients will have something to do with the appeal of different types of residential-care structures. Each residential-care facility has its own mission and goals. Some are simply providing clean, comfortable living arrangements for clients who are functioning well and may even be working. They need to return to a secure, stable environment and may have trouble with stress or too many challenges but essentially want as much autonomy as they can reasonably handle. Your role is to provide what is needed.

At the opposite end of the spectrum there are facilities in which you are called upon to physically restrain clients from time to time, partner them in personal-care activities, provide recreational and maintenance activities, and supervise and monitor behavior rather closely.

Presenting Issues.   The presenting issues that bring clients together in a residential unit may be more important to you than how long a client stays at your facility or how intrusive you are in your client's daily life. You may have a deep interest in the ability of people with Down's Syndrome to integrate into society. Or you may feel a strong pull to work with children who have been sexually or physically abused. A disease entity, a social problem, or a mental-health challenge may draw you to a client population to begin your career in residential care.

RESIDENTIAL CARE: A DEMAND FOR QUALIFIED STAFF

Residential care creates an enormous demand for staff. When you take the previously large capacity of medical and psychiatric facilities and break those living units down into smaller, house-sized communities, you can understand how the need for staff multiplies. In addition, most of these homes require what is called "awake overnight counselors" to be available to clients during the night and to monitor house activity. Day staffers can be involved in patient treatment plans, job counseling, and teaching a variety of daily skills and personal-care standards. It is challenging, demanding, and physically tiring work. It draws on staff members' ingenuity, patience, strength, and emotional reserves.

A PLACE TO BEGIN YOUR CAREER

Turnover in residential care is high, and that needs to be understood up front. Residential care is not career employment. Turnover is above normal because the job is demanding, generally salaries are not competitive, and there are many, many challenges. Professionals who hire for residential staff positions often *prefer* hiring the candidate who is "on the way" to something else. Many jobs are labeled "entry level," and the job announcement indicates that training and/or mentoring will be provided. A recent, typical job announcement said:

> *Residential Counselor.* Entry level. Responsible to help the residential manager establish and operate the residential home treatment program. She or he implements, as directed, the comprehensive treatment plan; provides appropriate support to youths in performing required tasks such as chores, homework,
>
> continued

continued

etc.; handles emergencies; and assumes responsibilities for all activities on shift and uses other resources as appropriate. Supervision and training provided. Requirements: Bachelor's degree in related field preferred; experience working with youth in a residential setting; preemployment drug screening; First Aid/CPR, DCF Medication Certification; Public Service License from the state required within thirty days of employment. Please submit letter of intent and resume to:

THE CHALLENGING REALITY OF RESIDENTIAL CARE

Most residential-care jobs are advertised as "counselor" positions. It may be, in fact, the job title that attracts you. Listed below are several entry-level positions that a psychology bachelor's degree recipient with an internship and part-time work experience under his or her belt would be eligible to apply for.

Assistant Residential Coordinator. B.A. and two years residential experience required. At least one year supervisory experience preferred. Please send resume and references to:

Mental Health Counselors. Work with mentally ill male adults. B.A. degree preferred along with at least one year related experience. Evening shifts include weekends. Driver's license a plus. Send or fax resume that MUST include salary requirements to:

Counselors. Providing residential and outreach services to a psychiatric population living independently in the community. B.A./B.S. in psychology, social work, or related field and a driver's license with a good driving record required; experience a plus. Send resume to:

Residential Counselor. Provide a nurturing, teaching, structured, and modeling atmosphere within the daily life experience of each child in a group home setting. Twenty-one years old, preferably B.A./B.S. in related field. Please send resume with cover letter to:

Residential Staff. Carrying a case load of extended residential patients and managing the therapeutic milieu for multiple levels

continued

continued

of care. B.A. degree and C.A.D.C. strongly preferred. Supervisory opportunities available for candidates with a master's degree. Fax resume to:

Residential Counselor. Two positions at group home for teen males. Live-in shifts run Tuesday night to Friday morning (B shift) and Friday morning to Sunday afternoon (C shift). B.A./B.S. degree with experience. Contact: . . . Or fax:

Residential Treatment Counselor. College degree in human service field, with emotional availability and a sincere commitment to youth. Excellent salary and benefits package provided. Please submit resumes to:

This group of actual job listings begins to highlight the range of duties required of residential-care workers:

- □ caring about clients
- □ creating a therapeutic atmosphere
- □ counseling
- □ assisting with daily living skills
- □ assisting with skill development
- □ effecting transitions
- □ integrating residents

In other words, case management. But there are many other duties that are also required:

- □ responding to emergencies
- □ handling public relations
- □ supervising staff members
- □ carrying out administrative duties

What's important in assessing these residential-care positions is: (1) your understanding of the duties and responsibilities and (2) your readiness to undertake this work. This is important work and it's critical that interested, qualified, and skilled people be in these positions.

Caring About the Clients

The work is, in a word, challenging. These jobs require the residential-care worker to have endless resources of patience and a caring, thoughtful attitude. Residents will present a variety of behaviors and abilities to manage independent living, and the residential-care worker will continually be required to draw on deep reserves of understanding and tact to help the clients become more adept at group living, interpersonal skills, and general life skills.

Creating a Therapeutic Atmosphere

House managers and their staffs are responsible for creating the proper therapeutic atmosphere to facilitate the growth and nurturance of residents. They are often responsible for the selection of new residents. They create house policy, educate residents on its implementation, and carry through the policies. How these duties are undertaken affects the atmosphere of the facility.

Counseling

Counseling is a process of connection and deep human involvement between people. There are many formal schools of counseling theory and technique, but individual counselors ultimately evolve a counseling technique that works for them and their clients. Often, for the clientele of the residential-care worker, the deeply empathic listening attention of the counselor is, in and of itself, therapeutic. Clients who have a caring listener who values them as individuals and to whom they can talk about their problems are able to begin their journey back to healthy living.

Assisting with Daily Living Skills

Residential care came about in large part because the ability of many of these clients to self-manage many daily living tasks was recognized. There is much they can do, and those who can master daily living skills find increased self-esteem and pride in their efforts. Most often in long-term residential settings, there may be some clients who are unable to carry out the basic daily care functions for themselves: feeding themselves, getting dressed, bathing, brushing their teeth, or taking care of their elimination requirements. Paraprofessionals oftentimes handle these activities, but you must be prepared to assist the residents as needed, striking a delicate balance between actual assistance and teaching.

Assisting with Skill Development

Residential workers assist residents with all sorts of skill development, from the art of negotiating turf issues, recreational choices, and music volume with their fellow residents, to practical skills in cooking, crisis management, medication administration, as well as educational plans.

Effecting Transitions

When residents leave to return home or to move on to independent housing arrangements, it is often the house manager who has helped to secure those new housing arrangements, acting as an intermediary to new landlords, neighbors, or the family to ensure an easy and stress-free transition for the resident.

Integrating Residents

Residential-care professionals also play a role in community education. It would hardly be helpful to neighbors, children, and the general public to be unaware of the inhabitants of residential-care facilities. Sitting on bright summer furniture and planting colorful bedding flowers may be enough activity for an elderly population that is not entirely mobile, but caring for other groups of clients, especially the mentally challenged, can involve far more activity.

Regular trips to shopping malls, the grocery store, pizza parties, or birthdays at the local McDonald's help the general public, in a low-risk, non-threatening way, to begin to understand and appreciate these people who are a part of their community. These same residents could effect no better demonstration of their similarities to their neighbors than being out on the lawn on a crisp, fall day raking and bagging leaves! Some things are the same for all of us.

Responding to Emergencies

Residential-care workers need to be ready to respond to emergencies as varied as power outages or resident conflicts. They may be required to obtain or administer medical assistance for residents, and that demands not only excellent record keeping but maintaining a clear, cool head in an emergency.

Many emergencies are no different from our own home crises: frozen water pipes, power failures, a personal injury. However, depending on the client population, some of these can be frightening at worst or overstimulating at the very least. Residential-care professionals need to be prepared and to anticipate problems.

Handling Public Relations Activities

In addition to managing the residence, residential-care professionals also serve as public relations officers and spokespersons for the residence to community groups, newspaper reporters, telephone inquirers, and neighborhood groups. This in itself can be a challenge because the psychiatric or community residence home can have difficulty being accepted in some areas.

Understanding and appreciating the public's objections and concerns is an essential step in beginning to respond to those concerns. Educating the public about the mission of your facility, profiling the residents as individuals, and not labeling them as a group are critical. Being out in the community and stressing their contributions at their jobs, their volunteer work, or the economics of residential care help the public understand the value of these residences.

Supervising Staff Members

Some residential-care workers are responsible for handling matters relating to staffing. They schedule the work rotations of ancillary staff and are principally responsible for their hiring, training, and evaluation. As with any management position, clear and consistent communication is important and that is magnified with twenty-four-hour shifts. Well-maintained duty rosters, detailed job specifications, frequent feedback, and staff meetings create an esprit de corps that staff members cannot fail to respond to.

Carrying Out Administrative Duties

House managers may collect rent and maintain accounting records for all residents. They also oversee the operating budget for food, house maintenance, and furnishings, and they will often supervise any outside contract workers conducting maintenance such as heavy cleaning.

Not every residential-care position will bring all of these requirements with it. Each will have its own unique combination of responsibilities and emphasis. Some professionals in the field have said, no matter what their principal duties, over the course of twelve months, they touch on each and every one of the elements we have just listed.

As a result, the psychology major looking for entry-level employment in his or her major and who wants a position that will not only challenge him or her to develop new skills but use existing talents in a new environment will find residential care worthy of the job search.

USE YOUR RESIDENTIAL COUNSELING POSITION TO GROW

What most typically happens in this career path is that, after you have worked in the residential-care setting, you will want to become more involved therapeutically in the care plans for these clients. Doing that will involve returning to school for additional coursework, training, and/or degrees. During this process, you will return to your experiences from your residential-care position again and again.

Leaving residential care for a new position in the helping professions, you will discover you are well situated for a number of openings in social and community service, therapy, administration and management, and counseling. Much depends on the particular emphasis in your residential experience and the particular role you played. Other chapters in this book outline a multitude of career paths for which residential care would provide an excellent jumping-off place.

Your responsibility is to ensure that, as you progress in your residential-care job, you are building a portfolio of success that will allow you freedom. Are you keeping samples of evaluation materials you designed for your staff? Have you typed up notes from your in-service training presentations and compiled a loose-leaf binder of programs you could present? If you've been successful in placing articles and news stories about residents and the home, have you collected those in an album? A personal journal or process notes on your therapeutic interactions will reinforce your memory and allow you to illustrate interview questions with anonymous but specific anecdotes about successful client interactions. Letters of recommendation can be collected from the many professionals in multiple disciplines you will work with on behalf of your clients. All of these efforts will help you in presenting your story to a new employer as you move forward in your career path.

WORKING CONDITIONS

Working conditions in residential care are interesting, to say the least. Do you remember, as a college student, going home for the weekend and trying to get that big paper written? Or perhaps you had your own apartment at college. The telephone, the television, the refrigerator, the CD player all proved to be hard-to-resist distractions. Sometimes, even taking the trash out or doing a load of laundry was preferable to writing that paper. You'll face similar issues and distractions in residential care.

Privacy

Living in and working at your job in a residential-care facility will cause you to think about how much privacy you need. It's your home (at least for many hours a week) *and* your place of work. Some residential-care managers have a separate apartment on the premises, but it can easily become everyone's space. And if your facility operates twenty-four hours a day, there are the comings and goings of each shift of care workers. It can be a challenge to carve out time for yourself or to separate your personal life from your work life.

Hands On

Residential care is hands-on, interactive care. Besides the possibilities that exist for actually assisting some of your clients in basic personal-care skills, this is not a good job for someone who wants to stand off in the distance and supervise or sit down and just talk. There is home maintenance to execute and organize, dishes to be done, meals to be prepared, spills to mop up, and bathrooms to clean—all the normal duties of running a house. Certainly, in most cases your residents will play the dominant role in these chores, but you need to be ready to pitch in and show how it's done or lend a hand when things need to be speeded up.

Teamwork

In most cases, your clients will be receiving other kinds of help. Depending upon their situation, this could range from drug therapy to rehabilitative services. You are part of a care team, and you will probably meet with many of these caregivers as you work with your individual residents. You will share your clients' progress, behaviors, and needs to ensure the team is functioning in the best interest of the client's.

Staffing in the residence itself is apt to be lean, although your facility may be staffed round the clock. There may even be periods where you are alone during the day while residents are out working or shopping or doing volunteer work or receiving therapy. You will need to have an outlet for your social instincts during your free time if your work unit is small or if you are by yourself.

TRAINING AND QUALIFICATIONS

Two factors are particularly important in terms of training and qualifications. Be sure to review each item carefully.

Your Motives Must Be Healthy

Attitudinally, residential-care workers must display the proper motivation for residential-care work. It is not to "rescue" or enable residents to feel dependent upon you. It requires a professional detachment that will foster the focus required to perform needs analysis and to create effective solutions that empower and strengthen each resident.

Expect Extensive Screening

Administrators charged with hiring residential-care workers are primarily concerned that the candidates themselves present healthy and appropriate psychiatric profiles, and they may request a psychiatric assessment be conducted by a consultant. Motivation, stability, and intentionality of the house leadership are all critical to the success of the residential-care program, so applicants are screened carefully and references assiduously verified. Prior academic and job performance are reviewed, as they tend to be reflective of future performance.

EARNINGS

Unlike some positions listed in the psychology career paths in this book, information on salaries for residential-care positions is fairly easy to obtain. To gain the best insight and most up-to-date figures, watch your major metropolitan Sunday want ads or check specialized job posting newsletters at your career office or public library. A good example of the specialized job announcement newsletter is *Human Services Career Connection*, serving the New England area with job listings for psychology graduates at every degree level in higher education.

Entry-level salaries for residential-care positions can range dramatically. Some of the highest salaries for entry-level positions come from corporate residential-care facilities. Independent social service agencies, church-affiliated outreach programs, or municipal programs may pay far less for the same work demands. While salary ranges given here are expressed as yearly amounts, in most cases you will find pay expressed as an hourly rate for these kinds of jobs. At the time of publication, entry-level salaries for residential (nonsupervisory) positions ranged from a low of around $20,000 to a high of about $25,000. Supervisory positions for bachelor's-degreed candidates who have approximately two years' experience in administration and/or supervision can jump to $28,000–$35,000.

Because entry-level salaries are modest, it's even more important that you complete the estimated monthly expenses worksheet suggested in the self-assessment chapter of this book. With a new job, and a demanding and potentially stressful one at that, it's important that it meet at least your *minimum* salary needs. As with any first job, although the salary may be more than you've ever made, you'll want to ascertain that it can cover your basic needs, including food, shelter, and transportation. You may be surprised at the sum total of your anticipated expenses, especially if a car loan or school financial aid payback expense is involved. Do a thorough expense analysis as we suggest, and you can be more specific with an employer about your minimum salary requirements. It is your responsibility, not the employer's, in accepting any job to be sure that the salary offered will allow you to support yourself. You would be very distressed to find you had underestimated your expenses and had to leave a new position due to lack of funds. Your short tenure in the position and reason for leaving could adversely affect your ability to secure new employment.

In positions where you are able to meet your minimum salary needs, but where the pay is still lower than you'd hoped for, don't overlook the value of the benefits package that may be provided. Many job postings indicate that excellent benefits are available. One benefit that you may be especially interested in is tuition reimbursement. Remember, this residential-care job begins your career, and you may be able to acquire some additional education you'll need to move on in your career path. The following are two typical job advertisements outlining benefits provided.

Residential Specialists. Bachelor's degree in psychology or related field required to join our residential services department, which offers a full range of housing alternatives for the mentally ill. We offer competitive salaries and benefits, which include medical and dental plans, life and disability insurance, a 403(b) plan, and tuition reimbursement.

Assistant Program Manager. Needed for community residence serving psychiatrically disabled adults. Bachelor's degree in social work or psychology required; prior experience preferred. Excellent benefit package and competitive salary.

CAREER OUTLOOK

The outlook for residential-care positions is excellent. According to the U.S. Department of Labor, Bureau of Labor Statistics (http://stats.bls.gov), the number of human-service workers, which includes residential-care positions, is expected to grow dramatically during the period 1998–2008. In fact, residential-care positions (under the general classification of social- and human-services assistants) is listed among the ten fastest growing occupations for the decade. The number of available positions is expected to increase 53 percent by 2008.

The outlook is positive for a number of reasons. First, with the increasing success of treatment for a variety of mental and emotional disorders in the homelike settings of residences, there is increasing appreciation and demand for this kind of treatment setting. Second, society in general is beginning to appreciate and recognize the value of including the mentally ill and handicapped in society. Third, the residential-care option means lower costs because patients sometimes share in home and group maintenance chores.

A Growing Appreciation for Residential Care

Although the objection to individual home establishments has not lessened in some communities, the number of residences continues to grow. As their acceptance increases and the notoriety of their presence fades, an increasing public acceptance and appreciation for their mission and work should follow.

Inclusion as a Societal Goal

Here on our campus, a number of individuals with mental retardation are employed. Some are engaged in grounds work year-round and, under the supervision of a crew chief, are conscientious and exemplary workers. Others work in the cafeteria or snack bar as food-service workers. They enjoy the contact with passersby, and campus residents see them in a new light as capable, productive, and fulfilling an important societal role.

A Need for Reducing Costs

A strong rationale for residential care is economic. Opinion is quite clear that these populations do not belong in hospitals or large mental health institutions, and they do far better in the secure and homelike milieu created by the group residence. Behavior improves, medication demands lessen, and patients add to their repertoire of coping skills and behaviors. Residential-care costs are easier to maintain and monitor and are appreciably less than larger institutions with higher overhead.

STRATEGY FOR FINDING THE JOBS

Your strategy for obtaining employment in residential care should include several tactics: taking relevant nonpsychology coursework, exploring and choosing a setting in which you would most like to work, gaining supervisory experience, promoting your degree in psychology, and making clear your aspirations for career growth beyond residential care. Before you are ready to begin this work, however, be sure to revisit the self-assessment you completed. It will be useful as you begin your job search. Residential care is deeply rewarding but makes commensurate demands on many personal attributes, including your energy, patience, cooperation, and decision-making abilities.

Take Relevant Nonpsychology Coursework

If you are still in school, you may want to use your elective credits or the option of a minor to build an area of specialization that enhances your credentials. If you have graduated, continuing education courses allow you the same opportunities. Skills and abilities that will interest potential employers may be in any of several fields, including leisure or recreation, business, or communications.

Skills in leisure-time use or recreation are important because residential workers often lead these types of activities. Facilities may offer arts and crafts, music, and recreation classes to provide a full leisure-time menu for residents so necessary to the therapeutic atmosphere of group living.

Some basic business courses that enhance the credentials you bring to the workplace include personnel and staffing, marketing, financial management, public relations, and business communications. Consider whether you are interested in building a knowledge base in this area.

Good communication skills are essential in working with residents, ancillary-care workers, and volunteers and in carrying out public communications with interested community groups. Courses may be offered in a communications, English, or business degree program. No matter where you decide to work, these communications skills will only enhance what you have to offer.

Choose a Residential-Care Setting

As you have read, the residential-care path has a wide range of work sites from which to choose. You may feel a little overwhelmed by the number of possibilities. Which would be best for you? Think back to your reactions as you read about different situations. There were probably some work environments in which you could picture yourself. You may have been particularly interested in the presenting issues that are addressed in a particular residential-care environment (for example, learning disabilities, mental retardation, or child abuse). Begin your job search by exploring a couple of the types of work settings whose client concerns will engage you.

You'll also want to talk with people working in the field. Use your college or university career network to identify a group of contacts or talk with professionals working at facilities in the geographic area where you live. In your conversations, ask people to explain in detail what their particular setting is like. What are the client demands? What kinds of presenting problems are evident and what are the particular challenges posed by these clients? Is it a quiet, clean, and neat setting? Is it a noisy and busy setting? Are necessary supplies easily obtained or are there ongoing funding issues? How often does the schedule rotation change? Begin to determine how this information meshes with what you learned about yourself in the self-assessment you undertook as a beginning step in the job-search process. You'll begin to see that there are some settings that "fit" better with who you are and what you want in a job. Begin your job search with opportunities available in these kinds of places.

Try to Gain Some Level of Supervisory Experience

Because staff turnover in residential settings is high, moves from a staff care-taker position to a supervisory position can take place fairly quickly. Those people with previous supervisory experience, no matter the specific setting, will be considered first for these positions. If, for example, you have experience in the food-service industry and you were able to move from a wait-staff position into a managerial position, you'll want to emphasize your ability to take on increasing responsibilities as you write your resume and as you talk with potential employers in an interview. We have already described coursework you may want to consider that will enhance your ability to supervise or manage a residential-care facility.

Promote Your Degree in Psychology

As you studied psychology, you built a strong foundation that will allow you to carry out the "helping" duties that are required in residential care *and* the many more administrative duties that are also required.

You'll have the ability to communicate effectively with other staff and multidisciplinary team members. You'll be able to handle public relations activities by writing clear and concise statements for the public and responding to verbal questions in an appropriate way. Your analytical skills can be used as you quickly develop an appropriate response to an emergency situation.

Add to this list and be ready to express *all* your talents as you write or refine your resume and talk with potential employers.

Express Your Hopes for Growth

Often, hiring committees will appreciate that someone seeking a residential-care position is simply beginning a career in mental health or a helping profession and is seeking increasing responsibility, possibly in the form of residential-care management. Those job candidates who are forthright and honest about expectations for career growth may, in fact, be perceived as the best suited, dispositionally, for this kind of demanding role.

Residential care is a fine opening to much larger vistas of work as a helping professional. It is demanding and draining, and it is expected that you will want to move on, enriched and strengthened in your career choice by this beginning.

POSSIBLE EMPLOYERS

Earlier, as described in the "Definition of the Career Path" section on page 121, you discovered that residential care has been defined according to three discriminates: duration of residence, structure, and presenting issues. In this description of possible employers we present a range of types of employers that highlights these factors.

Retirement Communities

Profile. Retirement communities represent a wide range of options for aging adults who no longer want to, or who cannot, maintain a household of their own. Some communities serve frail clients who can undertake very few efforts on their own and who require a great deal of assistance. Residential-care workers would be responsible primarily for meeting the physical needs of their clients: feeding, bathing, dressing, or moving within the facility. Other retirement communities present more of a social setting and the residential-care worker would be more likely to focus on providing leisure activities for residents.

Help in Locating These Employers. Two career guides that provide useful information on career paths that involve working with senior citizens are *Opportunities in Gerontology and Aging Careers* and *The Helping Professions! A Career Sourcebook*. Use the Yellow Pages to locate facilities within a given geographic area; look under headings such as retirement and life-care communities and homes. Organizations that will be able to assist you in locating facilities include local social and human services agencies that serve elderly persons, or contact the American Association of Homes and Services for the Aging in Washington, D.C. (www.aahsa.org).

Community Mental Health Providers

Profile. Community mental health residential facilities can house clients of every age and means, and there are a variety of facilities serving them. While some communities directly operate residential facilities for people who are dealing with issues related to mental and emotional health, others contract with for-profit or not-for-profit agencies to handle this need.

Help in Locating These Employers. A thorough review of related chapters in the NTC/Contemporary Publishing guide *Careers in Social and Rehabilitation Services* will prove to be invaluable in explaining the complicated mental health system. This book also contains professional associations and professional and trade periodicals. One particular journal specifically geared to this audience is *Community Mental Health Journal*, published by Kluwer Academic/Plenum Publishers. Since the first edition of *Great Jobs for Psychology Majors*, this journal has gone on-line and can be found at http://pinkerton.bham.ac.uk/titles/00103853.htm. The site includes one reasonably current issue completely free and on-line that can be downloaded and printed article. This site also contains free access to the table of contents of more than eleven past journal editions that can be purchased on-line. There is even a table-of-contents alerting service. If you enter your E-mail address, then you will be notified of the contents of forthcoming issues.

State Mental Health Providers

Profile. Every state provides support to its residents for handling issues related to mental health. Different states call their agencies by different names, but some of the more common ones include:

- Department of Mental Health and Mental Retardation
- Department of Health and Social Services
- Department of Health Services
- Department of Human Services
- Department of Mental Health
- Department of Institutions
- Department of Health and Rehabilitative Services

These agencies provide a variety of services, some of which the state directly provides, while other services are contracted out to both for-profit and not-for-profit agencies.

Help in Locating These Employers. Your telephone directory is a resource that lists state mental health agencies, or you can use a resource such as the *Piper Resources* guide to government-sponsored Internet sites at http://www .pipeinfo.com/state/states.html. Though each state's mental health department may be organized differently, most state sites have a search function on their home page that will help you easily locate where they place their department of mental health within the framework of their state agencies.

Substance Abuse Treatment Programs

Profile. Substance abuse, whether it relates to drugs or alcohol, cuts across all age, ethnic, and social groups. Many residential workers specializing in substance abuse work at halfway houses for recovering alcoholics. Emerging data show that treatment programs should differ given the age and gender of the client, so some treatment facilities may focus on a specific population. These programs may be funded by the state, community, or private organizations or some combination of these.

Help in Locating These Employers. The *Medical and Health Information Directory* contains three separately published volumes. Volume 3 lists clinics, treatment centers, care programs, and counseling/diagnostic services for many subject areas. Because the field is a changing one and often underfunded, the World Wide Web remains a more up-to-date source of information. The authors have found that a search under "addiction treatment" in www.looksmart.com leads to guides and directories, associations and support, clinics and treatment, and many related categories by addiction type. It's an excellent beginning resource.

Short-Term Youth Shelters

Profile. We saw advertisements for residential programs for abused, acting-out boys; runaway children; troubled children and youth ages seven through eighteen; substance-abusing youth; and youth involved in the criminal justice system. If you are interested in working with young people, this type of residential facility is worth your while to investigate.

Help in Locating These Employers. As with state and community mental health services, you'll want to network to discover the range of sites available in your area. Don't forget to scan your local Yellow Pages directory (at home or on the Web) under a category such as "social and human services." *The National Directory of Children and Youth Services* (at your college library or through interlibrary loan) also contains information on runaway youth centers. An excellent choice on the Web is the U.S. Government, Department of Health and Human Services, Administration for Children and Families home page at www.acf.dhhs.gov.

Schools for Students with Special Education Needs

Profile. Many schools that offer residential programs serve students who have special education needs. Because these students live at the school, staff are needed outside of class hours to oversee student activities. Residential-care workers help students pursue their studies; they take students on field trips; they oversee students' leisure and living activities; and they provide a safe and secure environment.

Help in Locating These Employers. Three resources that will help you locate residential programs that serve students with learning disabilities include *The Handbook of Private Schools, Boarding Schools Directory* and Peterson's website www.petersons.com, where you can find a comprehensive listing of independent secondary schools that offer programs and promote assistance to students with learning disablilities.

POSSIBLE JOB TITLES

You will see a range of position titles as you conduct your search for these kinds of jobs. The title reflects the level of supervisory capability the job requires. Review the list shown below and add to it as you identify sites at which you are interested in working.

Activities coordinator	Program manager
Assistant manager	Psychiatric residence staffer
Case manager	Relief worker
Case worker	Resident services provider
Child-care worker	Residential clinical director
Counselor	Residential counselor
Crisis worker	Residential specialist
House manager	Residential worker
House parent	Special school counselor
Mental health worker	Support worker
Program assistant	Youth-service worker

A growing movement considers the worker with a baccalaureate degree to be a professional. In the five career paths chosen for this book that is emphatically so. But be aware that the term *paraprofessional* is also used to indicate someone in the mental health field who has not had formal educational training beyond high school, so be sure to carefully review the required qualifications for each job listing you examine. You'll want to avoid gaining employment that underemploys you or that doesn't allow you to use your full range of knowledge and skills.

RELATED OCCUPATIONS

Residential-care workers utilize many skills that have been developed in academic programs in psychology and in various work settings. These counseling, integrating, and supervising skills can also be put to use in many other types of work. Consider the following list and explore related occupations described in this book as well as in other resources you've found useful in your job search.

Career counselor
College student-affairs professional
Community- and social-service worker
Human-resources worker
Job developer
Mental health counselor
Rehabilitation aide
Therapist
Social worker
Youth corrections officer

This list is just a teaser of the many related job titles that could be included here. Be sure to add to it as you study career possibilities that can use your psychology degree.

PROFESSIONAL ASSOCIATIONS

Many organizations that serve clients who may need residential care are listed below. Be sure to review each listing and decide whether the association offers services that may be useful in your job search.

American Association of Homes and Services for the Aging
901 E St. NW, Suite 500
Washington, DC 20004
Website: www.aahsa.org
Members/Purpose: Voluntary nonprofit and governmental homes, housing, and health-related facilities and services for the elderly; state associations; interested individuals.
Training: Provides educational program.
Journals/Publications: *AAHA Provider News*; directory of members.
Job Listings: See *AAHA Provider News*; job mart has job listings.

American Association of Mental Health Professionals in Corrections
c/o John S. Zil
P.O. Box 163359
Sacramento, CA 95816
Members/Purpose: Psychiatrists, psychologists, social workers, and other mental health professionals; individuals working in correctional settings.
Training: Sponsors workshops.
Journals/Publications: *Corrective and Social Psychiatry.*

American Association of Psychiatric Services for Children
1200-C Scottsville Rd., Suite 225
Rochester, NY 14624
Members/Purpose: Fosters prevention and treatment of mental and emotional disorders of the young.
Training: Sponsors educational programs.
Journals/Publications: AAPSC membership directory; newsletter.
Job Listings: See AAPSC newsletter; maintains roster of available staff positions.

American Federation of State, County, and Municipal Employees
1625 L St. NW
Washington, DC 20036
Website: www.afscme.org
Members/Purpose: AFL-CIO.
Journals/Publications: *AFSCME Leader*; public employee newsletter; women's newsletter.

American Mental Health Counselors Association
c/o American Association for Counseling and Development
5999 Stevenson Ave.
Alexandria, VA 22304
Website: www.amhca.org

Members/Purpose: Division of the American Association for Counseling and Development. Professional counselors employed in mental health services.
Journals/Publications: *AMHCA News*; *Journal of Mental Health Counseling*.
Job Listings: Job placement service for members.

Association of Halfway House Alcoholism Programs of North America
786 East 7th St.
St. Paul, MN 55106
Members/Purpose: Halfway house corporations, staff, board members, and individuals closely related to the halfway house movement.
Training: Offers workshops and conferences.
Journals/Publications: AHHAP membership directory; communications and services newsletter; conference proceedings.
Job Listings: Operates placement service.

Association of Mental Health Administrators
60 Revere Dr., Suite 500
Northbrook, IL 60062
Members/Purpose: Administrators of services for the emotionally disturbed, mentally ill, mentally retarded, developmentally disabled, and those with problems of alcohol and substance abuse.
Training: Sponsors educational workshops.
Journals/Publications: Journal; newsletter.

Child Welfare League of America
440 1st St. NW, Suite 310
Washington, DC 20001
Website: www.cwla.org
Members/Purpose: Privately and publicly supported membership organization devoted to the improvement of care and services for deprived, dependent, or neglected children, youth, and their families.
Journals/Publications: *Child Welfare: Journal of Policy, Practice and Program*; CWLA directory of member agencies.

Learning Disabilities Association of America
4156 Library Rd.
Pittsburgh, PA 15234
Website: www.lidanatl.org
Members/Purpose: Parents of children with learning disabilities; interested professionals.
Journals/Publications: LDA newsbriefs; learning disabilities.

National Association of Addiction Treatment Providers
501 Randolph Dr.
Lititz, PA 17543-9049
Website: www.naatp.org
Members/Purpose: Corporate and private institutional alcohol and/or drug dependency treatment facilities.
Training: Conducts seminars on marketing, management, and reimbursement.
Journals/Publications: *NAATP Review; NAATP Update;* salary survey.

National Association of Private Psychiatric Hospitals
1319 F St. NW, Suite 1000
Washington, DC 20004
Members/Purpose: Private psychiatric hospitals.
Training: Conducts continuing education for medical and administrative hospital personnel.
Journals/Publications: Journal; *Psychiatric Hospital;* psychiatric hospital directory.
Job Listings: Conducts personnel recruitment service.

National Association of Private Residential Resources
4200 Evergreen Ln., Suite 315
Annandale, VA 22003
Members/Purpose: Agencies that serve persons with mental retardation and other developmental disabilities; others interested in the field of private residential services.
Training: Offers workshops and seminars.
Journals/Publications: Directory of members; *LINKS; NAPRR News and Notes.*
Job Listings: Offers placement assistance.

National Association of Psychiatric Treatment Centers for Children
2000 L St. NW, Suite 200
Washington, DC 20036
Members/Purpose: Residential centers for emotionally disturbed children that have been accredited by the Joint Commission on Accreditation of Healthcare Organizations.
Training: Sponsors technical seminars.
Journals/Publications: Member facilities; *The Emerging Role of Psychiatric Treatment Centers.*

National Association of Rehabilitation Facilities
P.O. Box 17675
Washington, DC 20041

Members/Purpose: Rehabilitation facilities in the United States and Canada; agencies operating established medical and vocational rehabilitation facilities.
Training: Sponsors seminar and provides specialized education programs.
Journals/Publications: *Rehabilitation Review.*

National Association of State Mental Retardation Program Directors
113 Oronoco St.
Alexandria, VA 22314
Members/Purpose: State administrative personnel working with programs in the field of mental retardation.
Journals/Publications: *Capitol Capsule; Federal Funding Inquiry; New Directions.*

National Council of Community Mental Health Centers
121300 Twinbrook Pkwy., Number 320
Rockville, MD 20852
Members/Purpose: Community mental health centers, organizations, agencies, and interested individuals.
Training: Conducts workshops related to significant issues and changes in community mental health.
Journals/Publications: *Community Mental Health Journal;* community mental health salary survey; *NCCMHC-National Council News;* national registry of community mental health services.
Job Listings: See *National Council News.*

National Institute on Adult Day Care
c/o National Council on the Aging
409 3rd St. SW, 2nd Floor
Washington, DC 20024
Members/Purpose: Adult day care practitioners; health and social service planners; individuals involved in planning and providing services for older persons.
Training: Conducts workshops and training events.
Journals/Publications: *NCOA Networks.*

National Network of Runaway and Youth Services
1319 F St. NW, Suite 401
Washington, DC 20004
Members/Purpose: Community-based, human services agencies, programs, and coalitions dealing with the concerns of runaway homeless, and other at-risk youth.
Training: Sponsors educational programs.
Journals/Publications: *Network News; Policy Reporter*

National Woman Abuse Prevention Project
1112 16th St. NW, Suite 920
Washington, DC 20036
Members/Purpose: Works to prevent domestic violence and improve
services offered to battered women.
Training: Conducts educational programs.
Journals/Publications: *Exchange.*

CHAPTER ELEVEN

PATH 2: SOCIAL AND HUMAN SERVICES

Stop reading this book right now! Put it down and go visit a website such as www.socialservice.com, or look up "Social and Human Services" in the Yellow Pages of your telephone directory. No matter which source you use, there will be a significant number of agencies listed. Many you'll recognize immediately, such as The American Red Cross, your state legal assistance fund, The American Heart Association, or local and state family planning groups. But there will be other agency names unfamiliar to you that you'll find interesting, for example, your state's assistive technology and equipment center or a program of academic excellence. Other organizations are centered around issues such as helping people with AIDS or housing difficulties or fuel assistance. There will be programs offering abortion counseling or counseling for young people. Many agencies help people with disabilities. Investigate them all.

HELP: A WIDESPREAD NEED

As you explore social and human services websites or look through this section of the Yellow Pages for a large metropolitan area, there will be a staggering number of social service organizations listed. Not only will you be surprised at how narrowly focused some of the agency programs are, but you will also be surprised at the number of organizations listed under a particular heading. So, while you may be very interested to know there are workers concentrating on housing assistance issues, you may be even more surprised to see so many organizations listed under that heading.

These listings serve as symbols of both our social concerns and our social consciousness. They are clear signs of what is wrong in our society in the needs they express and what is right by the provision of an agency to help. It's fair to say that the size and breadth of these listings have as much to do with the size of the community as it does with the concern the community is expressing for others and the determination of those committed to the public good to found and operate organizations and agencies to help.

WHO RECEIVES SOCIAL AND HUMAN SERVICES?

The choice of populations and clients to work with is wide, indeed. Each group presents its own set of issues. Each group makes demands on and challenges the social and human services worker. Here's a selected list of some of the most prominent populations with a capsule description of relevant issues and statistics.

Aging

The need for social and human services generally increases with age, and the elderly population is growing in this country. Life expectancy in the United States rose dramatically during the twentieth century. In 1900, the average life expectancy was forty-seven years. By the end of the century, that figure increased to seventy-seven years. In the last decade of the 1900s, the number of people living to be at least one hundred years of age was just over 60,000. That figure is projected to exceed 800,000 by the middle of the twenty-first century. Not only has life expectancy increased, but the number of people reaching this age has also increased. By 1999, the number of people who were sixty-five or older reached 35 million, 13 percent of the total U.S. population.[1] Even though today's seniors may be more physically active or financially protected than their predecessors, there is still an increased need for physical therapy, transportation services, counseling for depression and emotional difficulties, and help coping with changes, including living circumstances and diet. Although some elderly individuals can afford to reside in planned communities, others live alone or in a variety of other settings. Some are in hospitals, nursing homes, or facilities that care for people with mental illnesses, including Alzheimer's disease.

Poverty

We not only continue to have significant communities of poverty across this wealthy country of ours, but our cities are filled with homeless and destitute

1. *The World Almanac 2000*, pp. 381, 891.

individuals and families. At the end of the twentieth century, the number of people in poverty was 34.4 million, representing 12.7 percent of the nation's population. More than one-third of the nation's poor were either under eighteen years of age or adults sixty-five and older.[2]

Some of these individuals, be they residents of Vermont or the barrios of Los Angeles, are on the federal welfare rolls, while others have fallen through the cracks in the system.

Poverty is not their only problem. Alcoholism, unemployment, drug abuse, illness, and a host of other social ills can be part of the picture for the social and human services worker fighting the battle of chronic poverty. The professional is not working alone as an agent for change. Government and private programs for jobs, housing, employment, and numerous preventative initiatives try to help as does an enormous network of other helping professionals.

Juvenile Delinquency

It appears that a variety of risk factors affect whether an adolescent finds his or her way to adulthood without becoming a member of the juvenile justice system. The factors include poverty, welfare dependence, absence of one or both parents, marital status of the parents, and educational attainment of the parents. One recent statistic indicated that on a typical day, nearly 106,000 juveniles were being held in a residential facility as a result of a law violation.[3] On an even more serious note, in that same year, approximately 12 percent of all murders in the United States involved at least one juvenile offender.[4] We know our penal institutions are not appropriate sites for remediation, and many job-training programs have discovered that they need to provide for follow-through for graduates to ensure employment. Working with juvenile offenders presents great challenges along with the possibility of equally large rewards for the community and social and human services worker.

Crime

During the last decade of the twentieth century, there were decreases in all categories of crime reported in the FBI's Crime Index. In contrast, the total number of prisoners under the jurisdiction of the federal or state adult correctional authorities hit a record high of more than 1.3 million.[5] The debate over punishment verses rehabilitation continues, but in the meantime, social

· · · · · · · · ·

2. Census Bureau Website (www.census.gov) Poverty, 1998.
3. White House Briefing, September 17, 1999.
4. Ibid.
5. *The World Almanac 2000*, p. 907.

and human services workers play an important role in the justice system. Some work directly with the prison population, while others assist with the inmate's reentry into the community.

Alcohol Abuse

Alcohol abuse remains largely hidden to the majority of the public, but the social and human services worker is all too aware of the pervasiveness of alcoholism and the great sadness and pain it can bring to families, relationships, employment, and most important, to the alcoholics themselves. Alcohol continues to be one of the most costly abused substances. The total cost of services, medical bills, lost earnings, automobile accidents, fires, and criminal justice expenditures was a staggering $167 billion.[6] We are learning more about treatment methods, the impact on children of alcoholic parents, and the role heredity may play in the predisposition to alcoholism. Considerable work is being done on several frontiers for alcohol abusers and their problems, but it remains an enormous social challenge.

Substance Abuse

Substance abuse remains a complex and challenging problem with a multitude of related issues. For the social and human services worker, addiction is a problem that requires the combined forces of both the medical community and other helping professionals. In the late 1990s, the Substance Abuse and Mental Health Services Administration's, Drug Abuse Warning Network (DAWN) reported an estimated 527,000 drug-related episodes in hospital emergency departments nationwide.[7] As with alcohol abuse, the costs are high: $110 billion.[8] Substance abuse can bring crime to support the habit and is as destructive of relationships as alcoholism. Unlike alcohol, the number and variety of substances available for abuse is ever-changing and can often present difficult challenges to the helping professional when the drug is unknown or unidentifiable.

Following detoxification, self-help programs, halfway houses, mentoring, and individual and group counseling are vital adjunctive therapies for the recovering addict.

Mental Illness

The general public is aware of and conversant in most of the social conditions we've been describing. We see these issues on the nightly news and in

....

6. National Institute of Health (NIH) Publication Number 98-4327.

7. *The World Almanac 2000*, p. 893.

8. NIH Publication Number 98-4327.

our morning newspaper. Less understood and more confusing is the world of mental illness. The National Institute of Mental Health has reported that severe mental illnesses are more common than cancer, diabetes, or heart disease. Twenty percent of families are affected by severe mental illness in their lifetime, and 21 percent of hospital beds are filled by patients with mental illness, the leading reason for hospital admissions.[9]

Mental Retardation

Many people also understand the distinction between a mental illness, such as depression, and mental retardation. Mental retardation is characterized by significantly subaverage intellectual functioning, existing concurrently with related limitations in two or more of the following applicable adaptive skill areas: communication, self-care, home living, social skills, community use, self-direction, health and safety, functional academics, leisure, and work. This definition was developed by the American Association on Mental Retardation. In 2000, approximately 2 percent of the U.S. population was classified as being mentally retarded.[10] We have seen increasing societal acceptance of people with mental retardation in terms of semi-independent and independent living, employment, and marriage. Their success in the community is supported by the social and human services worker.

Chronic Illness

Social and human services professionals assist individuals living with chronic illnesses and their families. Some of these illnesses include:

- Cancer
- Heart disease
- Kidney disease
- Liver disease
- Lung disease
- Alzheimer's disease
- Autism
- Cystic Fibrosis
- Epilepsy

··········

9. National Institute of Mental Health, Mental Health Information and Statistics.
10. American Association on Mental Retardation, Washington, DC, 2000.

- Juvenile Diabetes

- Leukemia

- Lupus

- Attention Deficit Disorder

- Burns

- Polio

- Neurological disorders and stroke

- Multiple Sclerosis

No matter which chronic illness affects an individual, the ongoing physical and often emotional challenges require attention and coordination. These conditions can and do occupy huge amounts of time to manage but need not relegate those affected to marginal lives. Dealing with insurers, caregivers, and service providers can become a preoccupation and can drain an individual of energy and spirit to accomplish more. As social and human services professionals assemble networks to provide services, opportunities for increasingly normal life patterns emerge for patients, families, and caregivers. This ability to provide an increased quality of life has been both a continuing challenge to professionals in the field and their greatest triumph.

EXPLORE THE RANGE OF ISSUES AND POPULATIONS OUR SOCIETY REPRESENTS

Although we have described, in some detail, a few of the larger populations receiving social and human services, there are many other groups that are served and issues that are addressed. The listing of types of services that follows is just the tip of the iceberg for the graduate looking to enter the social and human services field. Go down the list and think about which issues interest you. There may be some that surprise you or that you've never heard of. Each area is worth your exploration, and Internet searches, career books, magazines, and journals can provide you with information that you will find useful. In addition, we have listed at the end of this chapter a number of professional organizations that can provide helpful information.

Abortion-alternatives counseling
Abortion counseling
Adoption services

continued

continued

Athletic services
Battered spouses and children's services
Blind, organizations for the
Charity services
Child counseling
Children's services
Chronic disease services
Communicable diseases counseling and services
Community services
Consumer services
Crime victim services
Crisis intervention services
Day-care assistance
Deaf and hearing impaired, services for the
Developmentally disabled persons services
Disabled assistance services
Divorce counseling
Domestic violence counseling
Drug abuse and prevention services
Economic assistance services
Educational information services
Elderly persons services
Ethnic organizations and services
Family and individual services
Foster care services
Gay, lesbian, and transgendered organizations and services
Halfway houses
Health services
Home care services
Homeless persons services
Housing assistance
Human services
Immigrant assistance
Legal counseling
Medical relief services
Mental health services
Men's services
Philanthropic services
Pregnancy counseling and prevention information
Pregnancy and maternity services

continued

continued
Rape crisis services
Religious organizations
Sex information and counseling
Single parent's services
Suicide prevention services
Tenant's services
Traveler's assistance
Vocational services
Volunteer services
Women's services
Youth services

HOW CAN THE PSYCHOLOGY MAJOR FIT INTO THE PICTURE?

But what do all of these organizations and the people who work in them do? More important, as a psychology major with an undergraduate degree, is there a place for you? For the psychology major interested in social and human services, the problem is not *who* or *where* but *how* to choose among the many types of agencies that do exist. Each contains a world of specialized information, support networks, informational and financial resources, and dedicated professionals and paraprofessionals working to improve the human condition.

Social service is concerned with bringing people together with the information and tools they need to cope with and surmount challenges in their lives. Social-service workers help to bring harmony to strained lives and circumstances; to enrich lives that may be impoverished in any manner of speaking; and to teach people the skills and techniques needed so they can continue to find resources, work out solutions, and lead richer, fuller lives.

Any profession that deals with all of humanity and with the infinite number of human issues from birth to death cannot be limited to workers of one educational preparation or one kind of knowledge or experience. When issues as diverse as sexual abuse, disease, mental and physical disabilities, housing, insurance, education, crime, and alcohol abuse are part of the daily menu of problems presented in the environment, a range of educational backgrounds is required.

The field of social service draws from many areas of academic preparation: psychology, religion, counseling, medicine, health and nutrition, home economics, child care, law enforcement, political science, mental health, criminal justice, and, of course, social work. Social service involves seeking out the right information; the right resources for clients and connecting clients with the information, materials, and resources they require; and providing the assistance and support they may need to obtain such information and resources. In connecting clients with the many services and agencies providing assistance, the social-service worker is in a networking, communicating, bridge-building, role-modeling, counseling, and mentoring partnership role.

DEFINITION OF THE CAREER PATH

Let's begin the discussion of this career path by focusing on some entry-level community and social service want ads:

Intake Assistant. Screen potential clients, gather client data, schedule appointments, provide information about mental illness, provide family support, observe clients. Excellent interpersonal skills, flexibility, multiple tasking, B.A/B.S. psychology, social work, education, valid driver's license. Apply to (mental health services organization, Alabama)

Volunteer Coordinator and Socialization Group Leader. Ensure that volunteer services are provided to clients with disabilities. Develop and implement comprehensive volunteer program. Provide outreach for and lead semimonthy support groups for young adults with developmental and/or learning disabilities. B.A. or equivalent experience; volunteer management experience; ability to work comfortably supporting people with disabilities and chronic illnesses; knowledge of community resources; ability to work independently and as part of a team. Send resume and cover letter to (family and children's services organization, San Francisco)

Community Treatment Worker. Social-service agency seeks counselor for its reintegration service program in the Detroit office. Network to coordinate services and refer clients as appropriate. Bachelor's degree in social work or related field required. Send cover letter and resume to (recruiting firm, Michigan)

continued

---

continued

Districtwide Social-Services Worker. Provide short-term problem solving services; assist in translation and form completion; make home visits when necessary. B.S.W. or B.A. in social sciences, bilingual in Spanish. Send resume to (self-help for the elderly nonprofit organization, Texas)

Entitlements Specialist. Cutting edge, consumer-oriented nonprofit housing agency providing advocacy to adults with psychiatric disabilities is seeking someone to assess income needs and to direct entitlements (Social Security, public assistance, food stamps, Medicaid) for clients. Prefer prior experience with entitlements and advocacy. Excellent employee and generous time-off benefits. Forward letter and resume.

In breaking down these want ads into job components, several basic duties emerge: counseling, record keeping, assessing a wide range of conditions, networking, meeting immediate needs, referring, working with volunteers, interacting with multidisciplinary teams, and building a knowledge base. Each job presents some unique circumstances, and so these job components will carry a different weight depending on the position and the setting. Evaluate where your strengths are (you may want to refer back to the self-assessment you completed), and this will help guide you in determining how to choose the setting in which you may work most effectively.

Counseling

Counseling is a process of connection and deep human involvement between people. Certainly there are many formal schools of counseling theory and technique, but individual counselors ultimately evolve a counseling technique that works for him or her and the clients. Often, for the clientele of the social and human services worker, the deeply empathic listening attention of the counselor is, in and of itself, therapeutic. Clients who have a caring listener who values them as a person and to whom they can talk about their problems can be at the beginning on the road to healthy living.

Record Keeping

The social and human services worker must keep excellent records and may sometimes be responsible for determinations of financial assistance or other forms of aid. Frequently the social-service worker is called upon to explain local, state, or federal regulations or procedures to their clients and may actively assist them in their efforts to secure assistance.

Many new entrants into the field of social service work are overwhelmed by the amount of paperwork and telephone work. Hours and hours of each day are spent chasing people down by telephone or processing paperwork. Carrying out administrative duties can certainly create doubts about the "service" in social service work.

Assessing a Wide Range of Conditions

The types of human conditions seen in various settings are described in the advertisements. The social and human services worker can expect to become quite adept at recognizing the signs of alcohol abuse, delirium tremens, diabetes, hypothermia, malnutrition, or addiction, and will become skilled at assessing a client's self-help skills and willingness to change.

Networking

The new worker in this job will slowly build a network of contacts that he or she can count on for help: help in explaining the law, help in finding long-term housing, help in job training and employment, sources for food, clothing, medical help, and every other kind of assistance clients require. Social-service workers become very aware of the "hows" and "whys" of their clients' situations and the social fabric that contributes to their problems and the difficulties in solving them.

Meeting Immediate Needs

There is little time for psychological evaluation, and testing is seldom done by the social-service worker. There are more immediate and demanding needs to be met, such as shelter, food, and health care. Some clients can be assisted quickly; many others progress very slowly with much recidivism; and, sadly, many clients cannot be helped at all. The rewards are in the clients who *can* be helped. Social-service workers remain in the trenches, each day making a contribution, helping those who, if left alone, might not be able to do for themselves.

Referring

An important role is in trying to help clients such as the poor, those without housing, or those needing help with substance abuse in locating long-term shelters or permanent housing, securing jobs or job training, and the sometimes necessary attendant issues, such as finding day care or clothing. Connecting clients to agencies and sources of many of these basic needs is a first step in the helping and rehabilitative process. Some clients will need counseling and referral to treatment programs before other initiatives can successfully begin.

The adult client with cerebral palsy may need help connecting with someone who can advocate for him or her for appropriate and accessible housing. A referral to another agency may provide help in wheelchair maintenance or physical therapy. The client may need assistance in applying for food stamps or simply need a ride to and from the grocery store. Each client may need connections with a number of support services.

The job involves interviewing clients to assess the number and severity of their problems, making an evaluation, and determining specific needs and how those might best be satisfied. The social-service worker then begins to bring together all the necessary agencies, individuals, information, and resources to create some positive change. They will become well acquainted with the police station, the local stores, the court system, state aid, criminal elements in their locality, and the drug trade.

Working with Volunteers

Most social and human services organizations simply could not survive without dedicated, caring, and skilled volunteers. The reality is that the problems are widespread, the need is great, and the resources are very thinly spread. Volunteers help to bridge these gaps in service, staffing, and resources, and they do it with enthusiasm and sincere interest.

Volunteers often work only brief hours on irregular schedules. They require training and, as unpaid staff, need to be assigned activities and responsibilities in keeping with these considerations. The social and human services worker will spend some administrative time in scheduling volunteers, in training them on a continual basis, and in seeking to incorporate them in the organization's mission in a fulfilling manner.

Interacting with a Multidisciplinary Team

The human services client is often in receipt of help from a number of sources simultaneously. He or she may be receiving personal counseling from a therapist for sexual or physical abuse. Another client may be attending Alcoholics Anonymous meetings daily. You may have a client in personal therapy, jobs counseling, drug rehabilitation, under a physician's care for a chronic illness, and on probation all at the same time. You will have to help the client maintain these commitments and orchestrate the efforts of all these helping agencies to reduce conflict and maintain a comfortable climate for your client. Very often your clients will not be strong advocates for their own cases, and you can work with all of the professionals involved in your clients' care to devise a program that best suits their needs.

Building a Knowledge Base

Reading this, you begin to appreciate the time and focus entry-level social-service workers must bring to the job. All the while, as they improve their job performance (their ability to help), they are acquiring valuable information, knowledge, and skills in the setting and with the population they encounter.

The knowledge base builds almost imperceptibly, aided by in-service training, conferences, seminars, and a daily schedule of clients with their individual case histories. The caseworker finds his or her understanding of "the system" expanding, and the bureaucratic and legal aspects of assistance and support becomes clearer and more workable. You're becoming a professional. Laws and pending legislation can vary dramatically state by state, and there can be differences in implementation within states. To be an effective social and human services worker is to understand the system your clients find themselves in and to act as a guide in securing services for them. To do this well requires making contacts and connections, most often through your individual work for clients, and learning how things work in your locality.

Though you provide helping skills, much of your work depends on making connections with others and in advocating for the support and assistance for your client that the law entitles them to. Understanding and learning that takes time and experience.

WHY PSYCHOLOGY RATHER THAN SOCIAL WORK?

The short selection of job listings provided previously gives you some sense of the diversity of work present in social services, not only in the kinds of activities a social-service worker engages in, but also in the presenting problems of the people they work with and the age and gender mix of those populations The breadth and scope of social-service work and its initiatives result in an equally broad scope in the selection of candidates for social-service jobs.

What you took special notice of was the fairly generalized degree demands, in most cases, a bachelor's degree or a psychology degree, or some reasonably related degree. Most, for obvious reasons, would prefer previous experience so that the job candidate understands the job and the issues of the people the candidate will be working with.

While the generalized requirements may please some, others may be skeptical. Why don't they demand a social work degree? How can they be so loose in job qualifications when the work is so important? The answers lie in the nature of social-service work. It is enormously demanding, many would say taxing, of the social-service worker's energy, patience, time, and physical resources. Although the field has a range of pay for similar jobs, depending upon the employment setting, high salaries have not been a tradition of the social and human services field. The short answer may be that hiring officials who fill tough jobs paying less than top wages must draw from a wide pool of applicants.

There's another, equally valid, reason. When you look at the spectrum of problems social-service workers must wrestle with and the diversity of the human canvas that is placed before them, it is difficult to know where the talent may lie to help alleviate some of the struggle. Certainly, we have social workers who have studied the issues and earned a degree in the subject on the bachelor's, master's, and doctoral level. Others come to these same issues and concerns with as much to offer but a different, yet equally valuable, preparation in other academic areas and life experiences.

HOW CAN THE SOCIAL AND HUMAN SERVICES WORKER GROW?

Some students contemplating a career in social and human services wonder whether they can sustain a lifelong career in this field. They worry about burnout. There are three specific efforts you can make as you begin your career that will help you keep this issue in perspective. First of all, think about whether the skills you are using and the knowledge base you are building can be transferred to other populations and settings. Second, think about preparing for growth in a specialty. And third, take care of your own career needs.

Transferring Your Skills and Knowledge

One way you can progress in your career is to change work settings. You can consciously create some meaningful transitions by learning which skills and knowledge are valued in a given workplace. Some of the skills and knowledge that you acquire as you begin your career will be directly transferable to a different situation, while others will not relate to different settings. Look for the common threads. A position assisting homeless adults would provide some good experience in working with an elderly population, and that work can relate to a number of other, more stable eldercare situations. Or, work in adult substance abuse might prove sufficient to merit a move into an adolescent substance abuse clinic. A move from a facility servicing homeless adults to a residential center caring for child victims of sexual or physical abuse would, however, be more difficult to make. The type of facility and the type of client have changed, so fewer skills and less knowledge are transferable.

Preparing for Growth in a Specialty

You can also grow and develop in social and human services work by building a specific body of knowledge and helping skills; that, by necessity, suggests working with a particular population and learning the resources that exist for that group until you are proficient. Job growth may then come in the form of more supervisory responsibility for other caregivers, management control of a facility, or advanced or specialized education in your field.

Taking Care of Your Own Career Needs

It's no mystery that social and human services workers burn out. It's a tough, tough job, and some professionals simply get weary of the obstacles put in their clients' way or the recidivism that occurs among people whom they have tried mightily to help make some headway against serious obstacles.

You may act tired, you may get cynical, or you may want a job that is less physically and emotionally draining. Changing the population you work with is certainly one technique, especially if many of the issues are familiar ones to you. Growing within your speciality and taking an administrative or management position is yet another option.

Whatever you decide to do, make it an active choice. Don't let your career just "happen." You don't want your boss to take you aside one day and suggest you're overextended, tired, and no longer effective. Take your own career pulse from time and time and ask yourself, "Hey, how am I doing?" If you feel you need something different, make it your choice. Social and human services is a noble calling with rich rewards, but it makes equally insistent demands on your time and energy.

WORKING CONDITIONS

Social-service workers at every level of expertise (doctorate, master's, bachelor's, and paraprofessional) are employed in a number of different settings. The setting, in large part, dictates the types of activities in which the social-service worker is engaged, the jobs and duties they have, the types of clients and client needs they will encounter, and the ways in which they will practice their social service profession.

Some specific issues to consider include:

- Age of the population served
- Source of funding for agency/service
- Working hours
- Specific issues of the clientele
- Personal safety

Age of Population Served

Your interest in working with children, or your care and compassion for the elderly, may have been what drew you to work in social and human services. There are many agencies that serve specific age populations, so if age of your clientele is an important condition, be sure to target the appropriate agencies.

Some services are structured for particular age groups, so the activities, therapies, and atmosphere will combine to say to the client, "This is a for-you service." Shelters for adolescent males or senior-services centers are good examples. Other services are age blind and are built around a condition, disease entity, or problem. The HIV virus is age blind and a service supporting those afflicted would span all ages.

Source of Funding for Agency/Service

The stability of funding is an important consideration for any helping service. Funds that are not stable, that perhaps need to be renewed each year, can create a sense of impermanence affecting staff morale and services if refunding is delayed.

Other agencies may have relatively stable but require significant development work to continually raise money, and will call upon the social-service worker to assist in these fund-raising efforts. While necessary to continued viability, this fund-raising work can often be an additional burden on already overworked staff.

Some grant-funded programs ultimately end or program funding slowly drops and programs are disbanded, leaving workers to seek new employment. Other effects of funding sources can be on the physical facilities, location, type of support in terms of supplies, and quality of staff.

Working Hours

The variety of social and human services is not limited to age populations or need issues. Service providers work many different shifts and schedules especially in the areas of homelessness, drug and substance abuse, and sheltered care of all kinds.

There are standard rotating shifts, or there may be three full days on and four days off. There may be sleep-in accommodations with a need to be available twenty-four hours. There are traditional thirty-seven-hour weeks as well. You'll need to consider staffing hours carefully and think about how they will affect your personal life, your relationships, your avocational interests, and your well-being.

Specific Issues of the Clientele

Some substance abusers steal to support their habits. Many adolescent men and women have unprotected sex before marriage. Street people may sell blood for alcohol. The list of problems and behaviors goes on and on. Some of these may be inconsistent with your own value system.

Your clients need help, not judgment. As you explore possible work settings, it is important for you to ascertain how you feel about the issues facing the people with whom you choose to work. Compassion, caring, a sense of humor, and hopefulness are what your clients need, not lectures, censorship, or condemnation. Determine for yourself where you can be the most helpful and where you can commit to those you hope to serve.

Personal Safety

When people encounter great hardship and struggle in their lives, it can have pronounced effects on their temperaments. Anger, hostility, and violence may lie close to the surface, and from time to time, there certainly have been incidences involving threats to the personal safety of social and human services workers.

Most professionals would assure you that this is not a dominant concern in their workday lives. They exercise caution in their client relationships; they share concerns with coworkers; and they activate response systems, including police, if threats occur. In some settings, for example abortion clinics, overnight shelters, or disaster relief situations, tempers flare and outbreaks of violence may occur. In most cases, skilled personnel are well equipped to deal with this and do so effectively.

Think about your own ability to tolerate conflict and mediate violence. Consider your personal physical characteristics and the population you are interested in serving and talk to professionals now working in these areas for the best advice on how to cope with threats to your physical safety.

NETWORK TO GET INFORMATION AND ANSWERS

Because of your educational background in psychology and your possible hope of relating that education directly to social service, it's especially important for you to take the time and talk directly to some practitioners, even if their academic preparation was different from your own. Talking to people "in the field" will provide a reality check that no amount of reading can duplicate. It will bring home some truths about the job that you might not have expected.

You'll want to think carefully and examine your own interests, skills, and attributes before committing to service in a particular area. The self-assessment section of this book should provide a strong beginning exploration. Further talks with career professionals both in your career-counseling center and among the social-service community will help you decide if certain client groups, and their associated challenges, are interesting enough for you to work in as a career or at least to begin your career working with this group.

TRAINING AND QUALIFICATIONS

Be sure to review both the personal and professional qualifications we have outlined in this section and decide how they fit with what you have to offer.

Personal Qualifications

Mature	Communicative
Concerned for others	Teacher
Responsible	Idealistic
High standards	Ethical
Sense of humor	Sensitive
Good with people	Respectful
Dedicated	Good listener
Effective speaker	Productive
Discrete	Realistic
Objective	Innovative
Independent	Writer
Stable	Thoughtful
Empathic	Responsive
Resilient	

Social and human services work is so diverse that it would be foolish to try and create a comprehensive list or menu of necessary personal characteristics. The long list above is just suggestive of many of the personal characteristics that your profession will draw upon to a greater or lesser degree. The counseling techniques that may be effective in establishing rapport with young, unwed mothers may not serve the social-service worker in good stead when dealing with the chronically mentally ill. But there are some well understood qualities that are needed in many, many social- and community-services positions and the psychology major considering a career in social and human services needs to review this list and rate himself or herself on these criteria.

Concern for Others. One must be concerned for people and their problems. To engage the client and to assess the situation, the social-service worker needs empathy, sensitivity, an ability to establish and maintain rapport, and an appreciation of the wonderful diversity present in our population.

Working with a frustrated adolescent may require sitting with him or her for more than an hour before he or she begins to open up and talk to you about current problems. An elderly patient may begin to share fears and concerns more easily if you begin by letting the client show you a family album or some favorite pictures.

Appropriate Detachment. To be effective, however, there must be a maturity and ability to distance oneself enough to not take on others' problems as one's own. The social and human services professional will find no paucity of clients and many with problems that seem almost insurmountable. The work goes on and on, and sometimes progress is very slow.

For that reason, professionals need to pace themselves. They need to respect their own limitations and what they can accomplish. If you are exhausted, overwrought, allowing clients to call you at home or interfere with your personal life, you will eventually self-extinguish. What help can you be to the system if you are suffering from burnout?

True professionals in this field know their limitations and understand the importance of leaving work at work. They appreciate their own need for rejuvenation and restoration each day in order to be able to return and do effective work. Clients have problems you can help with, but they are not your problems.

Ability to Work the System. In addition, social-service workers must be quick studies in political systems to be able to marshal the necessary resources to help solve clients' problems. Referral networks, sources of financial aid, and housing entitlements all have their hierarchies, paperwork, and influential personalities. To do your best for your clients is to understand not only how the system "should" work, but how it, in fact, does work.

Flexibility. Flexibility is another key personal trait needed in social and human services work. Work hours or shifts may change constantly, the physical location where you carry out your duties may move, and members of a multidisciplinary team may be constantly changing given different schedule rotations. Assess your ability to be happy with the level of flexibility required for the types of positions you are considering and the types of populations you would be working with.

Professional Qualifications

Your Degree. Preprofessional and professional positions in social and human services work are largely determined by degree level and type of degree. Preprofessional positions are those undegreed or associates-degreed workers who are acting as aides or assistants to social and human services workers. Professional positions are those where the individual has at least a bachelor's degree in psychology, social work, or sociology that will satisfy the social service agencies' needs.

Licensure/Certification. Workers in the social and human services field have come under increasing public scrutiny. As in any area of human endeavor, there have been scandals and examples of unethical behavior. Laws and regulations surrounding the provision of services have increased exponentially, and many professional organizations publish detailed ethical guidelines for their members.

In addition to advanced degree attainment as an outward mark of professionalism, there is both licensure and certification in many states. Licensure has to do with the state ensuring certain educational standards and experiential standards have been met. It often involves some type of written examination. It helps the public know the individual has met some state-mandated criterion for professionalism. Licensing boards are then able to discipline unethical or fraudulent practitioners by revoking this license.

Certification through professional organizations promotes standards of education, practice, accountability, discretion, ethics, and visibility, and helps assure the public that the individual employee has met some established standards. Certification can involve testing or the documentation of professional development and years of practice. It is often issued for a limited period of time.

See your career office or talk with state officials for information on licensure and your applicable professional associations for certification information.

Knowledge of Other Languages. Frequently, an urban or metropolitan job announcement in social and human services will express the desire for fluency in Spanish, Chinese, Vietnamese, Cambodian, or another of those languages indicative of growing immigrant communities in our cities or districts of metropolitan areas. While the record of assimilation, especially in language acquisition, among these new citizens is remarkable, new arrivals and the elderly often cannot be effectively serviced without communicating in their native tongue.

EARNINGS

People interested in working in social and human services will take an interesting journey when trying to learn more about starting salaries. There is solid information on social work earnings and for doctoral level psychologists, but what can the newly-degreed psychology graduate with limited experience hope to earn? The answer comes in looking at a wide variety of actual job listings in social and human services. Although the Bureau of Labor Statistics (www.bls.gov) indicates those just starting out can expect to earn up to $30,000, you should expect a starting salary in the mid $20,000 range at best. Wages may vary slightly depending on the work site and the geographic region of the country. Because these figures may be lower than you anticipated, be sure to complete the "Calculate Your Economic Needs" portion of the self-assessment chapter to verify that you will be able to meet your basic economic needs.

CAREER OUTLOOK

Regrettably, the problems that face society do not abate, and each generation seems to encounter new and more challenging issues, such as the spread of AIDS or random acts of violence. In addition, natural disasters, fires, and other uncontrollable events occur without warning and also do tremendous damage to people's lives and well-being. Each type of problem precipitates the need for a core of services and a host of other support mechanisms.

Affordable health care, housing, and food should be controllable but remain out of reach for many people and with dire consequences. Social and human services workers will continue to be needed to help connect these people with services that are available to them.

The U.S. Department of Labor, Bureau of Labor Statistics projects that the number of human services workers will grow faster than the average through the year 2006. Fast-growing occupations generally have good employment prospects and conditions favorable for advancement.

STRATEGY FOR FINDING THE JOBS

As a psychology major interested in social and human services, you can undertake six tasks to enhance your job search. Be ready to:

- ❑ I dentify the social concerns that interest you the most
- ❑ Become very familiar with the required professional qualifications
- ❑ Identify the personal qualifications you possess
- ❑ Build skills and gain direct experience with a population that interests you
- ❑ Network with professionals working in the field
- ❑ Relate your psychology background to what the employer needs

Undertaking these activities, along with the other phases of the job search as outlined in Part 1 of this book, will put you on the right track as you begin to establish your career.

Identify the Social Concerns That Interest You the Most

As you have seen in reading this career path, many issues and concerns are addressed in social and human services work. You may have been drawn to major in psychology because of your deep interest in helping children or in promoting a cause such as affordable housing for all who seek it. No matter what your interests are, there are many, many places for the psychology major in social and human services, but only you can determine where you want to begin your career. This choice will help you create a focused resume, select appropriate employment sites to investigate, and interview in an effective way. You'll be able to relate your history to what the employer needs in a potential worker.

Become Very Familiar with the Required Professional Qualifications

Your job search begins with an in-depth awareness of the types and levels of skills and abilities that are really needed in social and human services work. In the job announcements we have presented for this path we have seen requirements for workers with experience with a specific population, creativity, sell direction, budget experience, ability to teach survival skills, flexibility, ability to work effectively on a multidisciplinary team, motivation, high level of energy, planning ability, implementation skills, and facilitator skills.

Begin to find the matches between your skills and experience, and those that many employers will need. You may have worked effectively in a food service team, you may have taught a lifesaving skill such as cardiopulmonary resuscitation, or you may have helped a professor plan a regional meeting. It is your job to make those experiences relevant to a social-service employer.

Identify the Personal Qualifications You Possess

In the "Training and Qualifications" section of this path, starting on page 162, we discussed some personal traits that the social and human services worker should possess. Those included concern for others, appropriate detachment, an ability to work the system, and flexibility. You may want to create a type of resume that will allow you to highlight the qualifications you possess and have to offer to an employer. A modified resume that includes a capabilities section allows you to enhance the way a potential employer reads and understands your relevant experience. For example, if you were to indicate on your resume three capabilities such as:

□ Empathic communicator

□ Effective resource provider

□ Flexible team member

the employer would read your work history section and look for the experience you've had that allowed you to build these skills.

Build Skills and Gain Direct Experience with a Population That Interests You

Go back and review the actual job listings shown in the "Definition of the Career Path" section for social and human services, starting on page 153. Two of the ads ask specifically for experience. You can begin gaining this experience through some combination of the following avenues: volunteer work, part-time work, full-time summer work, and internships. It will be important for you to get your feet wet as soon as you realize you have an interest in working in social and human services. You will get to test the waters to see if the work is a good fit given your interests and abilities, and you'll have that all-important experience to put on your resume.

If you are seeking volunteer work, it's certainly not hard to find. Review the list of social service organizations in your local Yellow Pages, contact organizations to see what their needs are in terms of volunteers, and also ask what training they provide. This can be a great way to enhance your skill base at no cost. These same organizations may also offer employment opportunities, but be sure to start your search early; there will be lots of competition for these jobs. If an internship is the type of experience you are looking for, check with the head of your psychology department and with your career office to find out about all of the opportunities available to you. Deadlines come early on some of these, so don't put off the research necessary for this undertaking.

Network with Professionals Working in the Field

No one can give you a more accurate accounting of what social and human services work is really like than a professional currently employed in the field. Start with the faculty in your psychology department and see whom they can recommend. You should also check with the career office and see who in your college or university alumni network may be a good source of information given your interests. Review the description of networking provided in Chapter 4, and prepare carefully to get the most you can out of this experience.

Relate Your Psychology Background to What the Employer Needs

As you progressed in your degree program, you took coursework that provided you with specific knowledge and skills that arc valuable in the workplace. You may have decided you were interested in working with victims of crime through a parole authority. Well, that introductory course you took in criminal justice that helped you gain a deeper understanding of the criminal justice system, combined with your coursework in abnormal behavior, gave you a background that will allow you to more effectively serve the victims of crime with whom you would be working. Generalize this example and see how your coursework relates to the population you want to serve. Consider adding a "Related Coursework" section to your resume, one that will pleasantly surprise the employer with additional knowledge you have added to your background.

POSSIBLE EMPLOYERS

In considering social and human services work, you should investigate a range of employers. These include:

❑ Nonprofit agencies

❑ Medical/health organizations

❑ Federal/state/local governmental agencies

❑ Corrections and rehabilitation

❑ Insurance companies

❑ Religious organizations

❑ Retirement homes/communities

The information provided below on each type of employer will help you begin your search.

Nonprofit Agencies

Profile. Nonprofit agencies offer an incredibly wide array of social and human services, and each hires workers to provide, oversee, administer, and manage these services. They need you, the psychology major, on their staffs. Whether you're working in consumer services, aid to the homeless, or immigration assistance, your skills in counseling, record keeping, and referring for services will be critical to your success.

Help in Locating These Employers. One excellent resource you will want to use to begin your job search is the website www.socialservices.com. This site lists positions by state for work in mental health, substance abuse, children and youth, medical social work, criminal justice, domestic violence, community organizing and outreach, homelessness, and others. A related site, The New Social Worker's Online Career Center (www.socialworker.com), has great links to a variety of job listings. A volume worth looking through is *Careers in Social and Rehabilitative Services*. And don't forget to check the Yellow Pages under "social and human services" for a listing of agencies in a given geographic area.

Medical/Health Organizations

Profile. These types of facilities serve a range of clients and assist them with issues relating to, among others, alcohol and chemical dependency, rape and violence, family planning, hospice care, health, or AIDS. The knowledge and skills you've built could be put to use in any of these settings. If, for instance, you were an AIDS outreach worker and your clients were deaf Americans, you would use your specialized knowledge in working with this type of client to educate them about the disease and work with those who had the disease to help them receive available medical as well as other services.

Help in Locating These Employers. Be sure to look at *Career Opportunities in Health Care; Medical and Health Information Directory; America's Top Medical, Education & Human Services Jobs;* and *Encyclopedia of Medical Organizations and Agencies* to gain valuable insights into working in the medical/health field. These references provide specific information on job listings and potential employer listings that you can use to enhance your job search.

Federal/State/Local Governmental Agencies

Profile. About one-fourth of what the U.S. Department of Labor calls human services workers, which includes some social and human services workers, are employed in corrections and public assistance departments. Corrections departments are growing faster than other areas of government, so social and human services workers should find job opportunities increasing. Public assistance programs have also been employing more social and human services workers in an attempt to avoid employing workers with more education who demand higher pay.

The U.S. government worker category that most closely resembles the social and human services work described in this path is 0187-Social Services. A couple job titles fall within this category, social services representative and social work associate. Three other worker categories to investigate include 0180-Psychology, 0181-Psychology Aid and Technician, and 0185-Social Work. Entry-level federal positions for college graduates are classified at the GS-7 or GS-9 level.

Help in Locating These Employers. Two volumes to start with are VGM's *Careers in Government* and *Opportunities in Government Careers.* Actual job listings for state jobs can be found on the Web by searching www.state._.us. Just insert the two-letter abbreviation for the state you want to explore. Then look for a link to state job listings. To look for U.S. government jobs, visit the Office of Personnel Management website at www.usajobs.opm.gov/index.htm. This site explains the federal employment process and lets you get general information, look at current job openings, and submit an on-line application. Select the option "Current Job Openings" and then "Choose a Specific Series." Enter one of the suggested codes described above (0180, 0181, 0185, or 0187) or select other options as a appropriate, and begin examining federal job listings.

Corrections and Rehabilitation (Federal, State, Local)

Profile. Social-service workers in corrections and rehabilitation at all governmental levels may have job titles such as child welfare caseworker, clinical psychologist, corrections counselor, parole officer, recreation leader, or social group worker. Psychology majors who have (1) taken related coursework or have an academic minor in a field such as criminal justice and (2) somehow gotten involved in gaining direct work experience (internship, part-time job, summer job, volunteer work) would be eligible for many of these types of positions.

Help in Locating These Employers. Several books provide a starting point for your exploration of a career in corrections and rehabilitation. VGM's *Opportunities in Law Enforcement & Criminal Justice Careers* and *Your Criminal Justice Career: Guide Book* are excellent starting points. Be sure to network with authorities in the relevant state and local agencies and use information contained in the previous section ("Federal/State/Local Governmental Agencies") to find current job listings.

Insurance Companies

Profile. Many health insurers provide managed health-care services to their members, and they employ psychology majors to fill positions in customer service, claims, and provider relations. You probably won't meet face to face with your clients, but you will assist them in obtaining the physical and mental health services to which they are entitled.

For a large employee benefit program, you might serve as a telemarketing resource, using computerized directory information to provide referrals to individuals seeking assistance. This is a sophisticated position, requiring excellent listening and questioning skills to determine need, and critical thinking skills to suggest a number of treatment options.

Help in Locating These Employers. *Career Opportunities in Health Care* and VGM's *Opportunities in Insurance Careers* both provide useful information on starting a career in the insurance industry. The Health Insurance Association of America, Washington, D.C. (www.hiaa.org) posts a list of members that includes accident and health insurance firms. Examine this list, contact the human resources department at companies where you believe you might want to work, and determine their application procedures.

Religious Organizations

Profile. Many religious organizations offer services to the community and provide trained and qualified personnel to assist those who ask for help. The organization may provide some type of center, or settlement house, where youth can come to use a gym or homeless people can come to sleep. Not all of the workers have specific religious training, although many of them do.

Help in Locating These Employers. Three resources that identify service agencies include: *Our Sunday Visitors Catholic Almanac*, the *Yearbook of American and Canadian Churches*, and the *American Jewish Year Book*. You might also want to review Gale's *National Directory of Churches, Synagogues and Other Houses of Worship*. Two job-listing newsletters include: *Y National Vacancy List* and *Personnel Reporter: Job Listings in Jewish Community Centers and YM-YWHAs*. You can access YMCA job listings by searching from the national website (www.ymca.net) and visiting Y sites for the cities where you're thinking of working. Jewish Community Center job listings can be accessed at the following website: www.jcca.org.

Retirement Homes/Communities

Profile. If you are interested in working in a retirement home or community, you can follow a couple of different paths. You may want to work in a counseling setting and you might be called a social worker, volunteer coordinator, leisure counselor, or rehabilitation counselor. Or, you may want to play an administrative role, in which case the job titles to look for are housing project manager, site coordinator, or administrator.

Help in Locating These Employers. The American Association of Homes and Services for the Aging posts some job listings on its website's (www.aahsa.org) "Job Mart" button. In addition, you can search for facilities that are members of this organization. Select the "Consumers" button and then enter search information to obtain the name and address of the member facilities in a given state. The *Mental Health and Social Work Career Directory* also contains valuable information relating to careers in gerontology that the psychology major may be interested in pursuing. Don't overlook a handy resource—your local Yellow Pages directory. It lists retirement and life care communities and homes in specific geographic regions that you can contact about employment prospects.

POSSIBLE JOB TITLES

You will see a wide variety of job titles associated with social and human services. Sometimes the word *counselor* is in the job title, and oftentimes these are considered entry-level positions. For those workers who have more experience, and for you that might mean part-time or summer employment, or an internship, the word *coordinator* might be used. Workers who have case management experience or who are responsible for supervision of other workers, facilities, or budgets will often have the word *manager, director,* or *supervisor* in their job title. Review the titles shown below and look for job listings that match your level of experience.

Care manager	Mental health clinician
Case coordinator	Milieu counselor
Case management supervisor	Parent counselor/educator
Case manager	Prevention counselor
Clinical coordinator	Project manager
Clinical director	Program coordinator
Clinical manager	Program director
Clinical supervisor	Program manager
Clinician	Psychologist
Community services specialist	Rehabilitation counselor
Community support clinician	Social worker
Consultant	Substance abuse counselor
Counseling coordinator	Women's counselor
Day treatment clinician	Youth specialist
Family counselor	Mental retardation and
Intensive case manager	mental health counselor

RELATED OCCUPATIONS

Many of the occupations that relate to social and human services work draw on the same talents and skills, but some also require a more specialized education than a bachelor's degree in psychology, or they may require certification or licensure. If any of the job titles shown below interest you, consult the *Occupational Outlook Handbook* (www.bls.gov/ocohome.htm) for details.

Activity leader	Music therapist
Admissions evaluator	Occupational therapist
Art therapist	Physical therapist
Employment services worker	Regulatory administrator
Expressive therapist	Religious worker
Health club manager	Social worker
Labor relations manager	

PROFESSIONAL ASSOCIATIONS

Because social and human services work takes place in such a variety of settings, we provide just an introduction to a smorgasbord of possible professional associations. Contact those that have titles that reflect populations you are interested in working with. Use the *Encyclopedia of Associations* or other references we have named to get additional information about why these associations exist and how they can help their members.

American Academy of Crisis Interveners
c/o Edward S. Rosenbluh, Ph.D.
215 Breckinridge Ln., Suite 102
Louisville, KY 40207

American Association of Homes and Services for the Aging
1129 20th St. NW, Suite 400
Washington, DC 20036
Website: www.aahsa.org

American Association of Retired Persons
601 E. St. NW
Washington, DC 20049
Website: www.aarp.com

American Association of the Deaf-Blind
814 Thayer Ave., 3rd Floor
Silver Spring, MD 20910

American Association on Mental Retardation
444 N. Capitol St. NW, Suite 846
Washington, DC 20001-1570
Website: www.aamr.org

American Council of the Blind
1155 15th St. NW, Suite 720
Washington, DC 20005
Website: www.acb.org

American Society of Criminology
1314 Kinnear Rd., Suite 212
Columbus, OH 43212

American Society of Directors of Volunteer Services of the American Hospital Association
One Franklin St., 31st Floor
Chicago, IL 60606
Website: www.asdvs.org

American Vocational Association
1410 King St.
Alexandria, VA 22314
Website: www.avaonline.org

Center for Immigrants Rights
48 St. Marks Pl., 4th Floor
New York, NY 10003

Consumer Federation of America
1424 16th St. NW, Suite 604
Washington, DC 20036
Website: www.consumerfed.org

Disability Rights Education and Defense Fund
2212 6th St.
Berkeley, CA 94710
Website: www.dredf.org

Foundation for Hospice and Home Care
228-7th St. NE
Washington, DC 20003
Website: www.nahc.org

Health Education Resource Organization
101 W. Read St., Suite 825
Baltimore, MD 21201

Housing Assistance Council
1025 Vermont Ave. NW, Suite 606
Washington, DC 20005
Website: www.ruralhome.org

Men's Rights
P.O. Box 163180
Sacramento, CA 95816
Website: www.mens-rights.org

National Abortion Federation
1436 U St. NW, Suite 103
Washington, DC 20009
Website: www.prochoice.org

National Adoption Center
1218 Chestnut St., 2nd Floor
Philadelphia, PA 19107

National Association for Crime Victims Rights
P.O. Box 16161
Portland, OR 97216-0161

National Association of Developmental Disabilities Councils
1234 Massachusetts Ave. NW, Suite 103
Washington, DC 20005

National Association of Public Child Welfare Administrators
c/o American Public Human Services Association
810 1st St. NE, Suite 500
Washington, DC 20002
Website: www.aphsa.org

National Association of Social Workers
750 1st St. NE, Suite 700
Washington, DC 20002
Website: www.naswdc.org

National Association of State Alcohol and Drug Abuse Directors
808 17th St. NW, Suite 410
Washington, DC 20006
Website: www.nasadad.org

National Charities Information Bureau
19 Union Sq. W, 6th Floor
New York, NY 10003

National Child Day Care Association
1501 Benning Rd. NE
Washington, DC 20002

National Coalition for the Homeless
1012 14th St. NW, #600
Washington, DC 20005-3410

National Commission on Youth Suicide Prevention
11 Parkman Way
Needham, MA 02192

National Council on Child Abuse and Family Violence
1155 Connecticut Ave. NW, Suite 400
Washington, DC 20036
Website: www.nccafv.org

National Legal Aid and Defender Association
1625 K St. NW, Suite 800
Washington, DC 20006
Website: www.nlada.org

National Lesbian and Gay Health Education Foundation
P.O. Box 65472
Washington, DC 20035

National Mental Health Association
1021 Prince St.
Alexandria, VA 22314
Website: www.nmha.org

National Organization for Women
1000 16th St. NW, Suite 700
Washington, DC 20036
Website: www.now.org

Single Parent Resource Center
141 West 28th St., Suite 302
New York, NY 10001
Website: http://singleparentresources.com

U.S. Athletes Association
3735 Lakeland Ave. N, Suite 230
Minneapolis, MN 55422

U.S. Conference of City Human Services Officials
1620 I St. NW
Washington, DC 20006

World Medical Relief
11745 Rosa Parks Blvd.
Detroit, MI 48206

Young America's Foundation
110 Elden St.
Herndon, VA 22070
Website: www.yaf.org

CHAPTER TWELVE

PATH 3: HUMAN RESOURCES

*S*tudents of psychology often feel that the human resources area of business and industry holds a strong application for their undergraduate degree. If you are among this group, you'll want to explore what this field has to offer, and what values, skills, and abilities it requires of its employees.

Human resources professionals are drawn from a number of undergraduate academic backgrounds, including psychology. An undergraduate degree in psychology does not necessarily provide an advantage in seeking human resources employment; it has more to do with (1) the student's understanding of the human resources function in business and (2) the orientation of the student's academic preparation in psychology. As with so many liberal arts degrees, the degree, in and of itself, does not suggest any special preparedness, and most employers will make no assumptions about the relevance of a candidate's degree to a potential job opening.

THE HUMAN RESOURCES FUNCTION IN BUSINESS

The workplace in general, and the human resources worker in particular, is primarily concerned with three types of development that create a cohesive work force and achieve the overall organizational mission and goals: (1) training and professional development, or developing key competencies in workers that enable them to carry out their duties; (2) organizational development, which primarily focuses on helping groups manage change; and (3) career development, which involves helping employees manage their careers within the organization.

Training and Professional Development

Most workers want to be proud of what they accomplish during the work-day and while they have the basic skills to do a good job, they may need additional training to be able to work at their full potential. A computer data-entry worker may need to learn database management. A new supervisor may need to develop some conflict negotiation skills. The human resources professional is responsible for making sure that employees either have or are able to develop the competencies they need to do the work they are assigned.

Organization Development

Organizations are undergoing stressful levels of change in order to mainsail their strategic advantage in the marketplace. Whether the organization is a nonprofit that coordinates emergency relief efforts or a for-profit manufac-turer producing the latest in computer chip technology, both have a need for employees who can handle changing needs. It is the human resources depart-ment that can help effect these changes through hiring procedures, employee training, and employee transitions within the organization.

Career Development

Job seekers face an ever-changing marketplace, one that demands flexibility to be able to handle organizational change. Human resources personnel help employees take concrete and specific steps to manage their own career within the organization, so that each person can produce work that allows him or her to use a full range of skills and abilities to meet the organizational goals.

PSYCHOLOGY AS AN ACADEMIC PREPARATION FOR HUMAN RESOURCES

Whether your college or university offers a standard, broad-based exposure to the discipline of psychology or concentration options in areas such as child or adult development, mental health, counseling psychology, or research design, your best bet would be to take those courses or elect those programs seen as most relevant to a human resources function. These would include all areas of adult development, learning, personality, and social psychology. Abnormal psychology, a popular concentration, would not hold particular relevance for a career in human resources; the workplace as a social organization relies on appropriate behavior. While some human resources programs do offer employee assistance programs (referrals and outplacement to helping professionals for individuals struggling with personal problems), it is not the province of the human resources area to either diagnose or treat these ailments.

Your academic program in psychology has also helped you build a critical set of transferable skills that are highly valued in human resources. You mastered them in the context of studying psychology, but now you must make them relevant to the human resources employer. These skills include your ability to set objectives, to evaluate, to coach, to interview, to manage time, to write, to manage projects, to master computer technology, and to plan Each of these skills is critical to functioning effectively in human resources

"Human resources" is an apt description because this area of the organization manages the resource of human productivity for the organization. Psychology could be an excellent preparation for a career in this area if you understand both how your degree will be used and the job you'll be doing.

WHO DOES HUMAN RESOURCES SERVE?

The essential dilemma for human resources professionals is *whom* do they serve: the organization or the worker? In the overwhelming majority of circumstances the answer is the organization, by maintaining the organization's expectations. In areas such as job design, pay grades and classifications, promotion and job enhancement, training and development, benefits administration, and the arbitration of grievances and employee policies, human resources professionals are not advocates of the employee but rather representatives of the employer, exercising the employer's mandate in the administration of the workforce.

However, that is not to say that the human resources professional cannot also be an advocate for the worker. Workers who grow in their jobs need to be reclassified to a higher rank. Oftentimes this happens because of, and aided by, the policies and encouragement of human resources professionals. Human resources personnel design creative and innovative programs for workers that not only improve their work performance and relationships but extend their influence to all aspects of life. Human resources programs, depending on their size and breadth, can touch on life changes, retirement, aging, and many life issues.

IS HUMAN RESOURCES REALLY YOUR INTEREST?

This discussion brings up an issue that should be of real interest to all psychology majors contemplating human resources work. If your interest in psychology is in human behavior, especially how individuals respond in groups, then human resources work may be of interest.

Maybe cognitive theory is your real interest. If so, research may hold more fruitful jobs for you. If you have studied psychology out of a love for and interest in developing and nurturing the human psyche, you might find a better fit in the areas of social and human services or therapy.

Though there's no doubt many of us credit wonderful opportunities for growth and personal and professional development to the programs and offerings of our human resources department, this is not the complete story of the work they do. You need to sit down and talk with a human resources professional about the amount of hostility they endure each day from employees angry over benefits administration or changes in work conditions, salary negotiations, or promotion opportunities. Hear the complaints and humiliation of a discharged employee who must be accompanied by a human resources official as he is checked out of every department (security, parking, credit union) before being discharged. There is the challenge of having to remove an employee with the help of security forces. To have the full picture of this "people" job, you need to hear both the positive and the negative.

DEFINITION OF THE CAREER PATH

Paying close attention to the news for even as little as a week's time will give you a very clear picture of the difficulties of the workplace today and the implications for human resources professionals. "Recurring motion syndrome" afflicts more and more workers using computers and there are lingering, unsolved questions about the low-level emissions from terminals. Gender issues are very much alive with continuing data on inequality in pay, and abusive and discriminatory behavior toward women. At the same time, the white male no longer dominates the workforce, and human resources professionals must build organizations from an increasingly diverse ethnic, racial, and religious population. There are corresponding challenges to assimilation, inclusion, and tolerance. Human resources professionals try to create understanding and, hopefully, appreciation and enjoyment of this diversity.

Your scrutiny of the news may have also made you aware of a large number of lawsuits between employers and employees. Issues of harassment, discrimination, illegal firing and layoffs, and workplace injury and stress have escalated recently and mean additional challenges for those working in the human resources area. Each lawsuit means documents are subpoenaed from human resources. They may include personnel files, records of vacation or sick days, training opportunities, formal commendations or reprimands, and many other kinds of legitimate requests for data. This can add a tremendous burden to an already busy office.

Economics play a large part in determining the fate of some organizations and you no doubt will have encountered stories of organizations moving their offices across town, across the country, or even out of the country! This has a profound impact on workers and their families. Likewise, many firms have reduced their staffs dramatically in an effort to stay viable and reduce costs.

Potential employees are more aggressively interested in the economic health of any organization they may be employed by and corresponding benefits that will be provided if they are let go. Employees no longer believe they will be with the same firm for all of their lives, and they also recognize the possibility that the organization may be bought or fail. Many of them want to know from human resources what contingency plans are in effect in any of these situations. Will there be severance pay, outplacement services, counseling, relocation assistance, or transfers to a subsidiary?

The possibility of job loss and frequent job change means workers will be more aggressive in extracting benefits and training and development opportunities from current employers. Human resources personnel may encounter increased and insistent demands for training and development opportunities, college courses, and spousal benefits. Employees as a group may demand resource acquisitions (gym or weight room, diet counseling, blood pressure checks, ergonomic consultations) and an accounting from the organization's management on money spent on staff development. As workers realize a need to be always ready to acquire new skills in preparation for new jobs, they will be more aggressive in utilizing every benefit opportunity. Utilization of benefits increases the work of human resources in administration and processing and the cost to the organization.

Health care issues dominate the press and, as the United States moves slowly toward more comprehensive health care, there will be dramatic effects on the workforce and the employer. Many of these are outlined in news analyses of health care issues. Workers who previously could not leave their jobs for fear of jeopardizing health benefits because of their own or a family member's "preexisting condition" are now being assured coverage. Part-time workers may not necessarily lose coverage under new plans. These changes may indicate that we will see greater worker mobility and less loyalty than in the past as employees are not benefit-tied to a particular employer. Because every change of employee is costly in out-processing a former employee and in-processing and training new talent, human resources professionals have much to be concerned about if worker mobility is no longer tied to health benefits.

Organizations are subtly affected in a positive way by the core of long-term employees who have experienced some history with the organization and have learned to work together as a team. If that team breaks up beyond a critical point, some of that efficiency and networking will be lost, to the detriment of the organization's ability to function as effectively.

WORKING CONDITIONS

For a job that supposedly involves people (the "humans" in human resources!), a lot of paperwork and data manipulation needs to be completed. In examining working conditions in the human resources area, it's best to look at the overall mission of a human resources department and how that, in turn, affects the activities of the department. Typical human resources functions include:

- Employment and placement
- Wage and salary administration
- Training and development
- Benefits administration
- Outplacement
- Research and information management

Review these four job descriptions for entry-level workers and notice the range of duties required of each.

Human Resources Assistant. HR assistant for sports newspaper publisher in downtown Manhattan. Incumbent will assist director in carrying out administration of benefits program and special projects as assigned. Must have bachelor's degree, proficiency with MS Word/Excel/PowerPoint. Familiar with ADP-PC/payroll a plus. E-mail resume and salary requirements to . . .

Hiring Coordinator. Requires college degree. Responsible for screening, interviewing, and hiring legal personnel for busy, fast-growing law firm. Establish relationship with managers, employees, and external recruitment sources. Must be a team player, organized, and enthusiastic. We offer fun and exciting work environment with tremendous benefits. Fax resume to . . .

continued

continued

Plan Specialist. One of Chicago's largest privately held companies seeks retirement plans specialist for its 401(k) savings and profit sharing plans. Maintain plan and system administration. Review and make recommendations to retirement programs. Ideal candidate will have excellent computer skills with proficiency in Excel and Word (Access and report writing desirable). Verbal and written communication, customer service, and technical skills required. You will be presenting complex plan materials to participants, and increasing awareness and participation in plans. Ability to handle multiple projects in fast-paced environment and work as team player. Bachelor's degree required. We offer comprehensive benefits package, tuition reimbursement, and continuous learning opportunities. Send resume and salary history to . . .

Human Resources Specialist. Bachelor's degree required, general knowledge of personnel, labor relations, and/or employee recruitment preferred. Submit cover letter and resume to . . .

We'll briefly discuss each of the various functions in the section that follows.

Employment and Placement

Many new human resources personnel are surprised and a bit disappointed when they realize their department does not make the actual hiring decisions for their organization. For most employers, hiring is done by the department needing staff. That department is best equipped to judge the qualifications of candidates for the job they seek to fill. Human resources departments, however, will often collect applications and resumes, assemble the candidates' files for the department, and perform credential checks and background investigations, as required. They often will conduct training workshops for supervisors and their staff on how to conduct interviews fairly and objectively and on other aspects of the hiring process. Except in cases of heavy demand for lower-level employees, the human resources department seldom hires anyone except someone for human resources.

After an employee is hired, it often is the responsibility of the human resources department to orient the new employee. This may include an actual tour of the employer's facility and will surely include a lengthy discussion of rules and regulations, policies and procedures, benefits, and compensation.

Most departments publish an employee manual, and it is often provided at this initial meeting. This is an exciting time for a new employee and a pleasant interview for the human resources professional, and it can represent the many rewarding aspects of employment with this particular employer.

But employers change over time. The marketplace may create new demands; products and services change; and outside economic conditions can create internal changes. Whatever the reason, most organizations are seldom static in terms of staffing needs, and the human resources professional is frequently asked to assess departmental needs for new personnel or to examine an area suspected of being overly supplied with workers. Consulting for this purpose, the human resources worker needs to understand the department and the various roles its workers play so he or she can offer effective solutions to staffing situations. Some employees may be transferred, while others face layoffs or termination. Because personnel costs often represent the largest consistent expense of an organization, the human resources professional's role here is critical to the financial success of an organization.

The psychology major will have little difficulty in bringing psychology studies to bear on the employment and placement activities of the organization. Issues of self-esteem, job definition and structure, and, most important, smooth entry into a new organization are all possible sources of anxiety for a new employee at any level. Your sensitivity to these issues will help you in working with department managers to better define job parameters, to plan for dignified and responsible interviewing procedures that give each candidate a fair chance, and to arrange for a first-day orientation and tour that says, "Welcome aboard."

Wage and Salary Administration

Our basic salaries, opportunities for wage increases, and deductions for various benefits are of crucial importance to all employees. We may not understand everything on our pay stub, but we notice if the total amount goes up or down! After all, pay is one of Maslow's basic needs, and it guarantees many of our lower-level demands, such as housing, food, and security. Understanding this, a psychology major will recognize how important it is to educate workers on their pay, how it works, and the reasons for any changes. They'll best appreciate the need to alert employees well in advance of possible change, and to anticipate questions and provide materials that satisfy those questions.

A psychology major in human resources appreciates how many people define their work by their salary level, make comparisons to others of similar employment level, and are on the alert for any discrepancies or hints of discrimination. Wages and salary are a sensitive and complex issue. The psychology major will understand and appreciate those ramifications and become a real asset to the human resources department.

Training and Development

Depending on the number of employees and the size of the human resources department, training and development may be conducted in-house or contracted out to other professionals. In most cases, it is a combination. In-house human resources professionals will offer workshops year-round on issues as diverse as retirement planning, safe driving, employee safety and health precautions, and effective use of employee benefits. There may be workshops on stress management, promotion opportunities, and new supervisor training workshops. Outside professionals may be called in to run cholesterol tests and education programs, as well as multicultural and diversity workshops. Here's an entry-level job advertisement that contains a training element:

> *Benefits Coordinator.* Excellent entry-level opportunity. Maintain group insurance and 401(k) plan records and assist employees with questions regarding internal forms and HR policies/ procedures. Conduct new hire orientation and training. Must be organized, detail-oriented, analytical. Excellent communication skills and MS, Excel, and Word required. E-mail resume to . . .

Staff development and training is rewarding both in the design and delivery of these training sessions. Workers value good on-the-job training and their feedback will often suggest further areas for enrichment. With issues facing the workplace such as the Americans with Disabilities Act (ADA), spousal benefits for same-sex partners, and a host of equally complicated issues, staff development and training not only builds a sense of employee cohesion and camaraderie, but it is often a quick and deliberate response to critical issues facing the workplace and its employees.

The psychology major looks out over the range and variety of employees in an organization and realizes that each person is at a different developmental and career stage. Some are young and ambitious, eager for change and growth, and able to be flexible with their time and life. Others are embarking on relationships or starting families and must, for the present time, concentrate their energies on these important life choices. Some may be continuing their education, others may be anticipating slowing down their schedules, working less and easing into retirement. Each is in a different place in his or her work life, chronological age, personal development, and identification with the organization.

Your appreciation of these differences can spark ideas and strategies for wonderful and varied training and development programs. "Managing a Two-Career Family," "Planning for Retirement," "Stress Reduction Techniques," and "Flex-Time or Work-at-Home-Scheduling" are just some of the training possibilities. You can help educate a workforce whose need for information about improving their jobs; managing work, careers, and home; and personal development is inexhaustible.

Benefits Administration

No human resources office is open for any length of time before the paperwork involved in the administration of benefits begins to accumulate. Requests for tuition reimbursement; worker's compensation; dental, medical, and optical care; pension planning; and 401(k)s pile up. The list is ever-changing as each organization offers a unique blend of employee benefits. Often, the menu changes depending upon the status of the employee. Full-time employees receive a full complement of benefits, and those who work less than full time often have their benefits prorated according to their percent-time worked.

It adds up to a mountain of paperwork. Some employees have horror stories to tell of how human resources mismanaged a benefit claim, but far more will speak of excellent benefits and thoughtful and caring benefit administrators who are sensitive and discreet in the processing of the ever-present forms.

New benefits are always emerging. Some of the newest at this writing include benefits for same-sex partners and supplemental health allowances. With the current governmental initiatives in health care, the area of benefits administration should remain vital and volatile. For example, many firms understand and deal with the issues of drug and alcohol abuse among their workers, and they have built programs that will refer these employees to off-site employee assistance programs for counseling and treatment. In the majority of cases, these employees continue working or return to full employment following a course of treatment.

Employers realize that the physical and mental health of their employees each plays a key role in productivity. Whether an organization provides exercise rooms or has a professional making mental health referrals, it knows it will see sharply reduced absenteeism, fewer claims on employee health and benefit programs, and increased productivity because of these benefits efforts. So, while the human resources promotional literature emphasizes enhanced benefits to the employee, the rewards for the employer are savings in dollars and cents.

Benefits administration could be a deeply rewarding job function to the psychology major, especially today as organizations become ever more sensitive to human needs and the relationship between satisfying those needs and work productivity. You can hardly function well at work if you're worried about retirement finances or the hospitalization costs for your child's chronic illness. Psychology majors employed in human resources work will have continuous opportunities to review benefit options and consider new proposals that might directly answer needs your employees have.

Outplacement

Most organizations now make provisions for helping their employees' transition out of the organization, regardless of the situation that might precipitate such a move. Even in the case of termination of employment, many employers provide an exit interview to allow the terminated employee an opportunity to express anger or disappointment and discuss the events and situations surrounding and leading to the termination.

When employers downsize their organization to respond to economic or market pressures and employees must be terminated regardless of their performance, more and more firms are providing the services of outplacement firms. These specialty organizations help the terminated worker through counseling, improving resume and interview techniques, and providing job leads to secure new employment. It is the human resources personnel who connect the employees with these types of firms.

It's interesting. Most successful employers don't have much experience in letting people go; they only have to do it infrequently. When they do have to fire someone, they are apt to do it awkwardly because of their lack of practice. They neglect to give their senior staff training in how to approach a termination meeting; they may not have follow-up counseling services in place or realize they have all the resources to put together an exemplary outplacement program. If you're a psychology major and you're reading this thinking, "I see an opportunity to make a difference," you'd be right. Understanding human behavior, and appreciating the difficulties of a job loss situation, the psychology major will look at his or her organization and help build a program that encompasses staff training, sensitivity, follow-up counseling, and a minimum of exposure and embarrassment for the terminated employee.

Research and Information Management

Requests for a history of worker's compensation claims, for average salary increases for middle management, or for any of a number of kinds of information having to do with employees, their numbers, cost, productivity, and changes over time are directed to the human resources department. Staff personnel need to be comfortable analyzing and providing data that will be useful to management in making personnel and strategic decisions.

The Americans with Disabilities Act (ADA), contract negotiations and arbitration, the Equal Employment Opportunity initiatives, fair wages standards, Occupational Safety and Health Administration (OSHA) guidelines, as well as an organization's own internal grievance process, all provide enormous amounts of paperwork in addition to the meetings, planning sessions, hearings, and presentations these issues generate.

To be prepared with this kind of information requires excellent record keeping with an eye to data retrieval. This is one of the many reasons why a human resources office is often very concerned about paperwork and administration and why many entry-level employees are disappointed to discover the human resources function is not as social as they had anticipated.

As a psychology major, you're ready for this task because you've not only had to deal with numerous research reports in your studies, but also have probably created some data yourself and had to transform that data into meaningful information for a paper or class presentation. Human resources work is no different. It might be salary equity among female managers of a certain rank, or uniform costs for certain employees; whatever the informational demands, you should find your major has prepared you well.

TRAINING AND QUALIFICATIONS

Having read the information on the functions and working conditions of a human resources department and still feeling strongly that you can bring your psychology education to bear on the work of such an office, you may be asking yourself, "Do I need experience in human resources to be considered for this type of work?" The answer is that there is much you can do to convince an employer you are ready for employment in a human resources position.

The foregoing discussion of human resources functions suggests many of the skills and attributes that will be important to a new human resources professional. But there are others that are important as well.

Communication

In both verbal and written communications, human resources professionals need to be very careful of their language, its accuracy, tone, and nuance. Notice the emphasis on communication skills in this ad:

Personnel Administrator. Local office of national CPA firm seeks enthusiastic, energetic person who has excellent interpersonal and organizational skills. Duties include recruitment activities,

continued

---

continued

orientation of new employees, maintenance of personnel files, benefits administration, etc. Ideal candidate will have bachelor's degree, one to two years business experience, and computer literacy. Most essential is ability to handle multiple projects simultaneously, to communicate effectively (written and verbal), and to project the friendly, professional image of the firm both in-house and throughout the community. Send resume and salary requirements to . . .

Most of the issues dealt with in human resources departments are critical to employees, and work conditions can be vital to an employee's sense of self-esteem and sense of identity. Change, even the suggestion of change, can provoke great anxiety among some employees, and how such change is presented is crucial to the success of any plan. Your communication skills will be called in to play again.

Let's say your firm has decided to purchase a new telephone system that requires each employee to "key in" their own identification number for every call. Prior to this, phone charges have been lumped by department for each extension number anonymously. The policy has been an unwritten one that reasonable numbers of personal phone calls (calls home, to your spouse, etc.) were okay. Now, with a new caller ID number, many employees will be frightened about the loss of that privilege. Knowing this, you may want to specifically address this in your memo and reassure staff members that reasonable personal calls are still allowed.

One-on-one conferences, small group and department meetings, memoranda, and policies and procedures manuals all need to contain language of the clearest and most direct sort to enable all staff members to understand and carry out human resources initiatives. An early independent project for the psychology major employed in human resources might be to collect and review literature and promotional materials from other public organizations for sensitive and clear language. Compare that to your own firm's written work. There may be some opportunities to improve your organization's presentation of material through careful editing.

Public Presentation Skills

For efficiency and because many human resources programs affect large groups of employees, you may be frequently presenting material to large groups. Professional staff need to have excellent public presentation skills, including the ability to plan, organize, and write a workshop or seminar, design and execute effective and appropriate visual materials, and design and execute forms for evaluation. Technical competency with audiovisual materials, including VCRs, video recording equipment, overhead projectors, and computerized presentations is certainly a plus.

If you've had some of this presentation and technical aids experience in your college years, be sure to feature that on your resume or in a cover letter. Skilled presenters are always in demand, especially when they are comfortable with a variety of technology that can be used to improve retention and communications.

Computer and Software Familiarity

As with all administrative units, the use of computers in a human resources department is pervasive. Database management skills are crucial for data analysis and retrieval as are word-processing skills, which are used for employee communications. This job description highlights the skills one employer is seeking:

> *Human Resources Position.* (Bank) is looking for a human resources generalist to assist the Director of Human Resources with all aspects of the function. Responsibilities will include recruitment, salary and benefits administration, personnel policies and procedures, and payroll. Qualifications: excellent verbal and written communication skills, Macintosh computer proficiency using Microsoft Word, Excel, and Filemaker Pro software. Organizational skills, high degree of accuracy, attention to detail, and the ability to maintain confidentiality are essential. Send resume and salary requirements to . . .

Many departments produce their own brochures and information pieces and rely on staff who have desktop publishing and Windows software capability.

Just as it is a safe assumption that all human resources staff at every level of management and seniority employ some degree of computer use in this exciting and demanding field, it is likewise a safe assumption that the entry-level candidate with strong computer skills stands a markedly increased opportunity for employment than the candidate who has neglected this technical competency.

Have you included your computer and data management courses on your resume? If not, be sure to mention them in your cover letter or during an interview. Reading about human resources, you've become aware of the vast amounts of data and detail that is going to be stored electronically. It's ironic, but true, that to perform your human resources task in a very human, connected manner with your employees, you need to be the very best at computer technology.

If you have a chance to meet and talk with a human resources professional (perhaps an alumni meeting arranged through your career office alumni connection), ask them about data technology. How much did they have coming onto the job and how much do they have now? How big a part of their day does computer technology play? Do they have human resources data analysts on their staff? Who inputs their data? A discussion about computer technology will help you put a new, and more realistic, face on human resources work.

Data Analysis

Human resources may be about people, but the paper can sure get in the way. To the rather tired and hackneyed statement heard from the young job candidate applying for a human resources position that he or she is "a people person," most hiring professionals might chuckle and say most days they could use a good data analyst. The reality is, as with so many issues, somewhere in the middle of those two extremes.

The effective use of and provision for the employment pool in any organization takes inordinate amounts of planning and analysis, and it demands staff comfortable with translating raw data into meaningful information for management to use in decision making.

For every human interaction—one-on-one meeting in personnel, public presentation to a department or group of employees, new staff orientation and briefing—much time is spent reading and analyzing data concerning staff. Overtime and associated costs, sick days and temporary help expenditures, vacation scheduling and conflicts, and use of benefits all need to be monitored and understood.

The psychology major knows enough not to confuse data with individual human interaction, but data do reveal trends and can indicate problems. Often, these data are warning signs that lead to conferences, meetings, and lots of human interaction as you seek solutions. The psychology major brings an ability to bridge the anonymous, cold data and the real, live human interactions the data represent.

EARNINGS

The Society for Human Resource Management conducts, in partnership with William M. Mercer, Inc., the *Human Resource Management Compensation*

Survey.[1] Their annual survey contains useful salary information for the entry-level types of positions we are discussing in this field. In the table shown below are entry-level position titles and salaries that fall in the 10th–25th percentile of the range. We believe these are realistic starting salaries for someone with the type of credentials the psychology major has to offer. Be sure to check with a regional association that can tell you how salaries vary in its area or check websites that show current salary information. One good example is www.wageweb.com.

Position Title	Base 10th Percentile Salary	Base 25th Percentile Salary
Compensation Analyst	$32,500	$36,000
Benefits Administrator	$31,000	$34,800
Associate Training Specialist	$30,400	$33,300
Compensation & Benefits Administrator	$27,800	$34,000
Entry-Level Generalist	$27,000	$31,300
Benefits Clerk	$22,000	$25,200
Human Resource Assistant	$21,300	$24,700

CAREER OUTLOOK

The number and types of positions in human resources vary dramatically, depending on the size of the organization, the current state of its fiscal health, and the emphasis the organization puts on its employees and their welfare. Human resources is not a revenue-producing department. Unlike the sales force whose high personnel expenses are offset by the generation of income for the firm, the human resources department is pure administration and is seen as overhead. Consequently, it is often earmarked during difficult economic times for trimming its staff or not rehiring empty positions to ensure greater profitability for the organization.

Entry-level positions are best selected from among midsize to large-size organizations and the largest corporations, and in those industries and economic sectors that are enjoying current profitability and growth. Demographic analysis indicates that the United States has an aging "baby boom"

··········

1. Information provided by William M. Mercer, Inc., 426 S. Fourth Ave., Suite 1500, Louisville, KY 40202-3415.

population that is going to stay in the workforce longer and more effectively than their predecessors. They are expected to enjoy healthier, more active, and longer retirements, suggesting future growth in industries relating to financial planning, medical institutions, planned retirement homes and communities, and geriatric services in general.

STRATEGY FOR FINDING THE JOBS

Entry-level human resources positions are filled by graduates who come from a variety of academic disciplines, so expect that the level of competition for these positions will be keen. We suggest focusing on a three-pronged strategy that will inform your job search in this field. You will want to be sure that you build some human resources knowledge and skills into your background, and suggestions for doing so are discussed below. You must be ready to relate how your psychology training has prepared you to work effectively in this field. Both your resume and your interview comments must highlight the relevance of this training. And finally, focus on an employment setting that seems like a good fit for you to begin your human resources career.

Build Some Human Resources Knowledge and Skills into Your Background

As you move through your college career, be sure to take courses that relate to human resources, and work to gain some actual experience in the field. Oftentimes, business departments at colleges offer courses in personnel or human/industrial relations. Minoring in one of these areas would be especially useful, but if that option is not available to you, take as much related coursework as you can. You may want to take a for-credit internship and get credit and hands-on experience at the same time.

In addition to your academic preparation, you'll want to explore two areas: (1) deepening your understanding of the current societal trends that affect the functions and mission of a human resources department and (2) becoming more knowledgeable about issues the human resources professional faces.

Deepen Your Understanding of Current Societal Trends. The discussion presented in this chapter will give you a basic understanding of human resources, but the related functions vary dramatically by organization, product or service, and even by geographic region. For example, many of our newer, cutting-edge technological firms have likewise instituted some of the newest and often most controversial employee benefit programs. Many have proven comfortable with work-at-home personnel, flex-time, and very loose organizational structures. Such policies might not succeed in a more traditional organization with a less-sophisticated or less-educated employment pool. Current newspapers and periodical business sections will often feature stories on various industries and a continued reading of these sources will help you to become conversant with trends that affect the current state of human resources administration.

Become More Knowledgeable About Legal Issues. Preparing yourself for seeking positions in this field is to become somewhat more knowledgeable about the legal issues and the issues with legal implications that increasingly dominate this field. Your reading of current literature will suggest many of these topics. More focused reading can be found in your local or university library or career office. There are also excellent websites such as the Society for Human Resource Management's HR Magazine (www.shrm.org/hrmagazine). Some of the topics you'll want to be familiar with include:

- OSHA
- Pension planning
- 401(k)s
- Medical claims/syndromes
- Ergonomics
- Arbitration
- Labor relations
- Negotiations
- Contracts
- Sexual harassment

You needn't become an expert on these topics, but they are important issues to human resources professionals. Your job search will be far more successful if you can demonstrate a competent awareness and appreciation for the challenges of these areas. In many cases, your knowledge of legal issues will overcome any hesitancy an employer may feel for a lack of direct experience. Your willingness to self-educate is, in and of itself, a strong employment consideration.

Use your summers or periods of part-time employment to find out as much as you can about working in human resources. If you are not employed in that department, network with the director or manager of personnel to let them know about your interests and to see if they can assist you in getting information or making contacts in the field. You may want to invest in joining a professional personnel or human resources organization (see end of chapter for suggestions) to continue your networking and to begin hearing about actual employment opportunities.

Be Ready to Relate Your Psychology Training Both on the Resume and in the Interview

Your psychology degree has helped you develop many skills important to working effectively in human resources (communication skills, public presentation skills, computer and software familiarity, data analysis). But those skills and that knowledge may not be readily apparent to a potential employer. Don't let them guess about how well qualified you are; show them on your resume and in your interview discussions. Point out your relevant training and tell them how you can help accomplish their human resources goals.

Focus on an Employment Setting That Seems Like a Good Fit for You

In the "Possible Employers" section that follows, a wide range of types of employers are described. You may be able to picture yourself working in some settings and also know immediately that you wouldn't feel comfortable in others. Review the following section, and make a decision about where you would like to begin your employment search. You may have to widen the scope of your search, depending on the geographic area where you live and the types of employers you decide to focus on first. But start with an industry that looks like the best fit.

POSSIBLE EMPLOYERS

Personnel, training, and labor-relations specialists and managers are found in every industry, from manufacturing to banking, from transportation to health care and education. We will begin acquainting you with some of the possibilities in the descriptions provided in this section, which include:

- ❏ Health care

- ❏ Service

- ❏ Education

- ❏ Manufacturing

- ❏ Finance and insurance

❑ Government

❑ Staffing companies

Your job search should begin with a review of all types of possible employers. After you have familiarized yourself with the range of possibilities, begin your job search by starting to network with professionals, and then apply for jobs in two or three industries.

Health Care

Profile. Health-care facilities employ doctors, nurses, technicians, food-service workers, maintenance workers, administrators, managed-care coordinators, social workers, and a host of other types of employees. The human resources professional can play a critical role in filling positions with the right people. If you would like to play an important role in this fast-changing industry, consider health care.

Help in Locating These Employers. Several resources you should review as you conduct your job search include: VGM's *Opportunities in Health and Medical Careers*, Gale's *Encyclopedia of Medical Organizations and Agencies*, and the Medical and Health Care Jobs website (www.nationjob.com/medical). Be sure to directly contact those health organizations you would like to work for, and do some informational interviewing or inquire about their procedure for advertising job openings.

Service

Profile. No matter where you go, whether it's in food retailing, household furniture and appliance sales, clothing sales, travel services, or business and professional services, personnel are available to assist you. Medium-size and large-size organizations have human resources professionals who help them hire people who are willing to work to support organizational goals and serve customers.

Help in Locating These Employers. Because the service industry is so large, we will present just a few resources that will be useful in your job search. Be sure to ask for recommendations from the other professionals you are working with, career counselors, and librarians. Depending on your interests, you may want to review: *Moody's Transportation Manual, American Bank Directory, Standard Directory of Advertising Agencies, O'Dwyer's Directory of Public Relations Firms, Ward's Business Directory*, and *Hoover's Handbook of American Business*.

Education

Profile. Higher education employers, including community and two-year colleges, four-year colleges, and universities, hire a variety of workers to help them achieve their educational mission and goals. Whether it is the custodian who keeps the facility in shape, the teacher in the classroom, the support or technical staff member, or the administrator, all are important, and the human resources worker helps find the right person for the right job.

Help in Locating These Employers. Resources that will be useful in identifying schools that have a need for human resources personnel include three of Peterson's (www.petersons.com) references: *Guide to Two-Year Colleges*, *Guide to Four-Year Colleges*, and *Guides to Graduate Study*. *The Chronicle of Higher Education*'s website (www.chronicle.com) contains job listings for you to review.

Manufacturing

Profile. Whether a company is manufacturing broad woven fabric, hats and gloves, wood office furniture, folding paperboard boxes, tires, abrasive products, farm machinery, sewing machines, automobiles, or costume jewelry, there are human resources personnel who have screened, processed, oriented, trained, and provided benefits to the labor force. As America fights to maintain its competitiveness in manufacturing, it needs competent human resources workers to assemble a well-qualified group of employees.

Help in Locating These Employers. Some resources to start with include *Moody's Industrial Manuals*, *Encyclopedia of American Industries: Manufacturing*, and Dun's *America's Corporate Families*. You'll want to become familiar with the Standard Industrial Coding (SIC) scheme, which groups manufacturers producing similar products, to find environments in which you are interested in working. Contact your local chamber of commerce for assistance in identifying manufacturing firms operating in your area.

Finance and Insurance

Profile. The finance and insurance industry includes commercial banks, savings institutions, and insurance companies. The psychology major can bring personal interest, general knowledge, and relevant skills, such as personal computer and software usage, to this sector of the economy.

Help in Locating These Employers. If you would like to begin generating a list of possible employment sites, begin by visiting websites such as www.bankjobs.com, www.banking.com, or A.M. Best Company's website (www.ambest.com). They connect you with industry news, employers, and associations. You may also find that companies in this industry have recruited on your campus—check with your career services office for a listing. And don't forget to check the Yellow Pages for organizations doing business in your area.

Federal, state, and local governments employ about 15 percent of the salaried personnel, training, and labor relations specialists and managers. Competition for entry-level government positions is keen, but don't let that fact deter you from exploring and pursuing career possibilities in the public sector.

Federal Government

Profile. The federal government competes with the private sector for well-educated, trained workers, including personnel managers. In order to attract more candidates, the government has made sweeping changes in how it provides information about the offices and agencies that carry out the federal government's charges and also in how it advertises job vacancies. The Office of Personnel Management (OPM) is the federal government's human resource agency. They ensure that the nation's civil service remains free of political influence and that federal employees are selected on the basis of merit and are treated fairly. The OPM maintains regional offices and a website (www.opm.gov) to assist potential and current employees. See the next section for help in accessing job listings. Some agencies, such as the Central Intelligence Agency, Federal Bureau of Investigation, Defense Intelligence Agency, and National Security Agency, are not required to hire employees through the OPM. They maintain websites that include their own job listings. Be sure to investigate each agency and find out what the current needs are for personnel managers. A list of OPM sites is included at the end of this chapter.

Help in Locating These Employers. Given the ease and availability of accessing the Internet, nearly every federal job is listed on the Web. A good place to start looking for actual job listings is on the OPM's website (http://www.usajobs.opm.gov/index.htm). This site explains the federal employment process, lets you look at current job openings, provides general information on federal agencies, and allows you to submit an on-line application.

If you select the option "Current Job Openings" and then "Choose a Specific Series," one of the options is "0201—Personnel Management." Select this option, search for "All" jobs, and a list will appear on your screen. Or, select the option for "Entry Level Professional" listings, then select the "Administrative" category for your geographic region. Positions are listed alphabetically by job title, so look for the "Personnel Management Specialist" jobs. Select any of the entries and a detailed job description is provided, including information on whom to contact for more information and how to apply for the specific positions.

State and Local Government

Profile. State and larger local governments offer human resources positions that help in staffing departments, including corrections, court systems, education, fire protection, health, highway and street construction, housing and community development, hospitals, libraries, natural resources, parks and recreation, police, sanitation, transportation, utilities, and welfare and human services. Your background in psychology has helped prepare you to process, test, and screen applicants who will be interviewed by the various departments.

Help in Locating These Employers. Begin your search on the World Wide Web. Use your favorite search engine and enter "State of (put state name here)." You will find references to state departments. Look for "Employment," "Personnel," or "Human Resources" headings, then look for job listings, opportunities, and so forth. For example, if you type "State of Arizona," several choices appear. Select "Arizona State Government," then choose "Welcome to the State of Arizona (Official state website)." Next, choose "Branches of State Government," "Executive Branch," "Human Resources Division," and "Employment." Arizona, like many states, makes a weekly job bulletin available. On the day this site was checked, a position for a Human Resources Specialist I was being advertised. On state websites, you will find application procedures and contact names. Some sites will allow you to apply on-line.

Printed resources such as VGM's *Opportunities in Government Careers*, Planning Communications' *Government Job Finder*, and Impact's *The Complete Guide to Public Employment* detail ways to work these government systems.

Staffing Companies

Profile. The importance of the role that staffing companies play in the workplace continues to grow. Almost 3 million people per day are employed by staffing companies.[2] Many organizations, rather than hiring a regular employee, will hire a field staffer (temporary employee) to "try out." If all goes well, the staffer will be offered regular employment.

....

2. American Staffing Association (www.natss.org) 2000.

The companies that fill these field staffing positions need professionals, including graduates with psychology degrees, on their own staffs. A psychology graduate might start out as a service coordinator and be responsible for interviewing and orienting applicants, testing them, making a decision as to whether the agency wants to work with them, evaluating job orders, locating and referring qualified applicants, and writing job advertisements. In this industry the service coordinator can move on into positions in sales, marketing, and management after they have "paid their dues" as a service coordinator.

Help in Locating These Employers.   One easy way to begin locating staffing companies is to review the Yellow Pages for the geographic area where you would like to work. Look under Employment Agencies, Employment Contractors-Temporary Help, and Employment Service-Employee Leasing. You will probably be surprised at the number of agencies listed. You may also want to contact the American Staffing Association, Alexandria, Virginia (www.natss.org), for more information.

POSSIBLE JOB TITLES

Because human resources workers can be generalists or specialists, depending on the size and complexity of the organization, you will see quite a range of job titles. Consider them all when deciding which positions you're qualified to fill or determining an area in which you would like to specialize.

Affirmative-action coordinator
Arbitrator
Benefits administrator
Benefits analyst
Benefits manager
Compensation manager
Compensation specialist
Education specialist
Employee assistance plan manager
Employee benefits manager
Employee development specialist
Employee relations representative
Employee welfare officer/manager
Employer relations representative
Employment interviewer
Employment specialist

continued

---

continued

Equal Employment Opportunity (EEO) representative
Grievance officer
Human resource information systems specialist
Human resources coordinator
Human resources manager
Human resources specialist
Industrial relations manager/director
Industrial relations specialist
International human resource manager
Interviewer
Job analyst
Job classification specialist
Labor relations specialist
Management analyst
Mediator
Occupational analyst
Personnel administrator
Personnel consultant
Personnel director
Personnel management specialist
Personnel officer
Personnel staffing specialist
Position classification specialist
Position classifier
Position review specialist
Recreation specialist
Recruiter
Salary administrator
Service coordinator
Staffing coordinator
Test development specialist
Trainer
Training and development manager
Training specialist

RELATED OCCUPATIONS

Some attributes of successful human resources workers include the ability to (1) communicate successfully in interactions with other people, (2) attend to details in completing necessary paperwork, and (3) accurately implement and utilize appropriate assessment instruments. Other professions that require the use of at least some of these same attributes include

Career planning and placement counselor	Operations manager
Counselor	Psychologist
Executive assistant, nonprofit organization	Public relations specialist
	Rehabilitation counselor
Labor relations manager	Sociologist
Lawyer	Teacher

Many other job titles could be added to this list. As you do your exploration, be sure to consider and explore these other titles you encounter.

PROFESSIONAL ASSOCIATIONS

If you are interested in pursuing a career in human resources, several associations serve this group of workers. Review the listings shown below and decide whether any of the groups can provide information relevant to your job search.

American Arbitration Association
335 Madison Ave., 10th Floor
New York, NY 10017-4605
Website: www.adr.org
Members/Purpose: Businesses, unions, trade and educational associations, law firms, arbitrators, and other interested individuals.
Training: Conducts workshops, seminars, conferences, and skill-building sessions.
Journals/Publications: *Arbitration Journal*; *Arbitration and the Law*; *Arbitration in the Schools*; *Arbitration Times*.
Job Listings: Regional offices sometimes have listings; contact AAA for regional office nearest you.

American Compensation Association
14040 North Northsight Blvd.
Scottsdale, AZ 85260
Website: www.acaonline.org

Members/Purpose: Managerial and professional-level administrative personnel in business, industry, and government responsible for the establishment, execution, administration, or application of compensation practices and policies in their organization.

Training: Organizes almost 300 seminars annually.

Journals/Publications: *ACA Legislative Scene*; *ACA News*; *ACA Perspectives in Total Compensation*; *ACA Resourecs—News You Can Use*.

Job Listings: ACA Career Bulletin.

American Society for Healthcare Human Resources Administration

c/o American Hospital Association
One North Franklin
Chicago, IL 60606
Website: www.ashhra.org

Members/Purpose: To provide effective and continuous leadership in the field of health care human resources administration.

Journals/Publications: *Hospitals*; *Human Resources Administrator*; directory of consultants.

Job Listings: Offers placement service.

American Society for Training and Development

1640 King St.
Box 1443
Alexandria, VA 22313
Website: www.astd.org

Members/Purpose: Professional association for persons engaged in the training and development of business, industry, education, and government.

Training: Maintains database on more than 100,000 public seminars, workshops, and conferences, and on courseware from more than 100 suppliers.

Journals/Publications: *Info-Line*; *Practical Guidelines for Human Resource Development Professionals*; *Training and Development Journal*.

Job Listings: Local chapters offer a job bank; see *Training and Development Journal* classified section.

College and University Personnel Association

1233 20th St. NW, Suite 301
Washington, DC 20036
Website: www.cupa.org

Members/Purpose: Professional organization made up of colleges and universities interested in the improvement of campus personnel administration.

Training: Sponsors training seminars.

Journals/Publications: *CUPA News*; directory, various salary surveys.

Job Listings: *CUPA News* classified lists upper management positions.

International Association of Personnel in Employment Security
1801 Louisville Rd.
Frankfort, KY 40601
Website: www.iapes.org
Members/Purpose: Officials and others engaged in job placement and unemployment compensation administration through municipal, state, provincial, and federal government employment agencies and unemployment compensation agencies.

Training: Conducts workshops and offers professional development program of study guides and tests.

Journals/Publications: *IAPES News.*

International Foundation of Employee Benefit Plans
18700 W. Bluemound Rd.
Brookfield, WI 53008-0069
Website: www.ifebp.org
Members/Purpose: Jointly trusteed, public, Canadian, and company-sponsored employee benefit plans; administrators, labor organizations, employer associations, benefit consultants, investment counselors, insurance consultants, banks, attorneys, accountants, actuaries, and others who service or are interested in the field of employee benefit plans.

Training: Co-sponsors the Certified Employee Benefit Specialist Program, a ten-course college-level study program leading to a professional designation in the employee benefits field.

Journals/Publications: *Employee Benefits Basics*; *Employee Benefits Practices*; *Employee Benefits Quarterly.*

Job Listings: Provides a job service.

International Personnel Management Association
1617 Duke St.
Alexandria, VA 22314
Website: www.ipma-hr.org
Members/Purpose: Public personnel agencies and individuals (personnel workers, consultants, teachers). Seeks to improve personnel practices in government.

Training: Sponsors seminars and workshops on public personnel administration.

Journals/Publications: *Agency Issues*; membership directory; *IPMA News*; public employee relations library; *Public Personnel Management*.

National Association of Personnel Services
3133 Mt. Vernon Ave.
Alexandria, VA 22305
Website: www.napsweb.org
Members/Purpose: Private employment agencies.
Training: Conducts certification program.
Journals/Publications: Membership directory; *Personnel Consultant*.

National Association of State Personnel Executives
c/o Council of State Governments
2760 Research Park Dr.
Lexington, KY 40578-1910
Website: www.csg.org
Members/Purpose: Personnel directors for state and territorial governments.
Journals/Publications: *State Personnel View* newsletter.

National Association of Temporary Services
119 S. Saint Asaph St.
Alexandria, VA 22314
Website: www.natss.org
Members/Purpose: Companies supplying workers to other firms on a temporary basis.
Joumals/Publications: *Con Temporary Times*; membership directory.

Society for Human Resource Management
1800 Duke St.
Alexandria, VA 22314-1997
Website: www.shrm.org
Members/Purpose:: Professional organization of human resources, personnel, and industrial relations executives.
Journals/Publications: *HR Magazine*; *HR News*.
Job Listings: See *HR News*.

OFFICE OF PERSONNEL MANAGEMENT ADDRESSES

OPM Job Information Center
1900 E St. NW, Room 2458
Washington, DC 20415
Website: www.opm.gov

OPM Atlanta Service Center
75 Spring St. SW, Suite 956
Atlanta, GA 30303
Website: www.opm.gov

OPM Chicago Service Center
230 South Dearborn St., DPM 30-3
Chicago, IL 60604
Website: www.opm.com

OPM Dayton Service Center
200 West Second St., Room 507
Dayton, OH 45402-1430
Website: www.opm.gov

OPM Denver Service Center
12345 W. Alameda Pkwy.
P.O. Box 25167
Denver, CO 80225
Website: www.opm.gov

OPM Detroit Service Center
447 Michigan Ave., Room 1196
Detroit, MI 48226
Website: www.opm.gov

OPM Honolulu Service Center
300 Ala Moana Blvd.
P.O. Box 50028
Honolulu, HI 96850
Website: www.opm.gov

OPM Huntsville Service Center
520 Wynn Dr. NW
Huntsville, AL 35816-3426
Website: www.opm.gov

OPM Norfolk Service Center
Federal Building
200 Granby St., Room 500
Norfolk, VA 23510-1886
Website: www.opm.gov

OPM Philadelphia Service Center
Federal Building
600 Arch St., Room 3400
Philadelphia, PA 19106
Website: www.opm.gov

OPM Raleigh Service Center
4407 Bland Rd., Suite 200
Raleigh, NC 27609
Website: www.opm.gov

OPM San Antonio Service Center
8610 Broadway, Room 305
San Antonio, TX 78217
Website: www.opm.gov

OPM San Francisco Service Center
120 Howard St., Room 735
San Francisco, CA 94105
Website: www.opm.gov

OPM San Juan Service Center
Torre de Plaza las Americas
525 F. D. Roosevelt Ave., Suite 1114
San Juan, PR 00918
Website: www.opm.gov

OPM Seattle Service Center
700 5th Ave., Suite 5950
Seattle, WA 98104-5012
Website: www.opm.gov

OPM Twin Cities Service Center
One Federal Dr., Suite 596
Fort Snelling
Twin Cities, MN 55111-4007
Website: www.opm.gov

EXCEPTED FEDERAL AGENCIES

The following is a partial list of federal agencies, bureaus, and departments you may want to contact:

Agency for International Development
Ronald Reagan Building
Washington, DC 20523-0016
Website: www.info.usaid.gov

Board of Governors of the Federal Reserve System
20th St. and Constitution Ave. NW
Washington, DC 20551
Website: www.federalreserve.gov

Central Intelligence Agency
Office of Public Affairs
Washington, DC 20505
Website: www.odci.gov

Defense Intelligence Agency
Civilian Staffing Operations
Division (DPH-2)
3100 Clarendon Blvd.
Arlington, VA 22201-5322
Website: www.dia.mil

Department of Veterans Affairs
(Health care occupations)
Veterans Health Services and Research Administration
Recruitment and Examining
Division (054E)
810 Vermont Ave. NW
Washington, DC 20420
Website: www.va.gov

Federal Bureau of Investigation
935 Pennsylvania Ave. NW
Washington, DC 20420
Website: www.fbi.com

National Security Agency
9800 Savage Rd.
Fort Meade, MD 20755-6000
Attention: M352
Website: www.nsa.gov

Nuclear Regulatory Commission
Office of Personnel
Washington, DC 20555
Website: www.nrc.gov

Postal Rate Commission
Administrative Office, Suite 300
1333 H St. NW
Washington, DC 20268-0001
Website: www.prc.gov

Tennessee Valley Authority
Employment Services, ET 5C 50P-K
400 West Summit Hill Dr.
Knoxville, TN 37902
Website: www.tva.gov

State Department
(Foreign Service positions)
Recruitment Division
P.O. Box 9317
Rosslyn Station
Arlington, VA 22209
Website: www.state.gov

CHAPTER THIRTEEN

PATH 4: THERAPY

The field of psychology is diverse with emphases ranging from clinical psychology to counseling psychology, developmental psychology to experimental psychology, and school psychology to social psychology. Each one of these subfields is, however, concerned with two things: behavior, and the data, facts, and observations relating to that behavior. Undergraduate psychology programs often focus on introducing the student to the full spectrum of behavioral fields, rather than on training the student to work in one particular subfield. Psychology departments are in the business of exposing and exploring the field of psychology and what the study of the human mind and human behavior represents as an academic discipline. They do not train students to diagnose symptoms of pathology and then treat them. Graduate programs in psychology provide this more specific training.

Your undergraduate psychology degree program presented you with texts, readings to digest, and papers to write that allowed you to explore facets of many subfields of psychology. You may also have had an opportunity to do behavior experiments with rodents or other animals. Perhaps, throughout your years of study, many interesting guest speakers visited your campus to talk on human behavior topics. Sometimes, an ambitious student or group of learners will have, with faculty supervision, created a survey or conducted an experiment with a consenting group of fellow students on some behavioral topic such as test anxiety or stress.

Some students gain some exposure to working with clients through counseling classes or developmental and industrial psychology courses. Others observe young children or work with residents of nursing homes, patients in hospitals, or workers in factories and corporations. Some academic programs require internships or fellowships in a counseling and psychological-services center or career-counseling office where students observe the counseling process in both individual and group settings.

Your academic, observational, and/or clinical training has awakened your interest in working in a therapeutic setting, and you're eager to learn more about what types of jobs await you in the world beyond college.

WHO ARE THERAPISTS?

The group of occupations that we label as therapists are those defined as working to treat and rehabilitate individuals who may present problems that are emotional, mental, or physical. The therapist works with a client to restore and develop function, to prevent the loss of capabilities, and to maintain an optimum lifestyle. An increasing number of therapy modalities, or mediums of therapy, are currently available to patients. Exercise, massage, counseling, music, heat, light, aroma, water, electricity, dance, ceramics, voice, and specific equipment are all employed in helping the client regain what has been lost, emotionally, mentally, or physically. These practitioners often work in or close to medically related institutions or programs where the therapy request originates. They are most often part of a larger team of helping professionals who rely on each other for diagnosis and treatment updates. Some of the more frequently encountered therapies are reviewed here.

Cognitive Therapy
Cognitive therapy focuses on recognizing and changing ingrained patterns of thinking or assumptions that are negative or counterproductive. It is a treatment modality often used to treat anxiety, specific phobias, drug and alcohol abuse, and mild to moderate depression.

Behavioral Therapy
Behavioral therapy focuses on recognizing and changing specific behavioral patterns. You may have read of its use in treating sexual dysfunctions, specific phobias, or anxiety states (such as a lawyer afraid to talk in court), and obsessive-compulsive symptoms. It may often be used in conjunction with medication.

Interpersonal Therapy
Interpersonal therapy focuses on interpersonal problems or other relationship difficulties in people with moderate depression. It does not explore past interpersonal dynamics.

Psychodynamic Therapy

Dealing with deeply ingrained internal emotional struggles and conflicts usually related to early childhood traumas and losses that continue to impair work productivity and personal relationships is the focus of psychodynamic therapy.

Psychoanalysis

Psychoanalysis is a more intense form of psychodynamic therapy that often involves meeting with an analyst several times a week. Regrettably, because of its exposure in literature, film, and humor, it is grossly misunderstood by the general public.

Family and Couples Therapy

Family or couples therapy deals with difficulties within the family or a couple's relationship, focusing on the interpersonal dynamics of the group or unit.

Expressive Therapy

Expressive therapy is a term undergoing some refinement in the treatment modalities available to therapists. It involves the use of creative arts, such as drama, art, music, movement, dance, or poetry. Expressive therapies (each of the expressive arts can be a therapy unto itself) are used in the treatment of a variety of populations (adults with chronic mental illnesses, sexual abuse survivors, youths at risk), in one-on-one sessions and in group treatment. There are practitioners labeled expressive therapists, as well as therapists in each of the expressive areas, for example, music therapists, art therapists, and dance therapists.

WHERE THE PSYCHOLOGY MAJOR FITS INTO THE THERAPY PICTURE

At about this point in the discussion, the undergraduate with a general psychology degree and an interest in working directly with clients might well ask, "Where could I possibly fit into this employment picture? I am interested in client contact and many of these modalities hold interest for me. But, I only have my bachelor's degree and am not yet ready to pursue higher education." The answer is interesting.

Psychology undergraduates are hired for some *preprofessional* therapist positions. They are not therapists, in the strict definition of that term, although many job specifications and advertisements will use that title. The positions themselves cover a wide range of duties and responsibilities. The American Psychological Association (www.apa.org), the preeminent professional group for psychology careerists in the United States, continually surveys the employment of preprofessionals in the area of therapy. They continue to find the overwhelming majority of these entry-level therapy positions to be working with the severely emotionally disturbed. Other large populations receiving therapeutic services from individuals with undergraduate psychology degrees include the neurologically impaired, the mentally retarded, and antisocial or acting-out populations. Consider these advertisements:

Activities Therapist. (Hospital) is currently recruiting for a part-time (thirty-two hrs/wk) activities therapist in psychiatry. Position is Sunday–Thursday, with six-hour rotation shifts (afternoon and evening hours). Be an integral member of multidisciplinary team approach to patient care; initiate and direct therapeutic recreation programs for mostly adult patients on this open unit where average length-of-stay is fourteen days. Bachelor's degree required, preferably in therapeutic recreation/ psychology; two to three years related experience preferred. Offer competitive salary and excellent benefits package. Please send resume to . . .

Rehabilitation Therapist. Part- and full-time positions. Develop and conduct prevocational-skills training and socialization groups in structured rehabilitation program for psychiatrically disabled adults. Bachelor's degree in psychology/human services preferred. Send resume with cover letter to . . .

After careful consideration, much discussion with professionals in the field, and a survey of job postings available to the bachelor's graduate in psychology, the authors have chosen to include therapist positions as one of the five psychology career paths. You will encounter the job title frequently in your job search. Before you make a job choice, we want to help you understand exactly what these positions entail, both the rich rewards and the very heavy responsibilities. To sum up

1. Therapy positions are advertised and do exist for undergraduate degree holders in psychology.

2. They are termed therapists, but are more accurately described as preprofessional positions, under the supervision of a therapist.

3. They do work with patients.

4. They do participate in a variety of therapeutic modalities or treatment plans.

5. All of this is under the close supervision of a degreed, trained, and licensed, certified, or registered therapist, and that therapist is probably part of an even larger care team headed by one or more medical doctors.

DEFINITION OF THE CAREER PATH

Securing and beginning your psychology career in a therapist position will be a challenge in and of itself. Fortunately, because the work is so rewarding, the effort is well worth it. The daily contact with clients and treatment interventions (activities) will help you build a history of experiences that you will draw from for the rest of your life. If you do begin your career in a therapy position, it is no exaggeration to suggest this will be a determining influence on your career in psychology.

However, challenges for baccalaureate-degreed therapists will continue to present themselves, especially in the form of the credentials, certification, and training issues. The therapeutic field is one that is under continuous scrutiny from the public, the government, insurers, caregivers themselves, the support networks of the clients, and even from its own professional organizations who are seeking to enhance the credibility and prestige of their profession. Questions of licensure by state officials, and certification programs by professional organizations provide a continuous dialogue in the popular press and in professional journals on ethics, standards, educational requirements, and professional criteria for all these therapies.

Professionally, we are witnessing an increased awareness by both the public and in the court system of issues surrounding the implicit legal and ethical contract between patient and therapist. For therapists, there are generally four elements to obtaining informed consent from their client: (1) client competency, (2) the disclosure of material information (does the client fully understand the treatment regimen), (3) the client's understanding of the presented material, and (4) voluntary consent.

There are more subtle controversies, as well. As this volume goes to press, public dialogue on the efficacy of long-term therapy has increased. Fueled in part by brief therapy proponents and practitioners, it has pointed up the lack of outcome evaluative measures for long-term therapy. How do we know if clients are getting better? Laws and regulations surrounding the provision for services have increased exponentially, and many professional organizations publish detailed ethical guidelines for their members.

In addition to advanced-degree attainment as an outward mark of professionalism, many states have both licensure and certification. Licensure has to do with the state ensuring certain educational and experiential standards have been met. It often involves some type of written examination and it helps the public know that the individual has met some state-mandated criterion for professionalism. Licensing boards are then able to discipline unethical or fraudulent practitioners by revoking this license.

Certification through professional organizations promotes standards of education, practice, accountability, discretion, ethics, and visibility. Certifications help assure the public that the individual therapist has met some established standards. Certification can involve testing or the documentation of professional development and years of practice. It is often issued for a limited period of time.

See your state officials for information on licensure and your applicable professional associations for certification information.

Consequently, the impetus is constantly on you to enhance your training, certification, and qualifications for the work that you do. If you find yourself fortunate enough to begin your career in a therapist position, you will want to take every opportunity your employer can provide or that you can yourself afford to enhance your training and skill package. Discover what is offered by local or state government agencies or professional associations in the form of workshops, seminars, and qualifying programs that will add to your professionalism and enhance your value to your employer.

AN EXAMPLE: EXPRESSIVE THERAPY

Perhaps you are interested in an entry-level position as an expressive or art therapist. Art, music, and dance are some of the major therapeutic avenues in what is termed *expressive therapy*. Generally, these modalities try to involve the client in creative, nonverbal (although there is vocal expressive therapy) expression to help with maladaptive behavior. Review the following advertisement:

Creative/Expressive Therapist. Seeking an innovative and responsible individual with experience in using art media as an expressive treatment modality. This is a full-time position. Our interdisciplinary rehabilitation team is dedicated to the provision

continued

---

continued

of quality patient care. Short-term rehabilitation, geriatric, and extended rehabilitation programming. Will provide individual/group sessions to facilitate communication and augment other therapies. Requirements: psychology/ counseling degree and expressive media experience working with various disabilities. Competitive salary/benefit package. 401(k) package. Send resume. . .

The expressive therapist is almost always grounded in one medium. The therapist may be a ceramist, modern dancer, or collage artist and believes strongly in the therapeutic qualities of that form and medium. It has been a salient and critical-feature of the therapist's own mental health. It ennobles them, lifts them up, and allows them to express themselves in a way they cannot otherwise. This belief in and personal grounding in the medium for their own self-improvement and revitalization is critical before they can use the therapeutic technique to help others. Incorporating your preferred medium with other possible creatively expressive approaches, you seek to help clients reach this same goal.

Art and expressive therapists are found in many clinical, educational, and rehabilitative settings, although their operating titles may vary. For a number of reasons, including medical school training, individual attending physician exposure, and some generational issues, the expressive therapies may not yet be among the modalities of first choice. The boundaries of this field and the research data to support it are not yet clearly defined.

"Art Therapy in a Socialization Program for Children with Attention Deficit Hyperactivity Disorder" is the title of an article in the August, 1998 issue of *Therapy*. A multimodal, integrated program sought to address long-standing programs with regard to peer, school, and family relationships among young children with ADHD is the focus of the article. Weekly sessions involving expressive art therapy allowed for the exploration of self-expression and awareness of self and others.

There is strong support available for expressive therapists that can be found in the training, graduate programs, and the certification standards established. Music therapists, for example, may apply for registration with the National Association for Music Therapy or certification by the American Association for Music Therapy. Qualified music therapists may become board-certified upon passing an exam given by the Certification Board for Music Therapists, an independent accreditation organization. Neither registration nor certification is required at the current time for music therapists to practice, incidentally.

Because most expressive therapists participate with other kinds of therapy treatments (occupational, recreational, and physical therapists) in a team approach for their clients and in institutional settings, they are covered by third-party insurance payments. As an individual, isolated therapy, even under referral by a physician, the patient may find that this therapy is not reimbursable by insurance providers.

WORKING CONDITIONS

Every therapy is different, every setting in which therapy is practiced is different, and every client is, of course, unique. Can we make any generalizations about your working conditions as an entry-level therapist paraprofessional? Yes!

Let's begin with clients, because your work begins with them. At any time in your practice, you are apt to have a roster of individual clients. Because you're working in one type of therapy, these clients may share, in a general way, some presenting issues (relationship difficulties, eating disorders, compulsive behaviors) but age, gender, and personality are all different. You'll have clients about to finish their course of therapy, either because of improvement or lack of benefits or finances. You'll have some clients right in the middle of their course of treatment and others just beginning to work with you on their issues. You're in a different place with each client, and as you move from appointment to appointment, you'll consciously have to shift gears and reassess your next appointment. Who are they and where are they in their treatment plan and what is your next step?

To answer these questions, you'll consult two sources: (1) your own process notes that you'll keep on your clients detailing what happened during your previous session and your thoughts and ideas for future sessions. You'll include any "homework" you gave your client for your next appointment and (2) the overall treatment plans for this client; you'll be directed in your efforts by the professionals on your team assigned to supervise and direct your work. As a paraprofessional, you'll be supervised quite closely, in most instances, until you have established a track record of trust, responsibility, and performance.

You'll be working to earn your client's trust and acceptance so that you can work with him or her in a productive manner and fulfill the protocols established for his or her therapy. You'll keep notes on your progress, and some of your sessions may be observed or even videotaped. You will be asked to contribute to evaluative reports on clients and documentation surrounding treatment plans for insurance purposes. You may also be asked to help write up case studies for research or publication purposes.

A number of elements of the therapist's working situation are discussed here.

Teamwork

The hallmark of the therapist is teamwork. Consulting with other paraprofessionals and professionals to ensure the most considerate implementation of the treatment plan for the client can be complicated with many intervening variables. If you are working with a recovering adolescent drug abuser who also happens to be profoundly deaf and whose speech is difficult to interpret, you may find yourself working closely with a speech therapist. Combinations and recombinations of team members are the rule, not the exception, and each member of the team is expected to maintain excellent communication, positive and energetic commitment to the client, superb and detailed record keeping, and a respect for scheduled appointments.

Group Settings

Oftentimes, because many clients share similar issues (early sexual abuse, eating disorders, or nonspecific anxiety), using the therapy in a group setting is appropriate and beneficial. Conducting group psychotherapy is a special skill that has many transferable applications to other employment settings, and if you are able to learn and observe some group counseling techniques (building cohesion, norming, consensual validation), you would be well-advised to take every advantage of the opportunity. You will draw upon that experience throughout your work life in almost any setting involving teams.

Family Involvement

Families often become involved in the therapy of one of their members. It may be a young boy acting out over his parents' divorce or an elderly patient who has become despondent about the death of a spouse. There will be consultations with the family about home life and there may be instructions to avoid certain behaviors or situations that are problematical for the client. Occasionally, family members may be asked to participate in the therapy.

Supervision

In all cases where paraprofessionals engage in many of the same treatment modalities as professionals, they are under the supervision of those more qualified and do not function with as much autonomy. Even as you establish a track record of performance and successful interventions with patients, you will be given very little freedom. This supervision protects the client and the professional from charges of malfeasance, mismanagement, and unethical behavior. If this supervision becomes too confining for you, it may be an excellent signal that the time has come for you to consider becoming a degreed therapist in your own right.

Length of Treatment

Therapists engage in both short-term and long-term treatment interventions. How long your clients stay in therapy may be important to you because it affects your interaction with them. At the extreme ends of the spectrum, in short-term, brief therapy, you will have a constantly changing population of clients seeing you for a limited number of sessions (often less than five). Short-term therapy has many proponents, including third-party insurers, and for some presenting issues, it can be effective. The pace may be rapid with much client diversity, and so there may be little closure.

Long-term therapy allows you to work intensively with clients and mark progress over time. Therapeutic options increase with the number of sessions as do the options for connection with your clients. On the other hand, many psychoanalysts (who may see their patients several times a week) will tell you there can be, as well, a corresponding static quality, with little dramatic change day-to-day and a numbing predictability.

TRAINING AND QUALIFICATIONS

Several training and qualification issues are extremely important for the therapist. They include possession of advanced degrees, licensure and certification, work experience, and certain personal qualifications.

Advanced Degrees

There is no question that the predominance of therapist positions begin with a demand for a master's-level clinician. However, the student with an undergraduate degree in psychology who earnestly pursues this particular career path will be rewarded by discovering a number of worthwhile positions offering the kind of client contact and caseload appropriate to his or her background and training. The position advertisement shown on the following page indicates a preference for someone with a master's degree, but will consider those candidates who do not have one; in the latter case, they probably will expect extensive experience.

> *Therapist.* Part time. Needed for residential treatment program
> serving adolescent females. Family, individual, and group
> therapy. Master's degree preferred. Will consider bachelor-
> degreed candidate with relevant experience. Please write to . . .

Licensure and Certification

Some of these therapies warrant reimbursement by third-party payers under
health insurance plans and others do not. Generally, in the case where
third-party payment is involved, licensure, certification, and degree attainment of the therapist become critical issues in the practice of these treatment plans. The overwhelming majority of therapy is prescribed by a
physician and the caregiver team. To ensure the continued professionalism
of therapy, licensure, certification, and degree attainment are welcomed by
most in the profession as ensuring their continued employment and demand
by the public for their services.

Work Experience

Even in positions that accept an undergraduate degree in psychology, there
may still be an expectation of work experience in the field. For example, an
addictions therapist position may be available for a bachelor's-degreed
candidate in psychology, but that candidate should provide evidence of two
years of outpatient counseling experience specific to drug and alcohol abuse
and rehabilitation. Some of that experience may be achieved through
well-supervised college internships and/or summer employment.

The work experience demand can be quite specific and often requires that
it be with the population described in the job advertisement. So, if the job
was for working with adults in a community residence, and your experience
has been with adolescents in a hospital setting, it may not be seen as appropriate preparation, given your degree level and lack of credentials.

Here is an advertisement for a cognitive therapist that is typical of its
undergraduate degree requirement with an expectation of significant other
experience with the client population (in this case, the disabled).

> *Cognitive Therapist.* We are a skilled nursing facility focusing in
> psychosocial rehabilitation. Bachelor's degree in
> speech/language pathology, psychology, or related field.
> Experience working with the disabled and knowledge of
> computer-assisted therapeutic programs helpful. Send resume to:

Personal Qualifications

There are important personal qualities required by the majority of these therapist positions, and you'll need to be candid and realistic with yourself in your work in the self-assessment chapter that begins this book. Some of the most important skills are discussed here.

Flexibility. Some therapists work independently, while others are part of hospital or nursing-home care teams. Because you are part of a team, there will be overlapping of efforts, communication difficulties, and all the variables one encounters when the number of people involved in a project multiplies. You'll need to stay poised to make changes on the spur of the moment with good grace and humor.

Patience. All therapist positions require enormous reserves of patience. It is often painfully slow work, with such small gains that only the therapist and those working intimately with the client can appreciate the patient's progress.

Record Keeping. Record keeping is critical and meticulous. Process notes (records of your appointments with clients) may actually be subpoenaed in case of any litigation. There may be overall evaluations on your client by the entire team to which you will contribute. Charts, forms, insurance documentation, and other records of a client's treatment and progress need to be thoroughly maintained.

Listening. We all can do this to some degree. Within the helping professions, where your client may or may not be able to communicate effectively or even authentically, you'll need well-developed listening skills to understand what the client is trying to tell you. To really listen to your clients, you need to care deeply about them and their needs.

Effective Communication. This is a frequently quoted skill on most individuals' resumes. Most college graduates feel they are effective communicators. You will be dealing with a variety of individuals, each communicating with you in a different way. Your communication not only needs to be clear and effective but "tuned in" to the person with whom you are working. You need to be sensitive to clients' understanding of you, the words they use, and what they mean to them.

Empathy. Listening and communicating with your clients involves understanding the world as they perceive it. Empathy means you share some degree of appreciation for what your client has experienced or feels. Truly understanding the other person's perceptions is a wonderful attribute for the helping professions.

Being Open. Understanding yourself and being able to express your own needs will help create trust and sharing. This does not mean you use the therapeutic situation to solve your problems but that you will be professional and open with your clients in your efforts to help them.

Acceptance. You may, in your work, come across individuals whose behavior is reprehensible to you or whose values are very different from yours. To be a truly effective helper, you need to keep from imposing what you believe to be right or good on others and concentrate on how you can help this individual. You don't have to agree or accept the behavior, but you must believe in the dignity of the individual as worthy of help.

EARNINGS

A review of current job postings and conversations with hiring personnel show that salaries for entry-level therapy positions can vary widely, depending on the geographic location, type of facility, degree of experience, and level of autonomy required. Positions that involve some therapeutic modalities (under strict clinical supervision) range from a low of approximately $10.00 an hour to salaried positions between $21,000 and $25,000 with most positions falling within that range. Many of the positions are available at health-care facilities, and most of them pay a differential for evening, weekend, and holiday work hours. This salary range may seem shockingly low to some job seekers, but keep in mind these positions are usually carefully supervised by highly qualified professionals. In order to obtain a higher level of income, additional education, experience, and certification credentials will be required.

As we discussed in other career paths, it is especially important for you, the job seeker, to determine if the salary an organization is offering will be enough for you to support yourself at the necessary income level. Complete the self-assessment as described earlier in this book to determine the level of pay you need to receive. And don't overlook the value of the benefits package, especially educational benefits, if you hope to grow in a therapy career path.

CAREER OUTLOOK

The field of therapy as a career for the psychology graduate needs to be seen as one they may enter only "on approval." Demands will increase for more and more specialization and an increasingly higher level of credential for anyone involved in direct patient therapy. In the not too distant future, it probably will be impossible to enter this field without an advanced degree.

The essential and very understandable reason for such a push toward specialization, both in treatment and in credentials of the caregiver, is the overwhelming responsibility these individuals have, in part, for the health and well-being of their clients. The organizations (hospitals, benefit providers, rehabilitation centers, and doctors) who are ultimately responsible for the treatment plan of any one individual are subject to the risks involved in group work. Litigation against participants in all kinds of health issues abounds, and awards become increasingly astronomical and can have serious repercussions on the integrity and stature of those involved, regardless of their culpability. One way of ensuring against this kind of risk is the very obvious one of demanding that the state set educational or professional criteria for the credentials of the participants. The future will only exacerbate this demand.

However, the psychology graduate who realizes this situation and who sees an immediate entry into the field as a paraprofessional therapist as an exciting and demanding way to begin a career in psychology, can use this first job as a platform to grow and gain the necessary education and credentials to ensure continued professional-level employment

STRATEGY FOR FINDING THE JOBS

Your job search strategy for therapy positions must be based on a certain level of experience. This begins with completion of an internship. In addition, you'll be working to gain additional direct experience, be aware of certification and licensure issues, work toward acquiring those that are important for growth in your career, and read and study on your own to enhance your knowledge base.

Begin Gaining Experience Through an Internship

Your own college career center website will undoubtedly contain both internship listings and links to other promising internship sites at colleges and universities around the country. An additonal resource may be one of the many internship directories published each year. A quick search on Amazon.com, using the keyword "internship," brought up 117 directories. One of the best is *America's Top Internships, 2000 Edition* (revised yearly) by Mark Oldman, et al. The following is typical of the variety and scope of the internship available:

National Sports Center for the Disabled
677 Winter Park Drive, P.O. Box 36
Winter Park, CO

General Information: Provides outdoor mountain recreational services to children and adults with disabilities. Established in 1970. Number of employees: Twenty-five to thirty-five. Division of Winter Park Recreation Association.
Internships Available: Five winter instructors: responsibilities include assessing and evaluating disabled students, teaching skiing one-on-one, assisting with adaptive equipment lab that administers a weekly program, and assisting the special events and projects. Duration is five months. Two summer instructors: responsibilities include assessing and evaluating disabled students; leading and teaching a variety of outdoor recreation activities, including mountain biking, rafting, fishing, and camping; and assisting with fundraising and special events and projects. Duration is three months.

Students pursuing these kinds of experiences often do so because of their strong feelings that they would like to work directly with a client population in a more clinical, therapeutic manner to effect positive change. These experiences are usually fully supervised, and the student receives valuable feedback. An internship such as the one cited above or any similar hands-on experience will give you a solid understanding of the problems and challenges facing various client populations, as well as building some specific helping skills.

Obtain Additional Related Work Experience

It appears that the key to working as a paraprofessional in a field dominated by professionals is to approach the job search with some specifically related work experiences. These need not all be paid positions. While still in college, you might consider volunteering at a mental health clinic or a drug halfway house. If your community has an Alcoholics Anonymous group that allows visitors (some do not), you might go and observe some meetings. Head Start, private and state rehabilitation clinics and hospitals, senior centers, and a host of other sites with differing populations and degrees of severity of problems may welcome your willingness to volunteer to help and may provide a broad range of participation. Some may have part-time paid employment that you can fit into your schedule while in college.

In either case, use an experience such as this to its fullest advantage. Meet and talk with as many of the staff professionals as you can. Let them know of your interests and career aspirations. They'll have excellent advice and tips for you on employment, job search, and job acquisition.

Stay Aware of the Certification and Licensure Issues

Talk with colleagues and read up on the current dialogue in your field of therapy on certification and licensure. What is the direction in your state and how far are you from attaining the necessary stature to ensure your continued employment? If your employer offers educational benefits, you may want to consider master's degree work at a nearby college or university.

To grow in your profession, both personally and in terms of your ability to act autonomously, to help design treatment programs, and to supervise other clinicians, you will eventually need to enhance your credentials with a master's degree. This will allow you to attain the kinds of licensure and/or certifications necessary to enjoy a broader range of employment possibilities and to enter private practice as well.

Read and Study on Your Own

Whatever milieu you find yourself in, don't be content with just your participation. Read and study what you can on the population and presenting problems. A site where you work on an internship or are employed part-time may house a professional library. Certainly the professional staff can provide you with insights on working with clients, and you have your own academic training and library resources to discover as much as you can, in addition to the training and exposure you are receiving in your work position.

POSSIBLE EMPLOYERS

If you are interested in working in a therapeutic capacity using your degree in psychology, be sure to explore the many types of organizations that may offer employment opportunities. Included here are medical institutions, schools, psychiatric facilities, private rehabilitation centers, residential care facilities, public and private mental health providers, nonprofit providers, and correctional facilities. Add to this list as you do your research, and be sure to network with administrators at the various types of sites where you would like to work.

Medical Institutions

Profile. One example of how the psychology major can put his or her interest in a therapeutic career in a medical institution to work is occupational therapy. Many occupational therapy preprofessionals work in hospitals under the supervision of registered occupational therapists. They help people who have a disabling condition (mental, physical, developmental, or emotional) learn or regain skills necessary for daily living and working. In occupational therapy, a variety of techniques are used to help a client, for example, someone who experienced a brain injury in an auto accident can be helped to enhance his or her functioning.

Help in Locating These Employers. Nearly every type of therapy modality is employed in the many medical institutions that are found in this country. The website, www.hospitaldirectories.com, can help you locate any hospital or medical facility in the United States. Career books on any of the specific types of therapies, including VGM's *Opportunities in Occupational Therapy Careers* or the *Mental Health and Social Work Career Directory*, will help you identify additional employment sites you may not have considered.

Schools

Profile. The August, 1998 issue of *Therapy* contained a poignant article by David Henley that reported on a therapeutic socialization program for young children with ADHD (Attention Deficit Hyperactivity Disorder). The program utilized expressive and specifically art therapy in concert with a number of behavioral, cognitive, psychodynamic, and medical approaches. Arts activities were used to explore various relational problems with peers, school, and families.

Music, art, dance, and many other types of therapy can help students express things that may be difficult to put into words, or these therapies can help channel aggressive behaviors in a positive format.

Help in Locating These Employers. There are many types of schools that hire various therapists, and the preprofessionals who work with them, to help their students reach their full potential. Be certain to review some of the excellent publications of the American Association for Employment in Education—formerly ASCUS—(www.ub-careers.buffalo.edu/aaee/college.htm), including their *National Directory of Job and Career Fairs for Educators, National Directory for Employment in Education,* and their annual *Report on Teacher Supply and Demand in the U.S.* Ask the career professionals and librarians you are working with for the names of additional references.

Psychiatric Facilities

Profile. The American Art Therapy Association describes their profession as one that offers an opportunity to explore personal problems and potentials through verbal and nonverbal expression and to develop physical, emotional, and/or learning skills through therapeutic art experiences. Art therapy can be used in rehabilitation counseling to help psychiatric patients prepare for greater participation in the community. Patients may be easily frightened by the demands of today's society as they begin reintegration, and art therapy can help these patients express their feelings and work to overcome them.

Help in Locating These Employers. The Web is your best bet for the most current information on mental health services. At the time of publication of the second edition of this book, www.looksmart.com was offering an on-line directory of mental health organizations and related associations listed nationally and by state. Two prominent associations you'll come across are the National Association of Private Psychiatric Hospitals in Washington, D.C. and the Association of Psychiatric Outpatient Centers of America.

Private Rehabilitation Centers

Profile. Massage therapy, or the art and science of applying the therapeutic properties of massage to restore function, relieve pain, prevent disability, and promote healing, is one therapy modality employed at private rehabilitation centers. A patient at this type of facility may receive massage therapy, along with several other types of therapy, on a daily basis as he or she recovers from one of a multitude of physical and/or mental conditions.

Help in Locating These Employers. An excellent introductory source that will, in turn, lead you to additional resources is the home page of the National Association of Rehabilitation Agencies (NARA) at www.naranet.org.

Residential-Care Facilities

Profile. Residential-care facilities often focus on a specific type of client they want to assist, and so the therapeutic modalities utilized will vary from location to location. Consider a residence housing women who have left abusive relationships or a home for the mentally retarded who need low levels of support. Each utilizes appropriate therapies given the philosophy of the funding agency and the talents of the staff members.

Help in Locating These Employers. The National Association of Residential Care facilities (NARCF) in Hartford, Connecticut, maintains a website (www.health-connect.com/narcf) that is a rich resource for the job seeker interested in residential-care programs for the elderly, mentally and/or physically impaired, or the developmentally disabled. Begin with this site, but you may also want to examine specific state residential-care sites such as the

Association of Residential Resources in Minnesota (ARRM), which maintains a very professional site with excellent links to others. It can be found at www.arrm.org. One particularly attractive feature of the Minnesota site is its list of advocacy links, including one to "Nikolinks," which is a social service network. Check it out!

Public and Private Mental Health Providers

Profile. Horticultural therapy is an emerging type of rehabilitative therapy that involves using gardening techniques for either vocational rehabilitation or for leisure purposes. A progressive public or private mental health provider might employ therapists and qualified preprofessionals who utilize this modality to work with substance abusers who enjoy working out of doors or working with their hands. This helps the clients to find concrete and enjoyable outlets for negative feelings that need to be rechanneled.

Help in Locating These Employers. The state-by-state directory listings of not only mental health organizations but also mental health professional associations found at www.looksmart.com is an excellent one-stop resource to begin your search for public and private mental health providers. Another comprehensive website is http://www.piperinfo.com/state/states.html, which allows you to access the directories of every state in the United States. Locate the department of mental health to appreciate the services provided in that state and then access the human resource department for current job listings.

Nonprofit Providers

Profile. Nearly everyone, at some point in his or her life, will experience at least a temporarily (as opposed to a permanently) disabling condition, and could benefit from working through one of the many types of therapies that are available. Quite a variety of nonprofit organizations provide funding or services that help people regain at least some level of functioning lost through a disabling condition or episode. Activities that employ drama therapy, or use the technique of psychodrama and dramatic productions to facilitate self-expression in clients, are funded by several nonprofit organizations.

Help in Locating These Employers. It would take you a considerable expenditure of time to thoroughly explore The Internet Public Library at www.ipl.org. Within this site, under "Business and Economics," you'll locate over six pages of resources for nonprofit organizations, including job listings.

nal Facilities

)ance, or movement, therapy is the psychotherapeutic use of move-
irther the emotional, cognitive, and physical integration of the indi-
)me preprofessional dance therapists work in correctional facilities
imates learn new ways to express themselves by using their bodies
in movement, rather than aggressive tactics that are self-destructive.

Help In Locating These Employers. General career books that provide valuable information on working in corrections include VGM's *Careers in Social
and Rehabilitation Services* and the *Criminal Justice Careers Guidebook* published by the U.S. Departments of Labor and Justice. Because correctional
facilities are run by governmental units, other resources to examine include
*Opportunities in Government Careers, The Complete Guide to Public Employ-
ment,* and *Government Job Finder.*

POSSIBLE JOB TITLES

Therapy job titles can range from generalist to specialist, depending on the
modality that is used. Review the list provided here, follow up on those that
sound interesting by talking with a career counselor and a provider of the
particular kind of therapy, and also contact the professional association serving that type of therapist.

Activity therapist	Dance therapist
Art psychotherapist	Day-treatment clinician
Art specialist	Drama therapist
Art therapist	Exercise therapist
Behavior therapist	Expressive therapist
Clinician	Family therapist
Creative-arts therapist	Heat therapist
Creative therapist	Horticultural therapist
Light therapist	Psychiatric rehabilitation
Manual-arts therapist	counselor
Marriage therapist	Psychomotor therapist
Massage therapist	Recreational therapist
Movement therapist	Therapist
Music therapist	Voice therapist
Occupational therapist	Water therapist

RELATED OCCUPATIONS

As you consider the many skills required of therapists, including flexibility, patience, record keeping, listening, effective communications, empathy, openness, and acceptance, you will realize that these same skills are valued in other types of workers. You'll be able to immediately name some, but review the sampler shown below to see if you've considered each of these job titles.

Community and social service worker	Project director
Credit counselor	Residential-care worker
Human-services worker	Safety coordinator
Mediator	Special-services supervisor
Negotiator	Teacher

Review the self-assessment chapter of this book and you'll probably be able to add to this list based on the deeper self-understanding you've built.

PROFESSIONAL ASSOCIATIONS

Some of the specific associations that oversee certification and licensing for some of the therapy modalities we've discussed are shown below. Each provides information on gaining specific training and education beyond the bachelor's degree, and will provide career information to those who request it.

American Art Therapy Association, Inc.
1202 Allanson Rd.
Mundelein, IL 60060
Website: www.arttherapy.org
Members/Purpose: Art therapists, students, and individuals in related
fields. Has established specific professional criteria for training art
therapists.
Training: Conducts seminars.
Journals/Publications: *AATA Newsletter*; *Journal*.

American Association for Marriage and Family Therapy
1133 15th St. NW, Suite 300
Washington, DC 20005
Website: www.aamft.org
Members/Purpose: Professional society of marriage and family therapists.

Training: Has accredited training centers throughout the United States.

Journals/Publications: Directory of clinical members and approved supervisors; *Family Therapy News*; *Journal of Marital and Family Therapy*; membership directory.

Job Listings: See *Family Therapy News*.

American Association for Music Therapy, Inc.

P.O. Box 80012

Valley Forge, PA 19484

Members/Purpose: Certified music therapists, students in music therapy, colleges and universities offering music therapy programs, and individuals interested in the field. Certifies music therapists.

Journals/Publications: *International Newsletter of Music Therapy*; *Music Therapy*; *Tuning In*.

Job Listings: Offers placement services; see newsletter.

American Dance Therapy Association

2000 Century Plaza, Suite 108

Columbia, MD 21044

Website: www.adta.org

Members/Purpose: Individuals professionally practicing dance therapy, students interested in becoming dance therapists, university departments with dance therapy programs, and individuals in related therapeutic fields. Develops guidelines for educational programs and for approval of programs.

Training: Conducts workshops.

Journals/Publications: *American Journal of Dance Therapy*; membership directory; newsletter.

Job Listings: See newsletter.

American Horticulture Therapy Association

909 York St.

Denver, CO 80206-3799

Website: www.ahta.org

Members/Purpose: Professional horticultural therapists and rehabilitation specialists; horticultural therapy students; institutions and commercial organizations.

Training: Conducts regional workshops and seminars.

Journals/Publications: *AHTA-Newsletter*; *Journal of Therapeutic Horticulture*; membership directory.

American Massage Therapy Association
820 Davis St., Suite 100
Evanston, IL 60201
Website: www.amtamassage.org
Members/Purpose: Massage therapists and technicians.
Training: Offers educational programs.
Journals/Publications: *Hands On*; *Massage Therapy Journal*; membership
registry.

American Occupational Therapy Association
4720 Montgomery Ln.
Bethesda, MD 20824
Website: www.aota.org
Members/Purpose: Registered occupational therapists and certified
occupational therapy assistants who provide services to people whose
lives have been disrupted by physical injury or illness, developmental
problems, the aging process, or social or psychological difficulties.
Journals/Publications: *American Journal of Occupational Therapy*;
Occupational Therapy Week.
Job Listings: See *Occupational Therapy Week*.

American Physical Therapy Association
1111 North Fairfax St.
Alexandria, VA 22314
Website: www.apta.org
Members/Purpose: Professional organization of physical therapists and
physical therapist assistants and students. Fosters the development and
improvement of physical therapy service, education, and research. Acts as
an accrediting body for educational programs in physical therapy.
Journals/Publications: *APTA Progress Report*; *Clinical Management in
Physical Therapy*; *Physical Therapy*; *PT Bulletin*.
Job Listings: Each chapter helps with placement activities.

American Psychoanalytic Association
309 E. 49th St.
New York, NY 10017
Website: www.apsa.org
Members/Purpose: Psychoanalysts who have graduated from or are
currently attending an accredited institution.
Journals/Publications: *Journal of the American Psychoanalytic Association*;
APA-Newsletter; roster.

Federation of Behavioral, Psychological and Cognitive Sciences
c/o David Johnson, Ph.D.
750 1st St. NW, Room 5004
Washington, DC 20002
Website: www.am.org
Members/Purpose: Scientific societies representing research scientists.
Promotes research in behavioral, psychological, and cognitive sciences
and their physiological bases and applications in health, education, and
human development.
Journals/Publications: Annual report; *Federation News*; science and public
policy seminar transcripts.

Institute for Expressive Analysis
c/o Dr. Arthur Robbins
325 West End Ave., 12B
New York, NY 10023
Members/Purpose: To provide professional training; moderate-cost
treatment services, including individual and group psychotherapy,
marriage and family counseling, and crisis intervention; consultative
services for mental health professionals, corporations, and community
agencies; research programs in applied psychology.
Training: Sponsors workshops.
Journals/Publications: *Journal of Rational-Emotive and Cognitive Behavior
Therapy.*

National Association for Drama Therapy
5505 Connecticut Ave. NW, #280
Washington, DC 20015
Website: www.nadt.org
Members/Purpose: Drama therapists and others interested in the field of
drama therapy, including those in psychotherapy, rehabilitation, and
education professions. Develops criteria and standards of training for
drama therapists; maintains a system of registration and peer review.
Training: Sponsors educational events.
Journals/Publications: *Dramascope*; membership list registry; proceedings
of annual conference.
Job Listings: See *Dramascope*.

National Association for Music Therapy, Inc.
8455 Colesville Rd., Suite 1000
Silver Spring, MD 20310
Website: www.namt.com

Members/Purpose: Music therapists, physicians, psychologists, administrators, and educators concerned with music in therapy. Aims to establish qualifications and standards of training for music therapists.

Journals/Publications: *Journal of Music Therapy*; *Music Therapy Perspectives*; *NAMT Notes*; NAMT membership directory.

Job Listings: Maintains placement services.

National Therapeutic Recreation Society
22377 Belmont Ridge Rd.
Asburn, VA 20148
Website: www.nrpa.org

Members/Purpose: Professional personnel whose full-time employment is directly related to the therapeutic application of recreation in clinical, residential, or community programs for people with disabilities.

Journals/Publications: *NTRS Newsletter*; *Parks and Recreation*; *Therapeutic Recreation Journal*.

Job Listings: See newsletter.

CHAPTER FOURTEEN

PATH 5: TEACHING

Perhaps the most familiar career path for those considering using their psychology education as a primary skill would be college teaching. It is certainly the role model for employment the student of psychology has seen most often and it may be that a particular teacher was the inspiration for the choice of major in college.

It is an attractive life to work with a body of information you love, and to share that enjoyment with countless students through the years. There is learning for the instructor, as well, which adds its own excitement. Most teachers readily admit that they enjoy being students, and good teachers come to the classroom as ready to learn from students as students arrive hoping to learn from their teachers. Good teachers maintain a regular program of professional development, continuing to learn new classroom techniques, improve their teaching methods, and add to their body of knowledge.

In any academic institution, there is a fellowship and camaraderie among teachers. They share anecdotes about techniques that have or have not worked in the classroom, and many can also share an interest in the growth and development of particular students they have interacted with through the years. Students often come back and visit their formative teachers and that brings its own rewards to the teacher.

Talk to psych professors you know and they'll tell you a surprising fact about their profession. They don't teach psychology, they teach students! The art of teaching and the skills required in handling the dynamics of student interaction are equally as important as knowledge of the course content. Your psychology classroom will be populated with many students majoring in psychology and your presentation of this material will weigh heavily in their consideration of continuing their studies in the major. But you'll also have many nonmajors who are taking your course as a general education requirement or for a minor, who represent different ages, cultural backgrounds, biases, and issues, and who sit in your class with dramatically different degrees of interest in the subject and the teacher. With all that in the way, simply having a love of psychology yourself is not enough, though that is certainly important and desirable. How could you begin to teach something you didn't truly enjoy and expect not to convey that disinterest through a mechanical approach to the subject?

Teaching something is an entirely different art beyond knowing something and demands additional skills. It has very little to do with your own proficiency in the subject. The world is full of extremely skillful practitioners who, for one reason or another and quite often inexplicably, cannot teach someone how they do it. The practice of something is very different from professing it in a classroom.

For example, planning for learning outcomes is critical. Teaching psychology within an established college curriculum means corresponding to some departmental goals and course outlines. Unless you've designed the course, there will be a written course description in the catalog. To accomplish this body of learning within a set time period requires judicious planning of the material. What will be done each day? How much time to allow between assignments, readings, and labs? What materials to require and what to only recommend? Scores of decisions must be made about how material will be introduced, presented, and ultimately delivered back to you for evaluation.

Add to this the fact that students learn in different ways; some are auditory learners who enjoy listening and gain most of their information in this way. If they are required to take notes *and* listen, something may have to give, and it may be difficult for them to retain the material. For others, auditory learning is less successful and they prefer a visual approach with board work, videos, handouts, their own notes, diagrams, books, and many visual materials. They retain these images and can call them up to remember the material.

Others need to participate through reading in class, role plays, team projects, and other activities that physically involve them. They learn best this way. These are kinesthetic learners, and they are often forgotten in planning and curriculum design. The professional teacher ensures that the class is satisfying the learning styles of all the students through judicious combinations of modalities in teaching. The professional teacher has analyzed his or her own teaching style and seeks to incorporate those other elements that come less naturally to ensure all students are reached.

The teaching and learning that takes place in a class is not static. The classroom is an emotionally charged environment for the student and instructor that may call into play questions of self-esteem and competency. People are exploring new definitions of themselves in relation to their capabilities, values, or achievements. A good teacher understands this and encourages a risk-free environment of mutual appreciation and participation. Both teacher and student are allowed to make mistakes and move on. The teacher strives to assist in establishing congruence between the self (who we know we are right now), the ideal self (who we want to be), and the learning environment being created in the classroom. Hopefully, the classroom will be a place where the student can rise up and begin to touch his or her ideal self.

Any mention of competency, self-esteem, or self-worth naturally suggests the subject of grading and the evaluation teachers provide. Grades are an expected and required part of many institutional academic settings. Establishing fair and consistent standards of evaluating your students and assigning grades is a significant challenge to many teachers who otherwise feel perfectly competent in the teaching role. Students, too, often complain about grading practices in teachers they, in every other respect, have positive feelings about.

The teacher of psychology is called upon to play other roles, too. Animating the class and inspiring attention and commitment to the material are all required in teaching. Part of this is the teacher's enthusiasm, part is teaching style, and part is effective use of ancillary materials and the ability to relate this material to a student's life. Psychology teachers, of course, present information and demonstrate schools of psychology, the psychology of developmental stages, and a variety of systems approaches to the diagnosis, treatment, and care of those people who have a mental illness or a handicap. They seek to raise relevant questions, prompt dialogues within the class, and develop within students the discipline of self-questioning. They clarify difficulties or obscurities in the material and draw parallels or find relationships between examples.

For a professional teacher, each class is not only an opportunity to teach the subject, but also to teach how to learn, as well. How to question, how to record information, how to be selective, and how to retain information is an ongoing lesson that takes place in every classroom to some degree.

Good teachers also use the class and the material to explain how this material reflects feelings. They will share their own agreement with or support of ideas or emotions in the material under study. Most of all, instructors will evaluate and, by example, develop the student's capacity for self-evaluation through careful, caring feedback about both in-class and out-of-class work. The instructors' own examples of preparation, organization, personal appearance, evaluation standards, student interest, and enthusiasm will remain examples long after the memory of the actual class content may have faded.

Teachers are very frequently cited as important factors in our choice of a career. Very often teachers will remember one or two of *their* teachers who were strong influences on their decision to teach. Much of that influence was a result of their presence in the classroom. They served as models of people enjoying what they were doing and doing it skillfully. They were professional and correct yet remained natural and approachable. We could watch and listen to them and think, "Maybe I could do that."

DEFINITION OF THE CAREER PATH

We'll focus on two levels of degree attainment in this teaching career path: the master's and doctoral degrees. Both degree earners will find employment in college settings; however, the doctorate in psychology is preeminently the degree of choice and will make the largest number of positions available to you. Even here, however, there are caveats because the specialization possibilities at both the master's and doctoral levels in psychology are dizzying, and many faculty position descriptions that we will presented in this section are specific in the research interests they hope an applicant will add to their faculty.

Areas of Specialization

Teachers of psychology can focus their research and teaching efforts in at least one of many different areas, including

Neuropsychology	Differential diagnosis
Forensic assessment	Cross-cultural psychology
Hypnotherapy	Industrial psychology
Humanistic psychology	Clinical psychology
Medical psychology	Community mental health
Counseling psychology	Psychology of aging
Adolescent psychology	Developmental psychology
History of psychology	Psychotherapy
Child/Family behavior therapy	Psychology of imagery
Psychiatric rehabilitation	Physiological psychology
Social psychology	Systems of psychology
Cognitive and human memory	Perception
Experimental social psychology	Environmental psychology
Developmental psychobiology	Applied psychology
Cognitive and mathematical	Learning
Psychology	Psychology of self

Some of these areas may be vaguely familiar to you from your undergraduate survey courses. Others are completely foreign. It can be a bewilderingly long list, and even if some of these specialties do seem interesting, you are probably asking yourself, "How do you become knowledgeable about these areas?" The answer in most cases is in the early days of your graduate degree work. You may be in a doctoral program that does not necessarily require a stopping off point at the master's level, or you may decide to begin with a master's degree and then reevaluate your position before launching yourself on the doctoral course. For many, there is a change of university affiliation between the master's and doctoral degrees that comes about in a search of a particular field of study or to associate with a department known for some research focus or simply to expose oneself to new faculty with new perspectives.

Teaching with a Master's Degree

Interesting enough, there are college positions for the master's-level degree holder in psychology. Review this job description, which presents specific demands for expertise within psychology as well:

Psychology Instructor. Master's degree in psychology. Neurological and cognitive psychology background. Expertise using statistical software (e.g., SPSS, Minitab, or SAS). Candidate must be prepared to teach all course offerings in psychology (general psychology, psychology of adjustment, human relations, and child psychology). Two years of college teaching. Experience with computerized instructional technology. Ability to employ new pedagogies and information technologies both in the classroom and at a distance. Candidates will be required to demonstrate teaching ability through a miniinstructional session during the interview process. Salary based upon degrees and previous experience, $36,045 to $67,237.

Similar positions, even those requiring a high level of specialization, can be found in community colleges or small enrollment schools. A rewarding teaching career in psychology at the college level with a master's degree is possible. Two-year and community college work can provide a long and productive career within the same institution or provide the opportunity for a lateral move to a similar type of institution. At the same time, however, it is important to caution you that if you are interested in moving from that type of institution to a four-year college or university, it may be difficult without an advanced degree, despite the fact that you may have years of teaching experience.

There are also some jobs teaching at the four-year college level with a master's degree in psychology. Nevertheless, the movement, expectation, and market demand would be for the doctoral degree, and it is that degree that will provide the most security of both employment and employment opportunities for a teaching career at the college and university level.

Teaching with a Doctoral Degree

The doctoral degree in psychology opens up the world of college and university teaching to the prospective educator. Competition here is keen for positions advertised in vehicles such as *The Chronicle of Higher Education* (www.chronicle.com) a weekly newspaper reporting on higher education issues and containing the most complete listing of faculty, staff, and leadership position openings for colleges and universities in the United States and some foreign countries. The following are ads from *The Chronicle* that would be of interest to a new Ph.D. in psychology.

Psychology. Tenure-track position in multicultural/Hispanic psychology: Department of psychology at Utah State University, Logan, Utah. Candidates should possess a Ph.D. and will teach psychology and research methods as well as upper level courses. See (website) or call . . .

Psychology. Assistant Professor, teach cognitive neuroscience, cognition, motivation and emotion, psychopharmacology, advanced physiological psychology lab, and introduction to psychology. Interest in cognition and study of neural processes in marine invertebrates desired. Ph.D. required.

Psychology. Experience teaching introductory to advanced undergraduate psychology classes generating consistently positive evaluations, and a willingness to innovate. Completed Ph.D. from APA-accredited clinical program, teaching excellence, strong liberal arts record, demonstrated scholarship, related experience desirable. Send letter of interest, three letters of recommendation, statement of research interest, and curriculum vitae to . . .

The road to a doctorate is fairly long and arduous. It is hard work. Along the way, you'll meet some wonderful people, some who'll be friends and colleagues the rest of your life. Even colleagues separated by long distances have the opportunity to revisit at conferences and symposia. Creating and maintaining this network plays an important role in the work of academicians.

The Earned Doctorate Versus ABD

All of these ads are interesting because they require an *earned* doctorate. To apply, you must have your degree in hand. Some advertisements will encourage the application of ABD (All But Dissertation) candidates who have not yet, but are soon, to complete their degree work. A position requiring an earned doctorate will pay more than an ABD position and will lead more directly and quickly to possible tenure and promotion. The ABD candidate will also have to decide how they will finish their degree (the dissertation often being the most time-consuming aspect of their academics) *and* hold down a full-time job.

Especially in psychology, because of the sensitive nature of the material being presented, colleges and universities of even modest size are going to seek the most credentialed and skilled faculty they can find and afford. Larger and more prestigious schools with significant research agendas will be even more demanding of the background of their faculty.

You'll have opportunities to write, teach, and perhaps publish—all before you finish your degree. Take advantage of these opportunities when you can. As the advertisements suggest, some of those kinds of qualifications will be asked of you. However, it is possible to become overly involved in some of these areas to the detriment of degree progress.

OTHER ISSUES FOR TEACHERS OF PSYCHOLOGY

Many of the ads we provide suggest issues important for both master's and doctoral degree holders.

- Demonstrating cultural sensitivity
- Documenting teaching effectiveness
- Developing a track record in research, publications, and presentations
- Providing community service

Position descriptions such as those provided throughout this path allow candidates to approach the hiring process with their eyes wide open.

Demonstrating Cultural Sensitivity

Some of the advertisements make demands for cultural sensitivity. This is prompted in part by the location of the particular school advertising for faculty. They may have a student body that is highly diverse. In other cases, it is a sincere attempt on the hiring institution's part to increase sensitivity and awareness of whatever diversity does exist on the campus. Here's an advertisement for a psychology professorship from *The Chronicle of Higher Education* that speaks specifically to the diversity possible in the classroom:

> *Psychology Instructor.* Master's degree in psychology, Ph.D. preferred. Primary responsibilities and interest must be in teaching at the freshman/sophomore level. Candidate must be able to teach a wide variety of courses in the field and have the ability and flexibility to teach students from multicultural backgrounds.

If you were teaching in a multicultural class with an Asian complement to the student body, it would be highly inappropriate and a good example of cultural bias to indicate in a class discussion on symptomatic behavior, that a failure to make direct and sustained eye contact with a physician was significant. Many Asian races do not make direct eye contact except to intimates and even more seldom to authority figures.

Gender-biased language, ignorance of cultures and customs, and inconsiderate choice of texts or illustrative materials from a diversity perspective only serves to impugn your teaching and undermine your credibility. It is in your best interest to broaden your horizons and ensure your class is an inclusive and welcoming one.

Documenting Teaching Effectiveness

In one ad, documentation of positive student evaluations is requested. This could come from graduate teaching assistantships done while working on the doctoral degree. Many students acquire this experience as part-time faculty, lecturers, or adjunct faculty at other colleges or programs. Summaries of student teaching evaluations that you received while gaining this experience can be used to document teaching success.

Developing a Track Record in Research, Publications, and Presentations

Some institutions of higher learning emphasize the teaching role and do not put excessive demands on faculty to "publish or perish." Other institutions place a high value on research and publications and a determined effort by faculty exists to find good research projects and then publish them.

What's more important to mention here is, regardless of the posture of your institution vis-à-vis research and publications, as a teacher, there should be an interest in sharing what you know with a larger audience. This may be accomplished through writing books, articles, or monographs. For others, it may be that public presentations at seminars, workshops, and conferences are the venue that suits their style best. In questions of promotion and tenure, your record of sharing your technical and professional expertise will be examined.

Providing Community Service

Colleges and universities have always been part of the larger communities in which they reside. Faculty and staff are often called upon to give back to the community that houses them. It can take many forms for the institution: an annual clean-up day or allowing local organizations to use performing spaces or open fields for special events.

For the psychology faculty, the need for outreach is very great. Local counseling hotlines may need staffers or someone to train the staffers. Any number of local shelters or halfway houses may need skilled volunteers to take client histories or do referrals with other helping agencies. Teen drop-in sexuality information clinics, local civic groups needing speakers, a variety of board of trustee opportunities—all of these could benefit from the psychology faculty member's involvement and attention.

HOW LONG DOES IT TAKE TO GET A DOCTORATE?

There has been considerable discussion in academic circles about the number of individuals who begin doctoral programs and do not see them through to completion. In fact, Neil Rudenstine, the president of Harvard University, coauthored a book that discusses the issue of improving and tightening up the time requirements to earn a Ph.D., particularly in the humanities.[1] His research dearly demonstrated that the timeline between initiating the

1. *In Pursuit of the PhD*, by William G. Bowen and Neil L. Rudenstine, Princeton University Press, 1992.

Ph.D. degree and earning it (elapsed time-to-degree[2]) in candidates earning a social science degree (which includes psychology) was among the longest of all degrees being sought. Not all students who begin a Ph.D. program complete it, so there is a correspondingly high rate of mortality that goes along with this issue of time-to-degree.

The important point is that doctoral work comes at a time in many young people's lives when, after sixteen or more years of education, no matter how fascinating the advanced study, distractions occur. They may be relationships, a strong biological imperative to begin a family, economic pressures to leave school and earn an income, or simply fatigue. Consequently, the dropout rate has been disappointingly high, especially when doctoral programs are not sufficiently explicit about requirements and the time it takes to complete a degree.

WORKING CONDITIONS

The working conditions for college teachers of psychology may vary somewhat according to the institution, but there is enough commonality of experience that we can make some generalizations. Many people consider a college teaching environment one of the most attractive work settings imaginable. There is less need to appease a number of outside publics. There is no school board to satisfy, no parents, no parent-teacher groups. Students are there voluntarily, and the upper-level classes are populated with psychology majors who love their subject and are interested in doing the work required to succeed in their courses.

Academic Freedom

The world of the college classroom is closed to outsiders. It is, in fact, rare to have a class interrupted by anyone outside of the room, so understood is this convention. Generally, the concept of academic freedom has allowed professors to express themselves within their class material with far greater pointedness than is the case in other teaching environments, and the system protects their right to do so. However, an increasing number of successful lawsuits and harassment claims are being made by students against faculty for what they perceive to be an improper use of the teaching platform. On campuses where this has occurred, concern and debate continue.

....

2. Elapsed time-to-degree: number of years between entry to graduate school and the awarding of the Ph.D.

Grading, evaluation procedures, numbers of tests, even the issue of whether to have textbooks or texts is entirely up to the faculty member, and if the rationale supports these decisions, the university would not interfere.

All of these conditions make the classroom environment and the relations of faculty and students very different than what has come before in the student's education.

Tenure

An added protection is the granting of tenure to established professors who have documented significant teaching histories and excellent student reviews, publications, campus committee work, and outreach to the community. The granting of tenure adds an additional degree of job security and further supports their expression of academic freedom. Colleges and universities have strict guidelines for promotion and tenure that may put strong emphasis and pressure on the faculty member to write, do research, deliver papers at professional meetings, and become involved in outreach to the community and in-college service in order to rise in academic rank or even hold their position at that institution.

Administrative Duties

In some departments the role of chair of the department is rotated, and all faculty are expected to serve a term. In other institutions, the chair is a hotly contested office.

Department-chair duties involve overseeing the scheduling of each semester's courses and assigning faculty responsibility for those course offerings. They may include hiring part-time faculty and adjuncts to meet demand or replace faculty on sabbatical. It may involve negotiations with other administrators for additional classroom space.

Supervision of the department budget is the chair's responsibility, and this includes monitoring expenditures for supplies, special events, faculty development, and travel. Faculty often lobby intensely for travel and professional development funds from the chair who must exercise impartiality and discretion in administering these funds.

Department meetings are called and run by the chair, who sets the meeting's agenda. These may be as frequent as every week and even in large departments will occur monthly.

Many colleges and universities hold a council of chairs to address issues such as curriculum changes, general education requirements, faculty standards, and other interrelated issues.

Facilities and Support

Facilities tend to be excellent, including laboratories, and there is usually adequate support staff to type materials, do copying, and prepare testing materials. A private office is usually provided, and a varied menu of faculty privileges may be available. Computers are usually provided for writing, research, library access, and data manipulation.

Work Schedule

The actual teaching time in a college or university setting involves about ten class hours per week. At an institution that focuses on faculty research, the teacher would be responsible for teaching two to three courses that each meet three to four hours per week. Schools that emphasize teaching rather than research require instructors to teach three to four courses for a total of nine to twelve hours of class meetings per week. These class hours and some mandated office hours for advising class students and general advisees are the principal requirements for attendance on the faculty member's part. But as the ads below make clear, there are other expectations:

Psychology. ABD. Doctorate completed by June 1 required. Prefer Ph.D. in psychology. Teaching responsibilities in the areas of research methods, advanced experimental, sensation and perception, and other undergraduate courses in an area of interest that matches departmental goals. Commitment to undergraduate research preparation of psychology majors is of primary importance. Interest in integrating multicultural and diversity issues into psychology courses and fostering a climate open to students from diverse backgrounds. Undergraduate advising. Additional responsibilities may include faculty advisor for Psychology Club/Psi Chi and coordinator of preprofessional focus. Send graduate transcripts, teaching evaluations, and evidence of teaching effectiveness to . . .

Psychology. Tenure-track position to start in fall. Child-clinical psychology with an ability to teach courses in developmental psychopathology, child therapy, general psychology, and other teaching as well as research and service to the academic community . . .

A college day is certainly not a rigid routine. Class schedules are the fixed element; beyond those, much is up to the involvement and activity level of

dual faculty member. Certainly, it can be busy and long. The college
ay feel institutional and professional pressures to fulfill certain roles,
ctual election of how to do that is up to the individual. Classes,
urs, meetings, and research work will be required. Because college
are often wonderful centers of art, music, and intellectual exchange,
frequently events to attend in the evening. Faculty members may act
as advisors to fraternities, sororities, campus newspapers, or clubs, and that
may also add to their day.

Teaching Introductory Courses

Most advertisements also indicate that the successful candidate will be teaching general psychology classes. Teaching introduction to psychology classes
is generally part of the teaching load of new college psychology faculty. Many
of these students will be taking introduction to psychology because it is a
college requirement for graduation and part of a general education core curriculum and not because they are psychology majors or have deliberately chosen the course. The psychology department performs a service to the entire
college in offering this course. Of course, for many students, regardless of
how they found their way to the class, this introductory course may prove
to be an exciting introduction to a field of study they had not considered
previously. Many majors are introduced through these generally required
courses. Even senior faculty will teach at least one offering of introduction
to psychology, though as you become more senior in the faculty you can take
on courses that are more directly related to your interests and educational
background.

Scholarly Research

In addition to courses and advising, scholarly research is an expectation even
of those colleges for whom tenure is not based on publication. All colleges
want their faculty to contribute to the scholarly dialogue in their discipline,
and this is reviewed by chairs of departments and academic deans periodi-
cally throughout the instructor's career. It may be a determining element in
granting tenure or promotion to that faculty member and may influence
issues such as salary negotiations and merit increases.

Committee Work

Committee work is also important because the faculty at most colleges are
the governing and rule-making bodies who determine and vote on governance
and program changes. Committee work can be issue oriented, such as a commission on the status of women or a female faculty pay equity survey; it may

be programmatic, such as a committee to study the core curriculum for undergraduates or to devise a new graphic arts major; it may be related to credentials as in a committee set up to prepare materials for an accreditation visit.

Some committees, such as academic standards, curriculum review, promotion and tenure, and planning and administrator-review committees, are permanent, though the members may change on a rotating schedule. Other groups are formed for a limited time or until completion of some task. These committees are essential and are one vehicle for guiding the direction of the school. Having the support of all the faculty and constantly fresh and interested members helps to ensure all voices are heard and many different opinions are considered in making what are often far-reaching decisions.

TRAINING AND QUALIFICATIONS

Most four-year colleges and universities would require that job candidates possess a doctorate in psychology and usually will, in addition, look for specialized areas of research, publication, prior teaching, and/or clinical experience. Occasionally, a college will hire faculty on a nontenured basis with less than a doctoral degree, but generally, the larger the institution, the less likely that this will be the case. Salary and assignments may be affected by lack of an earned doctorate.

If hired without an earned doctoral degree, there may be a stipulation in the contract at hiring indicating how much time can elapse before the degree must be earned. The difficulty here would then be your ability to finish the degree (for many the dissertation is the most challenging and time-consuming aspect of the degree) while holding down a full-time job. This certainly needs to be considered in your negotiations.

Seasoned scholars work with students at the very senior levels of graduate work for both master's and doctoral degrees. These scholars enhance their own unique areas of expertise as students pursue their degrees. Classes may be very small at this level, even at a large university, and the work is highly collaborative. Your teaching work at this level may be reduced to allow for pure research and writing in your areas of interest and scholarship, and you will be called upon frequently to speak to professional and scholarly groups about that research.

EARNINGS

The average faculty salary in 1998–99 for psychology positions in four-year colleges or universities was $55,633 at public institutions and $51,748 at private institutions. Instructors who are ABD or newly degreed Ph.D.s can expect to earn a salary in the $35,000–$40,000 range. Salary will vary by discipline taught and by geographic location of a given position. The American Pyschological Association's website (www.apa.org) makes available current salary information. After searching their site for salary surveys, one table revealed salaries for full-time faculty in the United Stated in master's degree departments by subfield, rank, and years in rank, Salaries for the 10 percent, 25 percent, 50 percent, 75 percent, 90 percent, and mean for each category were shown. The APA's website had a wealth of information to offer those students interested in pursuing a graduate degree and using it to teach.

CAREER OUTLOOK

As you consider employment in academe, one important trend worth researching is the increasing use of part-time faculty. In 1970, 22 percent of the professoriate worked part time. As we begin the twenty-first century, the figure has grown to almost 50 percent. There are many reasons for the shift, but the bottom line for you is that there is heavy competition for full-time positions in higher education.

Other factors worth researching are current trends in the use of tenure; population trends and the resulting number of students expected to attend college; whether a minimum faculty retirement age is currently required; and the number of individuals currently pursuing advanced degrees in psychology.

Given your investment of time and financial resources you have much to consider. Both the Chronicle of Higher Education's website (www.chronicle. org) and the American Association of University Professors' website (www.aaup.org) will have the latest information on these topics.

STRATEGY FOR FINDING THE JOBS

After you have invested so many years in acquiring the educational credentials required for teaching psychology in higher education, you will want to be sure to employ a useful strategy for gaining work. This strategy should include being prepared to relocate, getting your curriculum vitae in shape, using well-established job listings such as *The Chronicle of Higher Education*, networking with faculty colleagues, and attending professional meetings. Be sure to enhance your strategy as you decide on the area of psychology you will specialize in by talking with mentors and career development professionals.

Be Prepared to Relocate

Acquiring a college teaching position in psychology nearly always means that you will have to relocate to an institution other than where you received your degree. Higher education has limited openings at any one time. You increase your opportunities for securing a college teaching post as you expand the boundaries of where you will consider relocating.

Like many graduate students, you may have enjoyed some part-time teaching employment at your degree-granting institution. Often, there is an opportunity to teach as an adjunct faculty member for a limited period. Adjunct positions are used to staff introductory courses or to complete staffing shortages during national searches for permanent full-time faculty. Adjunct or part-time work is wonderful experience and will be an excellent recommendation to an institution considering your application. It is seldom, however, a guarantee of earning a full-time spot at your own school.

Most psychology departments have budget "lines" dedicated to full-time tenured faculty. That means that faculty who are hired in those budget lines are hired with the expectation they will become permanent members of the faculty and earn tenure and promotion when they are qualified.

Consequently, though there may be schools you would enjoy teaching at or areas of the country you would prefer to live, the supply and demand of college professorships dearly dictate you must follow the demand and relocate.

Though it may be disappointing to feel your job search is completely dictated by marketplace demands, if you talk to some of your own faculty mentors, you will learn how it was for them in their job search. Most of them have relocated as well. In our conversations with faculty colleagues, time and again they will mention their real pleasure at discovering a new area of the country new activities, and new awarenesses as they moved with their careers. College communities the world over tend to be centers of exchange, with speakers, arts events, celebrations, and a year-round calendar of activities for people of all ages and interests. Because of the college population, many have good shopping and excellent services. They are wonderful communities in which to live, raise a family, and retire.

Get Your Curriculum Vitae in Shape

Higher education places some different demands on the job seeker. In place of the resume, teaching candidates use a document called the *curriculum vitae*. It's a Latin term that means "the course of one's life." A curriculum vitae shares many similarities with the resume and some significant differences.

Many job seekers in higher education forget some of the resume, or in this case, curriculum-vitae basics as they begin their job search. Candidates tend to focus on their educational, teaching, research, and other experience so that they often overlook some of the very basic techniques that are important to use on this document.

The academic job search is competitive, and no matter how excellent your credentials, you still need to pay attention to assembling a package of materials that is professional, accurate, complete, and that will make an impact on the selection committee whose task it is to review these packets.

Ask yourself the following questions:

1. Have you customized your vitae for each position you apply for? If not, you should. Each advertisement reflects what type of background is important for that position, and your vitae should dearly announce, "I have the background and experiences you are seeking!" So, if multicultural awareness is mentioned as a need and you have served on a diversity task force, be certain that you list it on your vitae.

2. Is your document neat and easily read? Too much text with little white space or margins invites fatigue. You may have to go to multiple pages to create an inviting format.

3. Does your document look inviting or forbidding? Bright white paper with black lettering is hard on the eyes. Choose a soft cream or off-white to soften the contrast.

4. Will the selection committee be able to identify the categories of information you have included on your resume? Use **bold letters**, <u>underlining</u>, and indented sections to help accomplish this. Your campus career office can provide good guidance on these technical aspects of your curriculum vitae.

5. Have you organized and listed relevant coursework according to what the institution is asking that you be able to teach? Remember, readers of English read from top to bottom, and in scanning a vitae, committee members may only read the first couple items on a list, or the first phrase of a description. Always place the most salient information first.

We have included a sample curriculum vitae that might be typical for a newly minted Ph.D. in psychology seeking a first permanent teaching position in higher education. Your college career office will have many additional samples, and you can also review VGM's *How to Prepare Your Curriculum Vitae Second Edition*.

Exhibit 15.1

Sample Curriculum Vitae

WENDY PALMS
Curriculum Vitae

18 Main Street
San Francisco, CA 04131   (415) 555-5555

EDUCATION   Ph.D., Human Development & Family Studies,
2002
Cornell University, Ithaca, NY

Bachelor of Arts Degree in Psychology, 1995
Pomona College, Claremont, CA

SCHOLARSHIPS   NICHD Traineeship in Cognitive Development
& HONORS   Cornell University, 1994–1995

Mortar Board, Pomona College, 1994

TEACHING   Lecturer, University of Manitoba, 2000–2002
General Psychology, Child Development,
Adolescent Development

Teaching Assistant, Cornell University,
1999–2000
General Psychology

PROFESSIONAL   American Psychological Association
ORGANIZATIONS   • Division: Developmental Psychology
• Division: Teaching of Psychology

Society for Research in Child Development

PUBLICATIONS   Palms, W. J., Formal operational reasoning
and the primary effect in impression
formation, *Developmental Psychology*, 2001.

Will, J. P., and Palms, W. J., Social cognition
and social relationships in early adolescence.
*International Journal of Behavioral
Development*, 1992.

continued

continued

SUBMITTED FOR PUBLICATION   Palms, W. J., Who goes with whom? Early adolescent girls' perceptions of peer group structure.

PAPERS   Palms, W. J., Formal operational reasoning and the primacy effect in impression formation. Paper presented at the biennial meeting of the Society for Research in Child Development, 2000.

Palms, W. J., Formal operational reasoning and the primacy effect in impression formation. Doctoral dissertation, Cornell University, 2002.

Palms, W. J., Variables related to patterns of social exchange. Paper presented at the annual meeting of the American Psychological Association, 2000.

COMMITTEES   Graduate School Council, Cornell University, 1998–2000

Student Representative, Board of Trustees, Pomona College, 1994–1995

REFERENCES   Furnished upon request.

GO TO "THE SOURCE" TO REVIEW JOB LISTINGS

The Chronicle of Higher Education is the weekly national publication listing junior college, four-year college, and university teaching positions in psychology. Many of these advertisements are large display ads that detail in full the requirements and duties of the positions advertised. This publication is widely available on college campuses, and usually many offices have individual subscriptions. Your career center, department office, and college library will all have copies you can review each week. *The Chronicle* is also available on-line (www.chronicle.com).

Network with Faculty Colleagues

Another excellent resource for college-level positions will be the faculty colleague contacts you make as you pursue your advanced degree. There is a well-established network that becomes very active when schools are seeking to fill a position. Many search committees rely on the personal recommendation of a friend or former teaching associate to do the very best by the hiring institution.

This is a referral network, not a placement service. Your colleagues will be suggesting your name as an applicant. There are no guarantees, and all positions at this level must go through a search committee and interviews. Nevertheless, a recommendation to apply from a colleague is a strong beginning.

For this reason, it's important to ensure that your faculty mentors and colleagues are well aware of your teaching and research interests and geographic preferences so they can respond for you and move the process along if an opportunity presents itself.

Attend Professional Meetings

Professional meetings, seminars, and conferences allow you to meet and listen to representatives from many institutions. You become aware of research initiatives and many of the current issues in academe. Familiar faces will begin to appear as you continue on the conference circuit. Don't hesitate to submit your own proposals for presentations. It's a good way to share your scholarship and indicates your willingness to do outreach.

Interviews are also often conducted at professional meetings where recent job openings may be announced or posted in a conspicuous place at the registration table. As a graduate student, many of these conferences are available to you at substantially reduced fees, and you should take advantage of them for the professional content and the opportunity to meet representatives from the departments of other higher education institutions.

POSSIBLE EMPLOYERS

In teaching, the possible employers are well documented. There is no "hidden job market," and most schools advertise widely. We have identified resources that can provide the names of potential employers.

Directories

Some resources that can be used to identify schools if you are considering teaching psychology include *Peterson's Guide to Two-Year Colleges*, *Peterson's*

Guide to Four-Year Colleges, Peterson's Guides to Graduate Study, and *The College Board Index of Majors and Graduate Degrees*. Peterson's website (www.petersons.com) allows you to sort schools by specific majors offered, including psychology.

Career Office Postings

Career offices often carry national job vacancy listings, which include teaching positions. Some of these listings include *Current Jobs for Graduates in Education, The Job Hunter, Community Jobs, Current Jobs for Graduates,* and *The Chronicle of Higher Education.*

Many career offices also receive individual job posting fliers directly from institutions looking to hire psychology faculty. Be sure to find out if your institution receives these notices.

Psychology Department Postings

Sometimes when a hiring institution is seeking to fill a position under pressures of time, they will send notices of position openings to every school offering a graduate program in psychology. Be sure to find out where the psychology department posts these notices at your school. Often you'll find them on a bulletin board near the department chair's office or the department secretary's desk.

Professional Associations

In addition, be sure to carefully review the list of professional associations for teachers of psychology that ends this chapter. For several associations there is a line labeled "Job Listings," and any activities that the association undertakes to assist its members in finding employment are shown. These include professional meetings for sharing resumes, newsletters that contain job openings or positions wanted, and advertising space in journals.

POSSIBLE JOB TITLES

Job titles for positions relating to teaching and research in psychology will be fairly standard: teacher or researcher. Position descriptions will list areas of educational and research specialization required for the position. In both teaching and research, a specialization can be developed in one of the following fields.

Clinical psychology
Community psychology
Counseling psychology
Developmental psychology
Educational psychology
Environmental psychology
Experimental psychology
Family psychology
Health psychology
Industrial and organizational psychology
Neuropsychology and psychobiology
Psychology of aging
Psychology and law, and forensic psychology
Psychology of women
Psychometrics and quantitative psychology
School psychology
Social psychology

RELATED OCCUPATIONS

If you've earned a master's degree or Ph.D. in psychology, you have developed an extensive knowledge and skill base that would be welcome in many other employment settings. Advanced academic work in psychology is perceived as valuable because it is highly transferable. In addition to your degree work, you would want to be able to satisfy the employer's demand for excellent skills in both verbal and written communications. Your well-developed research skills will be difficult for a commercial employer to assess unless you take the time to learn about their research needs and how you might be able to use your skills in their environment. Consider the following job titles as a beginning list and investigate these and other positions that draw on the skill base you know you possess.

Business manager	Public affairs specialist
Consultant	Researcher
Health professional	Therapist
Human resources	Trainer
professional	Writer
Policy analyst	Salesperson

PROFESSIONAL ASSOCIATIONS

The primary information resource for someone considering a career in teaching psychology at the college or university level is the American Psychological Association. Students are eligible to join at reduced rates, and by doing so they can begin the ever-important tasks of networking and gaining an insight on working as a professional in this field. Review the other associations to see if you feel they can assist you in your job search.

American Psychological Association
750 First St. NE
Washington, DC 20002
Website: www.apa.org
Members/Purpose: Scientific and professional society of psychologists. Students participate as affiliates. Advances psychology as a science, a profession, and a means of promoting human welfare. Maintains forty-six divisions.
Training: Maintains an educational and training board.
Journals/Publications: *Behavioral Neuroscience; Clinician's Research Digest; Contemporary Psychology; Developmental Psychology; Health Psychology; Journal of Abnormal Psychology; Journal of Applied Psychology; Journal of Comparative Psychology; Journal of Consulting and Clinical Psychology; Journal of Counseling Psychology; Journal of Educational Psychology; Journal of Experimental Psychology* (animal behavior processes, general, human perception and performance, learning, memory, and cognition); *Journal of Family Psychology; Journal of Personality and Social Psychology; Neuropsychology; Professional Psychology: Research and Practice; Psychological Abstracts; Psychological Assessment; Psychological Bulletin; Psychological Review: Psychology and Aging; PsychSCAN: Applied Experimental & Engineering Psychology; PsychSCAN: Applied Psychology; PsychSCAN: Developmental Psychology; PsychSCAN: LD/MR; PsychSCAN: Neuropsychology; PsychSCAN: Psychoanalysis.*
Job Listings: Some journals contain classifieds.

American Psychological Practitioners Association
P.O. Box 1585
Cape Canaveral, FL 32920
Members/Purpose: Mental health and psychological practitioners, students, and interested others.
Journals/Publications: APPA directory/register; *Psychological Practitioner.*
Job Listings: Plans to institute placement service.

Association of State and Provincial Psychology Boards
P.O. Box 4389
Montgomery, AL 36103
Website: www.asppb.org
Members/Purpose: Alliance of state, territorial, and provincial agencies responsible for the licensure and certification of psychologists throughout the United States and Canada.
Training: Publishes materials for training programs.
Journals/Publications: *ASPPB Newsletter; Handbook of Licensing and Certification Requirements.*

Association for the Advancement of Psychology
P.O. Box 38129
Colorado Springs, CO 80937
Website: www.aapnet.org
Members/Purpose: Members of APA or other national psychological associations, students of psychology, and organizations with a primarily psychological focus. Advances psychology and represents the interests of all psychologists in the public policy area.
Journals/Publications: *AAP-Advance.*

International Council of Psychologists
c/o Patricia Fontes
P.O. Box 62
Hopkinton, RI 02833
Members/Purpose: Psychologists and individuals professionally active in fields allied to psychology. Advances psychology and furthers the application of its scientific findings.
Training: Conducts continuing education.
Journals/Publications: Directory; *International Psychologist.*

National Education Association
1201 16th St. NW
Washington, DC 20036
Website: www.nea.org
Members/Purpose: Professional organization and union of elementary and secondary school teachers, college and university professors, administrators, principals, counselors, and others concerned with education.
Journals/Publications: *ESP Journal; ESP Progress;* handbook; *NEA Today.*

Psi Chi, The National Honor Society in Psychology
825 Vine St.
P.O. Box 709
Chattanooga, TN 37403
Website: www.psichi.org
Members/Purpose: Honor society for psychology.
Journals/Publications: Handbook; *Psi Chi Newsletter*.

ADDITIONAL RESOURCES

ABI/ Inform on Disk
UMI-Data Courier, Inc
620 South Fifth St.
Louisville, KY 40202

America's Corporate Families
Dun & Bradstreet Information Services
399 Eaton Ave.
Bethlehem, PA 18025

America's Federal Jobs
JIST Works, Inc.
720 N. Park Ave.
Indianapolis, IN 46202
Website: www.jist.com

***America's Top Medical, Education, and
Human Services Jobs***
JIST Works, Inc
720 N. Park Ave.
Indianapolis, IN 46202
Website: www.jist.com

American Bank Directory
McFadden Business Publications
6195 Crooked Creek Rd.
Norcross, GA 30092

American Jewish Year Book
Jewish Publication Society
1930 Chestnut St.
Philadelphia, PA 19103
Website: www.jewishpub.org

Best's Insurance Reports
A.M. Best Co.
Oldwick, NJ 08858
Website: www.ambest.com

The Boston Globe
The Globe Newspaper Co.
135 Morrissey Blvd.
P.O. Box 2378
Boston, MA 02107
Website: www.thebostonglobe.com

The Career Guide: Dun's Employment Opportunities Directory
Dun & Bradstreet Information Services
899 Eaton Ave.
Bethlehem, PA 18025
Website: www.dnb.com

Career Information Center
Macmillan Publishing Group
866 Third Ave.
New York, NY 10022
Website: www.mcp.com

Careers Encyclopedia
VGM Career Books
NTC/Contemporary Publishing Group
4255 West Touhy Ave.
Lincolnwood, IL 60712
Websites: www.vgmbooks.com
www.ntc-cb.com

Careers in Government
Careers in Health Care
Careers in Social and Rehabilitation Services
VGM Career Horizon
NTC/Contemporary Publishing Group
4255 Touhy Ave.
Lincolnwood, IL 60712
Websites: www.vgmbooks.com
www.ntc-cb.com

Careers in State and Local Government
Garrett Parks Press
Garrett Park, MD 20896

Catholic Almanac
Our Sunday Visitor, Publishing Division
200 Noll Plaza
Huntington, IN 46750
Website: www.osv.com

The Chronicle of Higher Education
1255 23rd St. NW
Washington, DC 20037
Website: www.chronicle.com

The College Board Guide to Jobs and Career Planning
by Joyce Mitchell
The College Board
P.O. Box 866
New York, NY 10101
Website: www.collegeboard.org/index.html

College Placement Council Annuals
62 Highland Ave.
Bethlehem, PA 18017
Website: www.naceweb.org/about/

Community Jobs:
The National Employment Newspaper for the Non-Profit Sector
ACCESS: Networking in the Public Interest
50 Beacon St.
Boston, MA 02108
Website: www.accessjobs.org

The Complete Guide to Public Employment
by Ronald Krannich and Caryl Krannich
Impact Publications
4580 Sunshine Ct.
Woodbridge, VA 22192
Website: www.impactpublications.com

The Complete Mental Health Directory, 1999/2000
Grey House Publishing
Pocket Knife Square
Lakeville, CT 06039
Website: www.greyhouse.com

Credit Union Directory and Buyers Group
United Communications Group
11300 Rockville Pike, Suite 1100
Rockville, MD 20850
Website: www.ucg.com

Your Criminal Justice Career: A Guidebook
Prentice Hall
Upper Saddle River, NJ 07458
Website: www.prehall.com

Current Jobs for Graduates
Current Jobs for Graduates in Education
Current Jobs in Writing, Editing & Communications
Plymouth Publishing, Inc.
P.O. Box 40550
5136 MacArthur Blvd. NW
Washington, DC 20016

Dialing for Jobs: Using the Phone in the Job Search (**Video**)
JIST Works, Inc.
720 North Park Ave.
Indianapolis, IN 46202
Website: www.jist.com

Dictionary of Occupational Titles
U.S. Department of Labor
Employment and Training Administration
Distributed by Associated Book Publishers, Inc.
P.O. Box 5657
Scottsdale, AZ 86261
Website: http://stats.bls.gov/oco/ocodot1.htm

Directory of Adventure Alternatives in Corrections Mental Health and Special Populations
Association of Experiential Education
2885 Aurora Ave., No. 28
Boulder, CO 80303
Website: www.aee.org

Directory of American Firms Operating in Foreign Countries
World Trade Academy Press
50 E. 42nd St.
New York, NY 10017
Website: www.iteams.org

Directory of Bond Agents
Standard and Poor's Corp.
25 Broadway
New York, NY 10004
Website: www.standardpoor.com

Directory of Public School Systems in the U.S.
Association for School, College, and University Staffing (ASCUS)
c/o High School
1600 Dodge Ave., No. 5-300
Evanston, IL 60204
Website: www.ub-careers.buffalo.edu/AAEE

DISCOVER
American College Testing
Educational Services Division
P.O. Box 16
Iowa City, IA 52244
Website: www.act.org/discover/

Effective Answers to Interview Questions (video)
JIST Works, Inc.
720 North Park Ave.
Indianapolis, IN 46202
Website: www.jist.com

Encyclopedia of Associations
Gale Group
P.O. Box 33477
Detroit, MI 48232
Website: www.gale.com

Environmental Opportunities
Environmental Studies Department
Antioch/New England Graduate School
Keene, NH 03431
Website: www.antiochne.edu/prospects/esm/esmdept

Equal Employment Opportunity Bimonthly
CRS Recruitment Publications/Cass Communications, Inc.
60 Revere Dr.
Northbrook, IL 60062

Federal Jobs Digest
Breakthrough Publications
P.O. Box 594
Millwood, NY 10546
Website: www.jobsfed.com

Foundation Grants to Individuals
The Foundation Center
79 Fifth Ave.
New York, NY 10003
Website: www.fdncenter.org

Government Job Finder
by Daniel Lauber
Planning /Communications
7215 Oak Ave.
River Forest, IL 60305

Graduate Management Admission Test
Graduate Management Admission Council
P.O. Box 6108
Princeton, NJ 08541
Website: www.gmat.org

Graduate Records Exam
Graduate Records Examination Board
Educational Testing Services
P.O. Box 6000
Princeton, NJ 08541
Website: www.gre.org

Guide to Healthcare Market Segment
SMG Marketing Group, Inc.
1342 N. Lasalle Dr.
Chicago, IL 60610
Website: www.smg.com

Handbook for Business and Management Careers
VGM Career Books
NTC/Contemporary Publishing Group
4255 West Touhy Ave.
Lincolnwood, IL 60712
Websites: www.vgmbooks.com
www.ntc-cb.com

The Handbook of Private Schools
Porter Sargent Publishers, Inc.
11 Beacon St., Suite 1400
Boston MA 02108
Website: www.portersargent.com

Harrington-O'Shea Career Decision Making
American Guidance Service
4201 Woodland Rd.
P.O. Box 99
Circle Pines, MN 55014
Website: www.agsnet.com

Harvard Gazette
Harvard Office of News & Public Affairs
Holyoke Center 1060
Cambridge, MA 02138
Website: www.news.harvard.edu

The Helping Professions: A Careers Sourcebook
Brooks/Cole Publishing
511 Forest Lodge Road
Pacific Grove, CA 93950
Website: www.brookscole.com

Hoover's Handbook of American Business
The Reference Press
6448 Highway 290 E, Suite E104
Austin, TX 78723

Hospitals Directory
American Business Directories, Inc.
5711 S. 86th Cr.
Omaha, NE 68127

How to Prepare Your Curriculum Vitae, Second Edition
Acy L. Jackson
VGM Career Books
NTC/Contemporary Publishing Group
4255 West Touhy Ave.
Lincolnwood, IL 60712
Websites: www.vgmbooks.com
www.ntc-cb.com

How to Write a Winning Personal Statement for Graduate and Professional School
by Richard Stelzer
Peterson's Guide
P.O. Box 2123
Princeton, NJ 08543
Website: www.petersons.com

Human Service Career Connection
372A Broadway
Cambridge, MA 02139

Index of Majors and Graduate Degrees
College Board Publication
P.O. Box 2123
New York, NY 10101
Website: www.collegeboard.org/index.html

Infotrac CD-ROM Business Index
Information Access Co.
362 Lakeside Dr.
Foster City, CA 94404
Website: www.gale.com

Internships 2001
Peterson's Guide
P.O. Box 2123
Princeton, NJ 08543
Website: www.petersons.com

Job Bank Series:
Atlanta Job Bank
Boston Job Bank
Chicago Job Bank
Dallas–Ft. Worth Job Bank
Denver Job Bank
Detroit Job Bank
Florida Job Bank
Houston Job Bank
Los Angeles Job Bank
Minneapolis Job Bank
New York Job Bank
Ohio Job Bank
Philadelphia Job Bank
San Francisco Job Bank
Seattle Job Bank
Washington, DC Job Bank
Bob Adams, Inc.
260 Center St.
Holbrook, MA 02343

The Job Hunter: The National Bi-Weekly Publication for Job Seekers
Career Planning and Placement Center
University of Missouri-Columbia
100 Noyes Building
Columbia, MO 65211
Website: http://career.missouri.edu/

Job Listings In Jewish Community Centers and
YM-YWHAs
JCC Association of North America
15 East 26th St.
New York, NY 10010
Website: www.jcca.org

Job Seekers Guide to Private and Public Companies
Gale Group
P.O. Box 33477
Detroit, MI 48232
Website: www.gale.com

Manufacturing Directories
Tower Publishing
588 Saco Rd.
Standish, ME 04084
Website: www.towerpub.com

Medical and Health Information Directory
Gale Group
P.O. Box 33477
Detroit, MI 48232
Website: www.gale.com

**Million Dollar Directory: America's Leading Public and
Private Companies**
Dun & Bradstreet Information Services
899 Eaton Ave.
Bethlehem, PA 18025

Moody's Manuals
Moody's Investors Service
99 Church St.
New York, NY 10007

Myers-Briggs Type Indicator
Consulting Psychologists Press, Inc.
3803 E. Bayshore Rd.
Palo Alto, CA 94303
Website: www.cpp-db.com

National Ad Search
National Ad Search, Inc.
P.O. Box 2083
Milwaukee, WI 53201
Website: www.nationaladsearch.com

National Business Employment Weekly
Dow Jones & Co., Inc.
P.O. Box 300
Longmont, CO 80502
Website: www.dowjones.com

The National Directory of Children, Youth, and Family Services
Marion L. Peterson, Publisher
P.O. Box 1837
Longmont, CO 80502

National Directory of Churches, Synagogues, and Other Houses of Worship
Gale Research, Inc.
P.O. Box 33477
Detroit, MI 48232
Website: www.gale.com

National Directory of Private Social Agencies
Croner Publications, Inc.
34 Jericho Turnpike
Jericho, NY 11753
Website: www.croner.com

National Directory of State Agencies
Cambridge Information Group Directories, Inc.
7200 Wisconsin Ave.
Bethesda, MD 20814

National Human Service Employment Weekly
13137 Pennadale Ln.
Fairfax, VA 22033

National Job Bank
Adams Media Corp.
260 Center St.
Holbrook, MA 02343
Website: www.careercity.com

National Job Hotline Directory
Planning/Communications
7215 Oak Ave.
River Forest, IL 60305
Website: http://jobfindersonline.com

National Trade and Profesional Associations of the United States
Columbia Books Inc.
1212 New York Ave. NW, Suite 330
Washington, DC 20005
Website: www.columbiabooks.com

Occupational Outlook Handbook
Occupational Outlook Quarterly
U.S. Department of Labor
Bureau of Labor Statistics
Washington, DC 20212
Website: www.dol.gov

O'Dwayer's Directory of Public Relations Firms
J.R. O'Dawyer Co. Inc
271 Madison Ave.
New York, NY 10016
Website: www.odawyerpr.com

The 100 Best Companies to Work for in America
by Robert Levering and Milton Moskowitz
A Currency Book Published by Doubleday
Bantam Doubleday Dell Publishing Group, Inc.
666 Fifth Ave.
New York, NY 10103
Website: www.randomhouse.com

The 100 Best Small Towns in America
Houghton Mifflin Co.
222 Berkley St.
Boston, MA 02116
Website: www.hmco.com

Opportunities in Banking Careers
Opportunities in Gerontology and Aging Careers
Opportunities in Government Careers
Opportunities in Health and Medical Careers
Opportunities in Insurance Careers
Opportunities in Journalism Careers
Opportunities in Law Enforcement and Criminal Justice Careers
Opportunities in Occupational Therapy Careers
Opportunities in Sport and Athletics Careers
Opportunities in Television and Video Careers
VGM Career Books
NTC/Contemporary Publishing Group
4255 West Touhy Ave.
Lincolnwood, IL 60712
Websites: www.vgmbooks.com
www.ntc-cb.com

Patterson's American Education
Patterson's Elementary Education
Educational Directories Inc.
P.O. Box 199
Mount Prospect, IL 60056
Website: www.edudirectories.com

Peterson's Grants for Graduate and Post Doctoral Study
Peterson's Four-Year Colleges 2000
Peterson's Guides
P.O. Box 2123
Princeton, NJ 08543
Website: www.petersons.com

Places Rated Almanac (6th edition)
IDG Books Worldwide
919E Hillside Blvd., Suite 400
Foster City, CA 94404-2112
Website: www.idgbooks.com

Professional Career Series:
Careers in Advertising
Careers in Business
Careers in Communications
Careers in Computers
Careers in Healthcare
Careers in High Tech
VGM Career Books
NTC/Contemporary Publishing Group
4255 West Touhy Ave.
Lincolnwood, IL 60712
Websites: www.vgmbooks.com
www.ntc-cb.com

Professional's Job Finder
Planning/Communications
7215 Oak Ave.
River Forest, IL 60305

Security Dealers of North America
Standard and Poor's Corp.
25 Broadway
New York, NY 10004
Website: www.standardpoor.com

The Skills Search (**Video**)
JIST Works, Inc.
720 North Park Ave.
Indianapolis, IN 46202
Website: www.jist.com

Sports Marketplace
Sportsguide
P.O. Box 1417
Princeton, NJ 08542

Standard Directory of Advertising Agencies
Reed Reference Publishing
P.O. Box 1417
Princeton, NJ 08542
Website: www.redbook.com

Standard and Poor's Register of Corporations
Standard and Poor's Corp.
25 Broadway
New York, NY 10004
Website: www.standardpoor.com

Strong Interest Inventory
Consulting Psychologists Press, Inc.
3803 E. Bayshore Rd.
Palo Alto, CA 94303
Website: www.cpp-db.com

The Tough New Labor Market of the 1990s (Video)
JIST Works, Inc.
720 North Park Ave.
Indianapolis, IN 46202
Website: www.jist.com

**Volunteerism: The Directory of Organizations, Training,
Programs & Publications**
R.R. Bowker
121 Chanlon Rd.
New Providence, NJ 07974
Website: www.booksinprint.com

Wards Business Directory of Corporate Affiliations
Gale Research Inc.
P.O. Box 33477
Detroit, MI 48232
Website: www.galegroup.com

What Can I Do with a Major In....?
By Lawrence Malnig with Anita Malnig
Abbot Press
P.O. Box 433
Ridgefield, NJ 07657

World Chamber of Commerce Directory
P.O. Box 1029
Loveland, CO 80539

Y National Vacancy List
YMCA of the USA
101 North Wacker Dr.
Chicago, IL 60606
Website: www.ymca.com

Yearbook of American Canadian Churches
Abingdon Press
P.O. Box 801
201 Eighth Ave. S
Nashville, TN 37202
Website: www.sbingdon.org

INDEX